Justice and the Social Context of Early Middle High German Literature

Medieval History and Culture

Volume 5

STUDIES IN
MEDIEVAL HISTORY AND CULTURE

edited by
Francis G. Gentry
Professor of German
Pennsylvania State University

A ROUTLEDGE SERIES

OTHER BOOKS IN THIS SERIES

Justice and the Social Context of Early Middle High German Literature

Robert G. Sullivan

ROUTLEDGE
NEW YORK & LONDON

Published in 2001 by
Routledge
29 West 35th Street
New York, NY 10001

Published in Great Britain by
Routledge
11 New Fetter Lane
London EC4P 4EE

Routledge is an imprint of the Taylor & Francis Group.

10 9 8 7 6 5 4 3 2 1

Library of Congress Cataloging-in-Publication Data

Sullivan, Robert G., 1957–
    Justice and the social context of early middle high German literature / Robert G. Sullivan.
        p. cm. — (Studies in medieval history and culture)
    Includes bibliographical references and index.
    ISBN 0-415-93685-3
    1. German poetry—Middle High German, 1050–1500—History and criticism. 2. Religious poetry, German—History and criticism. 3. Justice in literature. 4. Holy Roman Empire—History—843-1273. 5. Holy Roman Empire—Social conditions. I. Title. II. Series.

PT221 .S85 2001
831'.209382—dc21

2001019649

Printed on acid-free, 250 year-life paper
Manufactured in the United States of America

Series Editor Foreword

Far from providing just a musty whiff of yesteryear, research in Medieval Studies enters the new century as fresh and vigorous as never before. Scholars representing all disciplines and generations are consistently producing works of research of the highest caliber, utilizing new approaches and methodologies. Volumes in the Medieval History and Culture series will include studies on individual works and authors of Latin and vernacular literatures, historical personalities and events, theological and philosophical issues, and new critical approaches to medieval literature and culture.

Momentous changes have occurred in Medieval Studies in the past thirty years in teaching as well as in scholarship. Thus the goal of the Medieval History and Culture series is to enhance research in the field by providing an outlet for monographs by scholars in the early stages of their careers on all topics related to the broad scope of Medieval Studies, while at the same time pointing to and highlighting new directions that will shape and define scholarly discourse in the future.

Francis G. Gentry

pour Meriem

Table of Contents

Preface

My intellectual debt to Francis G. Gentry will be obvious to anyone who reads the following pages, at least insofar as there is anything of value to be found there. Gentry has long pleaded for an ideal of medieval studies characterized by a cross-fertilization of traditionally isolated disciplines, particularly literary studies and social history. Such interdisciplinary scholarship is, of course, now scarcely as rare as when Gentry first advocated and practiced it, but its execution remains as difficult as ever. In my quest better to understand and historically situate Early Middle High German religious literature, I had frequent occasion to refer to extra-literary works and to consult historians of medieval society and law. While I hope that both legal and social scholars might in turn find something of use or interest here, I know too well that they may also object to my transgressing their fields. I make no claim to their specialist competence; instead, in my use of non-literary sources, I have deliberately tried to restrict myself to the traditional literary methods of the close reading of texts and the philological investigation of key words and concepts. To read legal documents and historical works as literature, so to speak, does not necessarily imply a philosophy in which all the world is text; this is certainly very far from my own view. The virtue of traditional close readings and conceptual analysis lies rather in their drawing attention to aspects of sources that had perhaps been neglected or overlooked.

In the interest of furthering interdisciplinary studies, I have translated all quotations in the body of the text from modern German into English, and I have provided translations of all medieval German texts in my notes. In the latter translations, which are often in themselves instances of interpretation, my aim has been to render these often difficult poems and prose works as literally as possible. I am painfully aware that with my literalness there comes a corresponding loss of felicity and good English style. I trust the relative accuracy for which I have striven may provide some compensation.

Beside my professional debt to Prof. Gentry, I owe to him and Edda Gentry a personal one for their kindness, generosity, and decency that I cannot possibly repay. I would like to acknowledge here, too, my thanks to my extraordinarily supportive colleagues at the Department of Germanic Languages and Literatures at the University of Massachusetts in Amherst, to the unfailing encouragement and inspiration of my parents George and Alyce Sullivan, and to my beloved children, Stephanie and Nicholas. May their world be one in which justice will finally reign supreme.

Abbreviations used in this work

ABäG		*Amsterdamer Beiträge zur älteren Germanistik*
Annales ESC		*Annales Economies Sociétés Civilisations*
BAW		*Bayerische Akademie der Wissenschaften*
BMZ		Georg F. Benecke, Wilhelm Müller, and Friedrich Zarncke.
		Mittelhochdeutsches Wörterbuch. 3 vols. Leipzig, 1854–1861.
CC		*Corpus Christianorum. Series Latina*
DA		*Deutsches Archiv für Erforschung des Mittelalters*
DTM		Deutsche Texte des Mittelalters
DVjs		*Deutsche Vierteljahrsschrift für Literaturwissenschaft und*
		Geistesgeschichte
FMS		*Frühmittelalterliche Studien*
GAG		*Göppingen Arbeiten zur Germanistik*
GRM		*Germanisch-Romanische Monatsschrift*
HdR		*Handwörterbuch zur deutschen Rechtsgeschichte.* Ed. Adelbert Erler
		and Ekkehard Kaufmann. Berlin: Schmidt, 1971–1997.
HJ		*Historisches Jahrbuch*
HZ		*Historische Zeitschrift*
LCL		*Loeb Classical Library*
Lexer		Matthias Lexer. *Mittelhochdeutsches Handwörterbuch.* 3 vols.
		Leipzig, 1872–1878.
MGH		*Monumenta Germaniae historica*
	Con.	Constitutiones et acta publica
	Cap.	Capitularia regum Francorum
	DChr.	Deutsche Chroniken
	Fontes Legum	Fontes iuris Germanici antiqui
	SS	Scriptores
NF		*Neue Folge*
NM		*Niederdeutsche Mitteilungen*
PBB		*Beiträge zur Geschichte der deutschen Sprache und Literatur*
PL		*Patrologiae cursus completus. Series Latina.* Ed. J. P. Migne
QF		*Quellen und Forschungen zur Sprach- und Kulturgeschichte der germanischen Völker*
RD		Friedrich Maurer. *Die religiösen Dichtungen des 11. und 12. Jahrhuderts.* 3 vols. Tübingen: Niemeyer, 1964–70.
SB		Sitzungsberichte
VL		*Die deutsche Literatur des Mittelalters. Verfasserlexikon.* Ed. Kurt Ruh. 1977 ff.
ZfdA		*Zeitschrift für deutsches Altertum*
ZfdP		*Zeitschrift für deutsche Philologie*
ZRG		*Zeitschrift der Savigny-Stiftung für Rechtsgeschichte*
	(GA)	*Germanistische Abteilung*
	(KA)	*Kanonistische Abteilung*

JUSTICE AND THE SOCIAL CONTEXT OF EARLY MIDDLE HIGH GERMAN LITERATURE

The Historical Context of Early Middle High German Literature

The following study is an attempt to understand the social and historical content and context of German vernacular works of the eleventh and twelfth centuries by focusing on their conception of *reht* or justice. This literature provides ample material to the literary historian. Aside from numerous fragments and significant prose works, it encompasses over 100 poems, ranging in length from 100 lines to many poems of well over 2,000 lines, and in the case of the massive rhymed chronicle of the emperors from Julius Caesar to Lothar III, the *Kaiserchronik,* to close to 20,000 lines. With the exception of Old English literature, there is nothing comparable in extent in any other vernacular European literature of this time, a fact that would in itself make these works of interest to medievalists. The themes of the works themselves are primarily religious, most often exclusively so, as their modern titles indicate, for example, the "Momento mori" or "The Heavenly Jerusalem."

Scholars typically refer to these works as "Early Middle High German religious literature." The characterization is drawn, of course, from historical linguistics and is not without its own difficulties, but I will continue to use it with slight modifications, less for its accuracy than for its ideological neutrality. In the following, "Early Middle High German" will refer to the language of those works written between roughly 1050 and 1200, that are religious in content and whose language is characterized by the gradual weakening in secondary syllables of the Old High German full vowels.[1] I have extended the usual terminal date of 1170 by some 30 years. The earlier date is in fact less influenced by linguistic criteria than by the beginning of a "courtly literature" as first evidenced in Heinrich von Veldeke's *Eneit* (1171). Simultaneous with this new thematic beginning in German literature, the older strain of Early Middle High German religious literature, however, continues to around 1200, unless one wishes to call "courtly literature" such works as *Das Anegenge* (ca. 1173-1180), the poems of Der Wilde Mann (ca. 1180), or Alber's *Tungdalus* (ca. 1190).

Until fairly recently, a discussion of the social views of the German religious poets of the eleventh and twelfth centuries would have seemed to many a contradiction in terms. Histories of literature once described the development of medieval German poetry and prose something like this: After a hopeful but sparse beginning in the Old High German or Carolingian period, German vernacular literature fell silent for a full century and a half, from around 900 to 1050. When it again found its voice in the second half of the eleventh century, its sound was alien and somber. Gone were the echoes of Germanic heroic songs which historians had delighted to hear in the "Hildebrandslied" and in parts of other Old High German poems. In their place was a veritable dirge.

This "new beginning" of vernacular literature was generally perceived as a regrettable reflection of the spirit and ideals of the great French monastic center Cluny, characterized by a fanatical religious asceticism, contemptuous of all art and education as well as worldly pleasure and honor and decidedly foreign to the essence of Germanic heroism.[2] One study from 1937 tells us: "In the classical period of Christian-ascetic culture, in the age of Cluny, the heroic spirit of the Germanic *Heldenlied* was forced into silence."[3] Not the least of the defects of this "Cluniac" poetry for nationalist historians was that its inspiration was French. It is thus not a little ironic that many of these same German scholars saw the return to proper German themes in the development of the courtly literature of the late twelfth century, the most famous examples of which were, with the exception of the *Nibelungenlied*, unequivocal adaptations and reworkings of French and Provençal originals.

Despite the occasional and sometimes even intense interest which this "Cluniac" religious poetry found among some of the greatest students of German literature, such as Scherer, von Kraus, Ehrismann, and DeBoor, the vernacular poems and prose written between around 1050 and 1170 were considered by most an embarrassing disappointment that was at best relegated to the realm of philologists and linguistic historians.[4]

Doubts about the accuracy and appropriateness of the Cluniac label were voiced early on, but it was only after the catastrophic collapse of the Germanic ideology at the end of World War II that the Cluniac characterization, or rather caricature, came under sharp critical scrutiny.[5] Although it still may be found in some popular literary histories, it has gradually lost favor.[6] In its place, new and sometimes contradictory pictures of the German vernacular religious literature of the eleventh and twelfth centuries have arisen, which up to the mid-1970s could be tied to the names of Friedrich Maurer and his disciples Heinz Rupp and Gerhard Meißburger, on the one hand, and Werner Schröder, on the other. The Freiburger Maurer school emphasized the basic continuity of medieval German literature. Maurer himself had argued that this continuity may best be seen in the metrical forms of the Early Middle High German religious poems, which he claimed were cast in the same long-line strophic verse best exemplified by the Old High German *Evangelienbuch* of Otfrid of Weißenburg.[7] He also posited an anticipation in the Early Middle High German religious poems of many of the ethical and moral themes of the literature of the high courtly period.[8]

Meißburger attempted to lay the intellectual foundation to Maurer's concept of formal continuity with his book *Grundlagen zum Verständnis der deutschen Mönchsdichtung im 11. und 12. Jahrhundert,* published in 1970. Drawing on the works of the historian Gerd Tellenbach and his students, especially Joachim Wollasch, Meißburger's goal was to demolish the traditional literary historians' view of the Cluny reform movement. He contended, first, that labels such as "extreme asceticism" and "anti-intellectualism" distorted the historical content of Cluny and second, that in spite of the sharp disputes among the various monastic reform movements, whether Benedict of Aniane, Cluny, Gorze, or Hirsau, there was a unified spirit underlying these movements. Early medieval German literature therefore reflected a clear and unified monastic tradition, ultimately based on the ideals of the Rule of Benedict, that transcended the different reform centers:

> Most histories provide no assistance in assigning a text to this or that reform movement.... We cannot expect to differentiate the reform movements according to their intellectual stances.[9]

The continuity of German literature from the Old High German period to the religious poems in Early Middle High German, finally, is assured, according to Meißburger, by the fact that the authors of these works were almost exclusively monks who therefore shared the common spiritual, cultural, and social goals of Benedictine monasticism, namely *pax, charitas, iustitia,* and *concordia*:

> The monastic movement of the tenth, eleventh, and twelfth centuries had not only the same source, Benedict of Aniane's reform, it also had the same goal: To lead a regulated life for one's own salvation as well as that of the world. ... Not as Cluniacs, but as Benedictines, on the basis of shared experience and responsibility towards one's neighbor, they taught the world that true salvation is to be sought not in the world but 'extra mundum.'[10]

Previous to Meißburger, Heinz Rupp's book *Deutsche geistliche Dichtungen des 11. und 12. Jahrhunderts* (first edition in 1958) had opened the door to a new aesthetic appreciation of Early Middle High German religious works by offering brilliant structural analyses of five of the most famous poems. Rupp had also argued against the Cluniac characterization by advancing a series of logically unrelated theses.[11] Like Meißburger, but without his deeper historical foundation, Rupp questioned the traditional Cluniac understanding of German literary historians.[12] Second, following Hallinger's studies, Rupp claimed that Cluny had had little influence on monastic reform in the Empire, the main source of which was rather the Lotharingian reform as diffused by the imperial proprietary monastery of Gorze.[13] Third, the German religious poems of the eleventh and twelfth centuries can by no means be characterized by self- and world-abnegation and asceticism.[14] Last, Rupp claimed that the authors of the German poems were in any case for the most part not monks, but lay priests.[15]

The cultural and intellectual level of these secular priests, according to Rupp, was quite low: "The German religious poems were composed by men of—so to speak—second and third class ability."[16] The result is that there is nothing of the new and sometimes radical reform spirit in the Early Middle High German works, rather "In general, the ideas contained in these works had belonged to the common property of Christian theology since the Patristic era."[17] This fact alone guarantees at least an intellectual continuity—albeit at a low level—between Old High German and Early Middle High German religious poetry. Rupp, following Maurer, also saw this continuity in the metric forms of the poems, but conceded that the evidence for this has to be deduced by hypothesis and cannot be empirically confirmed.[18]

As well as reaffirming Maurer's thesis of formal continuity, Rupp argued for the appearance of certain novel aspects in the Early Middle High German poems. The newness of the poems is not to be found in their content, but in their intricate formal structuring of traditional themes:

> The ideas are traditional; the achievement of the poets lies in their arrangement of ideas, and in this their independence and originality ought to be valued highly. They have not allowed themselves to be captured and oppressed by the religious literature before them. They have independently chosen themes and independently shaped them.[19]

Rupp traces this originality to the "Stilwille" or sense of style of the poets:

> The goal of the poets is not linguistic beauty, but a linguistic correctness. Ideas ought to be spoken in a German that is understandable and natural. To the poets this striving for linguistic correctness alone was appropriate for the ideas they wanted to express and the topics they wanted to treat.[20]

The suspicion that Rupp's thesis is close to an hypostatization of language is confirmed in another remark he makes about the traditional content of these poems:

> Nowhere are distinct contemporary political currents to be detected. There are good reasons for this. . . . The time was not yet ripe enough for allowing political ideas to become effective in German, in German literature. . . . In the eleventh and twelfth centuries, a work, even a poem, had to be written in Latin to be politically effective, for Latin was still the exclusive language of politics.[21]

Concepts like "sense of style" and "linguistic correctness" betray the influence of the Swiss critic Emil Staiger, whose book *Die Kunst der Interpretation* (1955), a metaphysically colored version of "New Criticism," played a dominant role in discussions of literary theory in the German-speaking lands throughout the late 50s and early 60s. The evident distaste with which Rupp discussed the possibility of any contemporary social or political content in the Early Middle High German poems no doubt had deeper roots in the political culture of his time. Rupp had rightly directed his readers' interest to structural and formal questions, but by describing their themes as the "common property of Christian theology," he in effect banned any extra-literary questioning of the poems.

Contemporary with Maurer's, Rupp's, and Meißburger's efforts were those of their harsh critic Werner Schröder. Schröder in two early essays had also rejected the Cluniac label, at least for most Early Middle High German works.[22] Schröder's later work, however, consisted mostly in critiques of other scholars and especially in numerous, sharp attacks on Maurer's thesis concerning the existence of a putatively Old High German long-line strophic form in the Early Middle High

German religious poems.[23] Behind Schröder's rejection of Maurer's arguing for formal continuity lay his espousal of a violent discontinuity between the Old High German and Early Middle High German periods. According to Schröder, there could be no talk of continuity in early medieval German literature for:

> Whenever and wherever German was written it had the air of an experiment and an exception in the mind of its authors, regardless of whether it occurred in true or only imagined isolation.[24]

In Maurer's, Rupp's, Meißburger's, and to a lesser degree, Schröder's work there was an element of consensus in the post-war understanding of Early Middle High German literature, namely an underlying rejection not only of the traditional "Cluniac-ascetic" label, but also of an appreciation of the historical and social content of Early Middle High German literature. Obviously, such historical questions as the influence of the monastic reform movement weighed heavily in these scholars' discussions. Yet by rejecting the influence of Cluny, however interpreted, they simultaneously eschewed an explanation of the historical background to the explosion of German vernacular literature in the second half of the eleventh century. Instead, post-war scholarship was content with either generally formulated intellectual history or with a concentration on purely aesthetic categories. Maurer, for example, spoke vaguely of "Salian religious poetry," while Rupp, as shown, was quite severe in his repudiation of any historical or political content in the poems. Meißburger's thesis of Benedictine monastic continuity remains quite nebulous despite his detailed historical research.[25] Schröder, finally, while ostensibly advocating an historical approach to the poems, emphasized their discontinuity and isolation to such an extent that he would sometimes seem to prefer the literary historical equivalent of "Just So" tales:

> The task of the historian and the literary scholar is to recognize and accentuate what is individual in a given work and not to trivialize and homogenize independent impulses.[26]

Schröder's concern for the individuality of each poet or poem is surely valid, but not at the expense of ignoring the larger picture. The student of early medieval German literature is confronted with the following facts: The years during which the Early Middle High German works were written, roughly 1050–1200, were times of tremendous upheaval for the German Empire, encompassing in turn the monastic and papal reform movements, the Saxon wars of Henry IV, the Investiture Conflict and the resulting increased feudalization of the Empire, the end of the Salian dynasty, the rise of territorial lords, the struggle between the Hohenstaufen and the Welfs for power and the control of the imperial throne, and the chaos following upon the sudden death of Frederick I. The British historian Geoffrey Barraclough was expressing a commonplace when he wrote of the period beginning in the last quarter of the eleventh century:

> Germany was divided into two camps, and a long generation was to pass before even the bare essentials of peace and settled conditions returned. But what was destroyed in these years could never be restored: the whole of subsequent

German history bears on it the marks of the conflicts which raged through Germany between 1075 and Henry IV's death in 1106.[27]

What is the connection between this history and Early Middle High German literature? Intuitively, one would think that this tumultuous age must have had some effect on the development and content of the literature, that history is needed to help explain these works. The religious poems, in turn, possess a unique status for the period, for as mentioned, they represent almost the only vernacular literature to have survived from this time, and thus they might also be valuable in illuminating history. In view of these facts, is the literary historian truly confined to posing questions of metrical and structural analysis, as did Maurer and Rupp? Or is the content of the poems really so meager that one must content oneself with such concepts as the vaguely described Benedictine spirituality, as Meißburger claimed, or are the Early Middle High German works in fact so isolated that one must follow Schröder's strictures on the uniqueness of each work and concentrate on the individuality of every poem at the price of discovering thematic regularities?

The nineteenth-century literary historians who first cleared the way for an appreciation of Early Middle High German literature did not think so. Wilhelm Scherer, for example, the first scholar to attempt to treat the Early Middle High German period as a whole, was quite open to the historical and social content of this literature, perhaps sometimes even too much so.[28] In the post-war period, varying efforts have also been undertaken to see the Early Middle High German religious poems and prose against their historical background, none more important and seminal than those of Hugo Kuhn. In his short essay "Minne oder reht" (1950),[29] Kuhn was being deliberately provocative in his choice of Noker's "Memento mori" to argue for the importance of history in Early Middle High German poems. This shorter work (ca. 1070) had been considered the perfect emblem of its epoch, and Noker's supposedly fanatic religiosity and *contemptus mundi* had thus been presented as representing in essence the spirit of Cluny as it was conceived by literary historians up through the 1950s.[30] Strongly rejecting the Cluniac label, Kuhn attempted to show that Early Middle High German poems were far from being examples of strained otherworldliness, but were in some instances eminently concerned with this world and even subtly political in their intent. By attempting to place the paradigmatically ahistorical "Memento mori" in the context of the Investiture Conflict and Henry IV's espousal of the Peace of God movement, Kuhn had implied that other Early Middle High German poems might have been equally mundane in their themes and concerns.

In a second essay, from 1953, "Gestalten und Lebenskräfte der frühmittel-hochdeutschen Dichtung,"[31] Kuhn included, at least in part, similarly historically grounded interpretations of the "Ezzolied" (Vorauer version, 1064-65), the *Vienna Genesis* (1060-80), and the *Annolied* (1077). In the case of the *Annolied*, the connection with very particular political events of the late eleventh century is undeniable; Kuhn, however, was more interested in a general appreciation of the poet's concept of history. The form of the poem is quite complex, but in essence it might be described as a saint's *vita* embedded in the wider context of salvation history, the relating of the divine plan of development with the course of terrestrial history whose middle point is the human being:

> duo deilte got sini werch al in zwei,   disi werlt ist daz eine deil,
> daz ander ist geistin: . . . .
> duo gemengite dei wise godis list   von den zwein ein werch,
> daz der mennisc ist,
> der beide ist corpus unte geist, ...[32]

The eponymous hero of the *Annolied* is the Archbishop of Cologne Anno II (died 1075) who was regent of the Empire during the minority of his ward Henry IV. The poem's unknown author is quite vivid in his description of contemporary events, and it is hard to reconcile the following lines with Rupp's comment, cited above, that "Nowhere are clear contemporary political currents to be detected" in the Early Middle High German poems:

> Dar nach ving sich ane der ubile strit   des manig man virlos den lip,
> duo demi vierden Heinriche   virworrin wart diz riche.
> mort, ruob unti brant   zivurtin kirichin unti lant
> von Tenemarc unz in Apuliam,   van Kerlingen unz an Ungerin.
> den niman nimohte wider sten,   obi si woltin mit truwin unsamit gen,
> diz stiftin heriverte groze   wider nevin unti husgenoze.
> diz riche alliz bikerte sin gewæfine   in sin eigen inadere.
> mit siginuftlicher zeswe   ubirwant iz sich selbe,
> daz di gidouftin lichamin   umbigravin zi worfin lagin,
> zi ase den bellindin,   den grawin walthundin:
> duo daz nitruite   bisuonin Seint Anno   duo bidroz une lebin langere.[33]

As mentioned, the particular historical details and political tendencies contained in the *Annolied* interested Kuhn less than general trends in the history of ideas. He concluded, for example, that the writers of the late eleventh-century poems

> yielded to the pressure to which all vernacular literature . . . would in the future
> be obliged. . . . The most pressing issue was the question of the salvation of the
> medieval cooperative existence, first that of the "empire," then society, knight-
> hood, and finally that of every estate and group of the late Middle Ages.[34]

Kuhn's view of the connection between the historical and social background of the poems thus remains quite general:

> German vernacular poetry of the eleventh century universally proclaims the new
> gospel: A generally binding history of mankind or the rule of law, under the sym-
> bolic seal of divine salvation, and that in the language of the people.[35]

Only in the case of the "Memento mori" did Kuhn see a connection with specific contemporary politics. Of the late eleventh-century poems that he discusses, it was the spirit of the "Memento mori" alone, namely its concern with the

"Rechtsordnung" or rule of law or justice that, according to Kuhn, would exercise notable influence in the twelfth century.

Kuhn's views remained without echo throughout the 1950s until Rudolph Schützeichel's monograph *Das allemanische Memento mori* appeared in 1962. Schützeichel shared Kuhn's belief that the "Memento mori" had definite social concerns that could be tied to contemporary events. But Noker's use of the concept *reht*, which Kuhn had understood as "justice" and which he connected with the imperially sponsored Peace of God movement in the late eleventh century, was eccentrically interpreted by Schützeichel as "sacraments." Schützeichel characterized Noker's criticism of the misuse of *reht* as a radical condemnation of simony and thus linked this criticism to the reform monastery of Hirsau in southwest Germany, the postulated home of Noker.[36]

In 1974, Gert Kaiser again raised the question of the historical content of the "Memento mori," admitting, as Kuhn had, that more was at stake than the interpretation of the "Memento mori" alone: "Admittedly, interwoven with the investigation of this text is the contentious issue of whether the Early Middle High German literature from 1050 to 1150 is Cluniac or not."[37] Noker's "Memento mori" thus again emblematically stands for Early Middle High German literature in general.

Kaiser rejected Rupp's ahistorical interpretation as well as Kuhn's and Schützeichel's vague historical appreciations. He also included in his discussion two contributions from the German Democratic Republic, which had been universally neglected in the West, only, however, to reject them in turn, as well.[38] Kaiser saw the historical content of the "Memento mori" against the background of what he described in Hegelian-Marxist terms as the new social mobility of the eleventh and twelfth centuries and the growth of the market and exchange economy.[39] This growth, according to Kaiser, led to a fundamental questioning of the traditional social order: "In the act of exchange all differences of status, which otherwise penetrate every sphere of existence, disappear.... [The "Memento mori"] shows a way to end inequality and at the same time the historical impossibility of this way."[40] Noker thus, claimed Kaiser, presents in his poem the problem of human inequality without being ideologically equipped to solve it.[41] Kaiser's admittedly eccentric interpretation is far removed from the disinterest in history shown by Maurer, Rupp, and Meißburger, but obviously strains the "Memento mori" with dubious interpretations of social and economic historians of the Middle Ages, whose own theses—however one understands them—were not beyond criticism.

A final instance of an attempt at mediation between Early Middle High German literature and its historical and social background is contained in two essays by Francis G. Gentry, also on the "Memento mori."[42] Gentry, like Kuhn and Schützeichel, sees the interpretative crux of the "Memento mori" in its middle strophes on *reht*, which he equates with the biblical and theological concept of *iustitia*.[43] He is more general than Kuhn in sketching the historical content of the "Memento mori," but he avoids the speculative hypotheses of Kaiser. Instead, his

approach is twofold: A structural analysis as advocated by Rupp and a close reading of the text, both combined with the question of historical context:

> While it is possible on the basis of an immanent reading of the text to determine
> what Noker is saying, the question as to why he is saying it, a question which
> should also occupy the critic, cannot be satisfactorily answered on that basis
> alone.

He concludes that "although Noker is making no direct political statement in his
poem, the answer must be sought in the historical and social background of his
era."[44]

Gentry views this background as "the state of political and social disintegration
which came into being as a result of the Investiture Contest . . . a time of crisis."[45]
Noker's key concern with *reht* or *iustitia* Gentry sees as part of a universal reaction to the confusion of the time:

> The concern with justice and peace and simply correct living was not the exclu-
> sive prerogative of either the king's or the pope's party. It was the common pos-
> session of all Christians and had been so since the earliest days of the church.[46]

The historical content of the "Memento mori," according to Gentry, can be
found in Noker's championing of justice in the face of injustice. Gentry argues
that Noker's advocacy of justice is an appropriation of a traditional and central
Christian category to solve the conflicts surrounding him, and thus the poet revi-
talizes a particular tradition for a particular historical situation.

It seems to me that Gentry's method, combining a close reading of a work with
the historical question of what the poets may perhaps be responding to, provides
the most sensible approach to the question posed above, namely what is the connection between Early Middle High German literature and the historical period
in which it arose? There are, of course, significant constraints on this approach.
First, the historical question must often remain inexact since the provenance and
dating of the poems are often highly uncertain.[47] Equally difficult is the related
question of authorship: Almost all of Early Middle High German literature is
anonymous, and as we have seen, scholars are uncertain if the authors were monks,
lay priests, or laypeople. Gernentz's economic and social reductionism and Kaiser's
tenuous connection of the poems with sociological studies of the eleventh and
twelfth centuries are, aside from any other methodological considerations, inappropriate for it is simply impossible directly to tie most Early Middle High
German poetry and prose to quite specific political or ideological movements.

Second, Schröder was quite right to argue that the Early Middle High German
works do not necessarily present a unified program. But there is no need to
explain this lack of thematic unity solely in Schröder's terms of the authors' individuality and the discontinuity in the development of German literature. I have
found it more useful to try to underline the differences among the poems and
prose works in terms of the genres they represent. Unfortunately, however, here
too there has been little consensus among scholars as to how these different genres should be described. The classical categories of lyric, epic, and drama are woe-
fully inadequate for categorizing these religious works, and one is therefore forced

to use more contextual categories, which are in turn often unclear.[48] A poem like the *Vienna Genesis* would seem adequately described by the term "biblical epic," yet large portions of it are in the form of moral sermons commenting on the biblical text. The frequently utilized concept of "Reimpredigt," or rhymed sermon, for such poems as the "Memento mori" gives a good first impression of the tendency of many of the poems, but ignores the fact that the traditional sermon is usually prefaced by a specific biblical pericope or theme, which is lacking in the case of poems like the "Memento mori." "Liturgical hymn" has been used for such works as the "Ezzolied," but again, one would hesitate to argue that such a vernacular work was actually used in the context of the liturgy. "Sündenklage" or lamentation for sins might be useful for some Early Middle High German works, but its meaning seems stretched when applied to any work in which a poet mentions his feelings of guilt.

The assignment of Early Middle High German works to a given genre transcends any desire for literary-historical tidiness. Important differences among these works appear to have their source in the constraints of genre, however broadly one wishes to conceive this,[49] which is no more than to claim that a liturgically influenced poem on, for example, Noah's curse of his son Ham will probably treat its theme differently from the manner in which a preacher concerned with castigating his audience's turpitude would treat the same topic.[50]

In view of the difficulties many of the proposed genre classifications cause, one ought perhaps best be content with fairly broad and flexible categories of genre, which neither constrain their objects too severely nor distort the peculiarities of each work. Perhaps the best classification of Early Middle High German works has been offered by Gisela Vollmann-Profe in her review of the Early Middle High German period. She divides the poems into three "main types," according to their relation to the work of salvation:

> "The completion of salvation" (Das Heil im Vollzug), [including] encomium, prayer, credo, and confession of sin, "teaching through salvation" (Belehrung durch das Heil), [including] sermon, rhymed sermon, theological-motivated natural history, and "narrated salvation" (erzähltes Heil), [including] various, further subdivided types of biblical and historical literature.[51]

These terms are of course unwieldy, and in the following I will instead use the adjectives "liturgical," "sermonic," and "epic" as equivalents to Vollmann-Profe's three main types. A fourth category, "meditative," might also be added under which I think some of Vollmann-Profe's "confessions of sin" are more correctly subsumed.[52] The adjectival usage should at the same time underline the fact that very few of the Early Middle High German poems can be exclusively assigned to any one genre: The *Vienna Genesis*, as mentioned, is both epic and sermonic in content.

In addition to the difficulties of uncertain dating and authorship, and restrictions and emphases imposed by genre, there is a third and more complex constraint on the study of Early Middle High German literature that involves the relation in the poems between tradition and innovation. It is indeed true, as Rupp forcefully argued, but scarcely surprising, that the Early Middle High German poems and prose are very much dependent on traditional Christian theology.[53] Except in rare cases, however, the poems reveal no one single and definite source. Rather, their authors appear to have selectively drawn on different strands of tradition. Instead of "sources," therefore, scholars rightly prefer to speak of "parallels" between the ideas or motifs expressed in the poems and traditional or contemporary Latin works.

The Early Middle High German works are usually not translations; nor are they merely centos built of theological commonplaces, as Rupp argued and as David A. Wells's comments initially seem to imply:

> Theological literature is, of course, lacking in originality. For the Germanist, its interest lies chiefly in its presentation in the vernacular of a certain chain of thought which may mean that the content, from the standpoint of theology is full of commonplaces.[54]

Wells qualifies this statement, however, by adding:

> Only the thorough assessment of the tradition which flows into vernacular literature will allow us to see if and to what extent the German author takes issue with the theological sources at his disposal.[55]

It is obviously imperative to examine each theological idea in the poems in the light of tradition, to decide which traditions are used, which ignored, which are determined by genre restrictions and which flout such restrictions, and finally to determine if and when and how the Early Middle High German authors change or criticize tradition to adopt it to their own concerns.

The failure to consider tradition results in anachronistic interpretation. Noker's "Memento mori" again provides a good example. The following lines from Noker's poem, in particular, have evoked serious misunderstandings:

> Got gescuof iuh alle, ir chomint von einem manne.
> to gebot er iu ze demo lebinne mit minnon hie ze wesinne,
> taz ir warint als ein man, taz hant ir ubergangen.
> habetint ir anders niewit getan, ir muosint is iemer scaden han.[56]

This idea of the unity of humankind based on Adamic descent is of course biblical, and as such, its evocation is not uncommon in the Early Middle High German period. The anonymous author of the "Scopf von dem lône" (ca. 1150), for example, writes with regret of the division of this primal unity due to Cain's killing of Abel:

> wir solton all enein varin: so nesin wir leidor so geborin:
> doch daz ein wib wære, diu uns erist gebære,
> diu truoc misselichiu kint, also die afterkomin ie noch sint.
> einen sun siu getruoc, der sinen bruodir ersluoc.[57]

Closer to the wording and arguments of the "Memento mori" are some lines from a secular epic, *König Rother* (? ca. 1150–1160). King Constantine's wife pleads with her husband to release Rother's men who are languishing in prison:

> "waz wnderis wiltu an in began?
> Ir vader hiez Adam,
> dann wir alle quamin.
> Du soldes gothis schonin
> ander uil armer diete."[58]

And in the Ermlitzer Fragment of *König Rother*, someone—unfortunately it is not clear who—says in a line almost identical to the "Memento mori": "Wan wir chomen alle von einem man."[59]

The notion of common Adamic descent is used by Noker to justify his call to his audience to live in love and justice. A similar argument can also be found in the oldest French vernacular "rhymed sermon" from the beginning of the twelfth century, the Anglo-Norman "Grant mal fist Adam":

> Dunc puis jeo prover,
> e raisun mostrer,
> qu'il sunt mi proceain
> quant d'un sol lignage
> sunt e fol e sage
> corteis e vilain.[60]

Without corroborating evidence, the idea of the unity of humankind as expressed in the "Memento mori," can scarcely be placed in a "revolutionary" context.[61] Nor does it represent an incipient egalitarianism.[62] Rather, this biblically-founded idea has clearly become a *topos*, in the case of the "Memento mori" probably derived from Saint Augustine, as Gentry has convincingly argued.[63]

To recognize the weight of tradition and to state that an idea is a *topos* or commonplace of that tradition, is not, however, to deny that it can be historically and socially significant. The idea of the unity of humankind, for example, can indeed take on revolutionary tones in certain situations and depending on how it is used,[64] but it is never used in such a way in the Early Middle High German period.

The Early Middle High German poems and prose are expressions of medieval Christianity and, as such, participants in Christian tradition. Like other religions with authoritative, divinely sanctioned texts and traditions, however, progress and innovation and regression and reaction occur in Christianity by the selective reappropriation and reinterpretation of holy tradition. To the protagonists of change, there is, of course, nothing new under the sun, nothing new, at least, that is at the same time true. Change is always seen as a reinvigoration of the original sacred revelation. Tradition is thus actualized in each new situation, and in this respect Christianity is no different from Judaism, of which Gershom Scholem wrote in a classic essay on the relation between tradition and innovation:

> "Tradition," in the sense of an understanding of the efficacy of the Word, is constituted in each concrete situation into which a . . . society enters. A process begins in which the question is posed of how revelation as a concrete message can be preserved and transmitted from generation to generation . . ., with ever growing immediacy the question also arises of if and how this revelation can be

applied. And thus a spontaneous element breaks into a tradition that is constituting itself.[65]

Nor is Christianity in this respect any different from Islam, in which according to the anthropologist Michael Gilsenan, the preservation of revelation is:

> . . . a creative process. It had to be. . . . Belief and practice that are regarded as eternal, unchangeable in essence if not in every detail, and as given by a higher and non-human power still have to be carried on. They have constantly to be re-created in social life. Even if the pious fiction is that things are just as they were and that the sacred tradition is unaltered, the myths unchanging, the genealogies fixed forever, we know that in fact things do change.[66]

Thus when Rupp states of the author of the "Memento mori": "No idea is new to him, not even fundamentally new in formulation, and—this needs to be expressly recognized—no idea is formulated more sharply, strongly, more threateningly than in previous [authors in the Latin tradition]"[67] and when he says of Hugo Kuhn's efforts to link the "Memento mori" to the circle of the Emperor Henry IV on the basis of Noker's use of the concepts of "reht" and "minne" that such efforts are "not provable, especially because precisely these ideas have played an important role in Christian thought at all times"[68] then one must ask if these remarks, too, are not examples of "pious fiction." Is Noker's use of *reht* really no different from its biblical, patristic, or Carolingian meaning? Is the centrality of *reht* in the "Memento mori," for which in different ways Kuhn, Schützeichel, and Gentry argued, really unmotivated by the circumstances in which Noker wrote? To answer these questions in the negative is to condemn Noker's poem to absolute historical irrelevancy. Any attempt, on the other hand, to prove that Early Middle High German literature can indeed be historically and socially situated must answer these questions by continuously striving to mediate between the connections between history and the traditions selectively chosen and modified to depict, confront, and perhaps even change this reality.

With these constraints in mind, I will undertake such an attempt to place the Early Middle High German works within an historical context. My purpose is not to treat this literature as simply untapped historical documents for an understanding of German history in the eleventh and twelfth centuries. Rather, I should like to show that without this historical contextualization, one cannot understand and appreciate Early Middle High German literature itself. Clearly, any such attempt must be selective and restricted to certain themes. Following Gentry's contention that the key to understanding the "Memento mori"—and by implied extension many of the Early Middle High German works—is in Noker's use of *reht*, I will limit myself to an investigation of the Early Middle High German poets' concept of *reht* to discover what the poets and sermon writers understood by *reht* and then ask, in Gentry's words, "why they are saying it."

This concentration on *reht* must itself be justified and its usage in the eleventh and twelfth centuries explained with the help of philological, legal, and theological studies. Only then may we turn to its particular use in Early Middle High German literature.

NOTES

1   Cf. Hans Eggers, *Deutsche Sprachgeschichte*, vol. I, *Das Althochdeutsche und das Mittelhochdeutsche* (Reinbeck: Rowohlt, 1986), 296-300, 307-311, and Gerhard Meißburger, *Grundlagen zum Verständnis der deutschen Mönchsdichtung im 11. und 12. Jahrhundert* (Munich: Fink, 1970), 109.

2   See, for example, Werner Schröder's remarks about the spirit of Cluny ("Der Geist von Cluny und die Anfänge des frühmittelhochdeutschen Schrifttums," *PBB* [Halle] 72 [1950], 321-386):"Askese war die Losung" (327). "Das reformatorische Mönchtum hat die klassischen Studien aus den Klöstern verbannt" (330). ". . . de[r] besonder[e] Charakter des Cluniazensers . . . ist bildungsfeindlich aus Prinzip" (332). Schröder wrote further of the "Ezzolied," which he argued predated the influence of Cluny: "Es ist, als hätte eine kindlich erwartungsvolle und sorglos vertrauende Frömmigkeit hier noch einmal ein deutsches Herz ganz erfüllt, bevor der cluniazensische Stachel ihm den frommen Sinn mit unauflöslichem *zwîvel* beschwerte" (324). With the advent of Cluniac ideas in the Empire, however, "Das deutsche Volk erlebte so etwas wie eine nochmalige Bekehrung, und diesmal wurden auch die breiten Massen davon ergriffen wie von einer Krankheit" (386).

      I quote from Schröder at length because he was one of the first scholars seriously to question the appropriateness of the Cluniac label to German religious literature written after 1050, and his later work is usually far removed from nationalist cant. Indeed, he shortly revised some of the comments quoted above in a second article published five years later: "Mönchische Reformbewegungen und frühdeutsche Literaturgeschichte," *Zeitschrift der Universität Halle. Gesch.-Sprachw.* 4,2 (1955), 237-248.

3   Gertrud Schmidt quoted in Cornelius Soeteman, *Deutsche geistliche Dichtung des 11. und 12. Jahrhunderts* 2nd ed. (Stuttgart: Metzler, 1971), 6.

4   See Soeteman, 1-10, 14-18, for a review of scholarship up to 1950. Essential to any study of Early Middle High German literature is Francis G. Gentry's *Bibliographie zur frühmittelhochdeutschen geistlichen Dichtung* (Berlin: Erich Schmidt, 1992).

5   Historians proper had also began to question the older view of Cluny and its influence on Germany that had been mostly based on Ernst Sackur's study, *Die Cluniacenser in ihrer kirchlichen und allgemeinengeschichtlichen Wirksamkeit bis zur Mitte des 11. Jahrhunderts*, 2 vols. (1892/94; rpt.: Darmstadt: Wissenschaftliche Buchgesellschaft, 1965). Sackur's view was substantially revised by the works of Gerd Tellenbach and Kassius Hallinger's study *Gorze-Cluny*, 2 vols. (Rome, 1950/51). English-language scholarship has followed Hallinger. See H. E. J. Cowdrey, *The Cluniacs and Gregorian Reform* (Oxford: Oxford University Press, 1970).

6   See, e.g., H. A. and E. Frenzel's *Daten deutscher Dichtung. Chronologischer Abriß der deutschen Literaturgeschichte* (Munich: DTV, 1980), I, 4-9. More recent literary studies are more circumspect. See, for example, Max Wehrli, *Geschichte der deutschen Literatur.* Vol. 1. *Vom frühen Mittelalter bis zum Ende des 16. Jahrhunderts*

(Stuttgart: Reclam, 1984) and Dieter Kartschoke, *Geschichte der deutschen Literatur im frühen Mittelalter* (Munich: DTV, 1990).

7   See Friedrich Maurer, "Über Langzeilen und Langzeilenstrophen in der ältesten deutschen Dichtung" (1950) and "Langzeilenstrophen und fortlaufende Reimpaare" (1959) both reprinted in *Dichtung und Sprache des Mittelalters* (Bern: Franke, 1963), 174-194 and 195-213; see also the introductions to volumes I ("Die Formen der religiösen Dichtungen des 11. und 12. Jahrhunderts," 1-60) and II ("Vorwort,"VII-XXXI) of Maurer's *RD.*

8   Maurer, "Salische Geistlichendichtung" (1953), reprinted in *Dichtung und Sprache*, 168-173.

9   Meißburger, op. cit., 127-8, 141, fn. 275.

10   Meißburger, 168; 149-150.

11   Unrelated in the sense that if, for example, Rupp's statement that Cluny had little influence on the Empire is true, then it is irrelevant to the historian of German literature whether the traditional Cluny picture is true or not.

12   Heinz Rupp (Bern/Munich: Francke, 2nd. ed., 1971), 261-266.

13   Rupp, 264-265.

14   Rupp, 266-271.

15   Rupp, 272-275. Rupp writes: "Seelsorge [which he sees as the purpose of the Early Middle High German poems] ist nicht Aufgabe des Mönchtums; außerdem widerspricht es der benediktinischen Haltung, ausgerechnet in deutscher Sprache und in dichterischer Form solche Anschauungen dem *Laien* zugänglich zu machen. . . . Die Seelsorge ist Aufgabe des Weltklerus" (272).

     One need not accept Meißburger's arguments for the monastic authorship of the poems to agree with his rejection of Rupp's historically untenable thesis, to which a good part of Meißburger's book is devoted. Cf. also Thomas L. Amos: "Monks and Pastoral Care in the Early Middle Ages," in Thomas F. X. Noble and John J. Contrenti, eds., *Religion, Culture, and Society in the Early Middle Ages* (Kalamazoo, MI: Medieval Institute Pubs., 1987). Amos writes: "Even Gratian, who took a dim view of most forms of monastic pastoral work, conceded that monks could preach if they wished" (175).

16   Rupp, 274.

17   Rupp, 276.

18   Rupp, 283-284.

19   Rupp, 293. Note that Rupp is referring here mainly to an aesthetic restructuring of tradition and not to a production of new thoughts or arguments on the basis of traditional ideas.

20   Rupp, 293.

21   Rupp, 278.

22   Schröder argued that the traditional Cluny label, which he initially, if somewhat critically accepted, was inappropriate to the literature it purported to describe. Among the Early Middle High German authors, Schröder limited the influence of Cluny to Noker, Heinrich von Melk, and the Arme Hartmann (Schröder, "Der Geist von Cluny").

23   Werner Schröder, "Zum Begriff der 'binnengereimten Langzeile' in der alt-
       deutschen Versgeschichte," in *Festschrift Josef Quint*, ed. Hugo Moser et al. (Bonn:
       Emil Semmel, 1964), 194-202; "Zu alten und neuen Theorien einer altdeutschen
       'binnengereimten Langzeile'," *PBB* 87 (1965), 150-165; and "Versuch zu
       metrischer Beschreibung eines frühmittelhochdeutschen Gedichts mit einer
       forschungsgeschichtlichen Vorbemerkung," *ZfdA* 94 (1965), 196-213, 244-267.
       See also Werner Hoffmann's brief, but thorough discussion of the controversy
       between Maurer and Schröder: *Altdeutsche Metrik* (Stuttgart: Metzler, 1967), 46-
       53.

24   Schröder, "Kontinuität oder Diskontinuität in der Frühgeschichte der deutschen
       Literatur," *ZdfA* 100 (1971), 196.

25   Cf. Schröder's criticism: "Der seit dem 6. Jh. im Abendland wehende benedik-
       tinische Geist vermag so wenig ihre Einheit [of the Old High and Early Middle
       High German poems] zu konstituieren wie eine von Karl dem Großen bis zu
       Friedrich Barbarossa reichende Kontinuität zu begründen." (Schröder,
       "Kontinuität," 222).

26   Schröder, "Kontinuität," 210. To be fair to Schröder, one must admit that his pos-
       tulate of discontinuity is usually restricted to the differences between the Old
       High German and the Early Middle High German periods (see, e.g., 196-197),
       a thesis which one can more readily accept than that of a synchronic discontinu-
       ity within the Early Middle High German poems themselves, which he also
       sometimes seems to have advanced (see, e.g., 212-213).

27   Geoffrey Barraclough, *The Origins of Modern Germany* (New York: Norton,
       1984), 110.

28   See *infra*, Chapter III.

29   Hugo Kuhn, "Minne oder reht," reprinted in *Dichtung und Welt im Mittelalter*
       (Stuttgart: Metzler, 1969), 105-111.

30   Even the sharp critic of the Cluniac label, W. Schröder, excepted, as mentioned,
       the "Memento mori" from his reinterpretation of the Early Middle High
       German period and granted that the "Memento mori" was indeed an example
       of the Cluniac spirit, a position he even later refused to change (See Schröder,
       "Kontinuität," 200).

31   Hugo Kuhn, "Gestalten und Lebenskräfte der frühmittelhochdeutschen
       Dichtung," in Kuhn, 112-132.

32   Friedrich Maurer, ed., *RD*, vol. II, 2, 3-6. "God divided all His creation into two:
       this world is one part, the other is spiritual. . . . God's wisdom combined from the
       two one creation, the human being who is both body and spirit."

33   Ibid., 40, 1-11. "Afterward the evil conflict began in which many lost their lives
       when this empire was thrown into confusion for Henry IV. Murder, robbery, and
       arson destroyed the churches and lands from Denmark to Apulia, from France to
       Hungary. No one—if they would faithfully remain together—could resist those
       who organized great military campaigns against their own relatives and *familiae*.
       The entire empire turned its weapons on its own viscera, and with victorious
       sword-hand it so conquered itself that bodies of Christians lay everywhere

unburied as carrion for the howling gray wolves. When Saint Anno saw that he could not amend this, he grew weary of living longer."

Whether the passage refers to the Saxon wars or the Investiture Conflict depends on the date one assigns to the poem. Kuhn thinks of the Saxon wars ("Gestalten," 125), while Eberhard Nellmann thinks it could refer to either: *Das Annolied*, Ed. and trs. by Eberhard Nellmann, 2nd ed. (Stuttgart: Reclam, 1979), 113-114.

34 Kuhn, "Gestalten," 129.

35 Kuhn, "Gestalten," 131.

36 Schützeichel was probably led to this interpretation by some remarks in Herman Jacobs's detailed study *Die Hirsauer* (Cologne: Böhlau, 1961), 229-232. Jacobs had criticized Rupp in passing for brushing over the importance of the reform movement for the vernacular works of the eleventh century: "All dies wird von Rupp teils nicht erwähnt, teils unterschätzt. Das "Memento mori" des Noker von Zwiefalten [?] könnte beispielsweise sehr wohl für Laienbrüder im Kloster gedichtet worden sein" (231). Jacobs's judicious remarks on the uniqueness of the monastery of Hirsau within the reform movement should be remembered when considering Meißburger's sometimes undifferentiated picture of the monastic reform movement.

37 "Das Memento mori. Ein Beitrag zum sozialgeschichtlichen Verständnis der Gleichheitsforderung im frühen Mittelalter," *Euphorion* 68 (1974), 337.

38 Hans Joachim Gernentz, "Soziale Anschauungen und Forderungen einiger früh-mittelhochdeutscher geistlicher Dichter," *Weimarer Beiträge* 3 (1957), 402-428, and Ewald Erb, *Geschichte der deutschen Literatur von den Anfängen bis 1160* (Berlin [East]: Volk und Wissen, 1964), I, 2.

Gernentz's article is in effect a restatement of the old Cluniac-ascetic inter-pretation with a vulgar Marxist twist, according to which "der Asket (wird) in seinem Bemühen, die Welt seinem himmlischen Ideal anzupassen, zum Revolutionär. Allerdings liegt der Schwerpunkt der umstürzlerischen Absichten nicht auf politischem, sondern auf sittlich-religiösem Gebiet. Aber der betonte Hinweis auf die ursprüngliche Gleichheit der Menschen und die Aufforderung an alle, in gleicher Weise vor den Verlockungen des Diesseits zu fliehen und ein Leben nach mönchischen Idealen zu führen, ist eine Kampfansage an das System der feudalen Klassengliederung und der hierarchischen Kirche" (407). Erb in his official literary history had little use for such historically unfounded hypotheses.

39 Kaiser relies heavily on the works of Theodor Meyer and Karl Bosl to justify this view. On Meyer and Bosl, see Chapter II.

40 Kaiser, 362 and 365.

41 Kaiser, 369-370.

42 "*Vruot . . . verdamnot?* Memento mori, vv. 61-62" *ZfdA* 108 (1979), 299-306 and "Noker's *Memento mori* and the Desire for Peace," *ABäG* 16 (1981), 25-62.

43 Gentry, "Noker," 43-53. Schützeichel had also translated *reht* in the "Memento mori" as *iustitia*, but as mentioned, he understood this to mean "sacraments."

44 Gentry, "Noker," 53-54.

45 Gentry, "Noker," 62.

46   Gentry, "Noker," 61.

47   In most instances I follow the *opinio communis* as presented in the *Verfasserlexikon*.

48   See Soeteman, 33-38 for a review of the problem of genre in the Early Middle High German works.

49   Cf. Sybilla Mähl's comment on Carolingian Latin theological works: "Ein Motiv, ein Schema kann sich im Gefüge der verschiedenen Gattungen—wobei wir den Begriff nicht zu eng fassen wollen—in jeweils sehr unterschiedlicher Bedeutung präsentieren. Die Gattungen unterscheiden sich ja nicht nur in Stoff, Form und Denkmethode, sondern auch in ihrer Herkunft voneinander. Ihre Kontinuität und Eigengesetzlichkeit bestimmt in erstaunlichem Maße die Aussagen über ihren Gegenstand und wiegt oft schwerer als die persönliche Eigenart der einzelnen Schriftsteller." *Quadriga virtutum. Die Kardinaltugenden in der Geistesgeschichte der Karolingerzeit* (Cologne: Böhlau, 1969), 3.

50   See Chapter II.

51   See Gisela Vollmann-Profe, *Von den Anfängen bis zum hohen Mittelalter. Wiederbeginn volkssprachlicher Schriftlichkeit im hohen Mittelalter (1050/60-1160/70)*, Vol. I, Part 2 of *Geschichte der deutschen Literatur von den Anfängen bis zum Beginn der Neuzeit*, ed. by Joachim Heinzle (Königstein/Ts: Athenäum, 1986). The succinct summary of Vollmann-Profe's categories is quoted from Hartmut Freytag's review in *ZfdA* 117 (1989), 134.

52   I am referring especially to such works as the "Vorauer" and "Millstätter Sündenklagen," which are quite different in form and purpose from the smaller "Beichten." Similarly, the concept "meditative" seems better to describe long passages of Frau Ava's works, whose general form, however, is epic. "Meditative" is used here in the sense in which R. W. Southern discussed the "Meditations" of St. Anselm. Southern contrasted the traditional prayers of the Carolingian epoch with the novel aspects of Anselm's meditations, including an "immense elaboration" of traditional forms, a "much greater sense of the independent agency of the saints in the work of salvation, and a new emphasis on the inexplicable primacy of the will" (R. W. Southern, *Saint Anselm and his Biographer* [Cambridge: Cambridge University, 1963], 44).

53   Whether one should therefore rely like Rupp only on Patristic and Carolingian theologians as exponents of this tradition is, however, doubtful. In an exemplary and detailed study of the Early Middle High German poem known as the "Summa theologiae," Hartmut Freytag noted that Rupp's citing from the works of Alcuin and Hrabanus Maurus as parallels to the ideas expressed in the poem is unjustified and comes at the expense of generally ignoring the German poet's near contemporary Honorius Augustodunensis: "Die Nähe der 'Summa Theologiae' zu Honorius bleibt am auffallendsten" (Freytag, *Kommentar zur frühmittelhochdeutschen Summa Theologiae* [Munich: Fink, 1970], 29).

54   David A. Wells, "Die Erläuterung frühmittelhochdeutscher geistlicher Texte," in L. P. Johnson, et al., eds., *Studien zur frühmittelhochdeutschen Literatur. Cambridger Colloquium 1971* (Berlin: Erich Schmidt, 1974), 161.

55   Wells, 161.

56   Maurer, ed., *RD*, I, 255, ll. 7, 1-4. "God created you all; you stem from one man. He commanded you to live in this life with love, but you have ignored that you were one man. Even had you done nothing else wrong, you would have to suffer for this transgression."

57   Maurer, *RD*, II, 267, ll. 1, 4-7. "We should live and act as one. Unfortunately we have not been born so. There was one woman who first bore us, she gave birth to two different children and so their progeny have ever since been. She bore a son who murdered his brother."

58   *König Rother*, eds., Theodor Frings and Joachim Kuhnt (Bonn/Leipzig: Kurt Schroeder, 1922), ll. 1198-1202. I have added modern punctuation and capitalization. "What strange thing do you want to do to them? Their father was called Adam, from whom we all come. You should remember God in these wretched people."

59   Ibid., Ermlitzer Fragment, page 47, E, b.

60   Hermann Suchier, ed., *Reimpredigt* (Halle, 1879), strophe 30.

61   As Gernentz, for example, argued, 406.

62   As Kaiser maintained, 363 and 367.

63   Gentry, "Memento mori," 40-41.

64   See, e. g., the problems with which American slave-holders were confronted in view of the biblical Adamic unity: Thomas Virgil Peterson, *Ham and Japeth: The Mythic World of Whites in the Antebellum South* (Methuen, N.J., 1978).

65   Gershom Scholem, "Offenbarung und Tradition als religiöse Kategorien im Judentum," in *Über einige Grundbegriffe des Judentums* (Frankfurt a. M: Suhrkamp, 1970), 96.

66   Michael Gilsenan, *Recognizing Islam: Religion and Society in the Modern Arab World* (New York: Pantheon, 1982), 28.

67   Rupp, 25.

68   Rupp, 278.

CHAPTER I

Early Middle High German *reht*

In an older study on the social demands and views of the Early Middle High German poets, Maria Mackensen underlined the ubiquity of the concept of *reht* in the Early Middle High German poems: "The idea of *Recht* is known to all religious poetry beginning with the Memento mori."[1] Rupp, too recognized this in numerous comments on the works although, as shown, he argued that this *reht* should not be historically specified, for it plays an important—and one assumes identical—role "in the Christian thought of every time."[2] The centrality of the concept of *reht* in these poems has never been seriously debated. But what is the Early Middle German understanding of *reht*?

One should not expect any theoretical discussion of what *reht* means from the Early Middle High German authors themselves, although opportunities were available. The *Tnugdalus* (ca. 1160–1190), for example, by the Regensburg priest Alber, is one of the few Early Middle High German works[3] for which an unequivocal source can be named. Alber's ca. 2,200-line poem is a translation/adaptation of the monk Marcus' *Visio Tnugdali* (1149), a very popular account of the Irish knight Tundalus' vision of Hell and Purgatory experienced during three days while he lay in apparent death.[4] Like a twelfth-century Dante, Tundalus is shown in vivid detail the pains and torments of the condemned souls of murderers, traitors, the proud and avaricious, thieves and rapists, etc. Tundalus himself suffers many of the same pains as the sinners in the course of his tour of Hell. In the Latin original, he finally asks of his Virgil, an unnamed angel, why he and the sinners have to suffer such miserable torments. How can one speak of God's mercy in the face of such misery? The guardian angel responds with a concatenation of biblical and theological commonplaces on the relation between God's mercy and justice: "God, although he is merciful, is nonetheless just. Justice renders to each what he has deserved; mercy forgives many offenses deserving punishment."[5] God would not be just, says the angel, if he left sin unpunished, yet there can be no justice without mercy and no mercy without justice. The angel then explains this paradox:

For if those sinners who are not penitent are mercifully spared while in the body then they must suffer here [in Hell] according to the dictates of justice. Although earthly comfort is denied to the just in the body for their excesses, when they leave their bodies a lasting treasure will be mercifully granted to them with the angels.[6]

Justice and mercy are thus balanced through the dispensing of the one in this life and the other in the life to come. Compared with St. Anselm's wrestling with the paradox, of course, this is not terribly sophisticated.[7] Yet Marcus at least gives definitions of justice and mercy and attempts to reconcile them with some degree of abstraction.

In Alber's vernacular version of *Tnugdalus*, the concept of *iustitia* disappears, except in its negative form "unrehte," and the poet instead concentrates on *misericordia*, which is not, however, so much defined as described. The angel's answer to the Irish knight's question about God's mercy is very forthright: mercy to the penitent, punishment to the incorrigible:

> grôze genâde got begât,
> iedoch sî niht enstât
> über ander deheinen,
> wan über den einen
> der mit riuwen wirt bevangen,
> des er zunrehte hât begangen,
> unde des widerkêret
> als uns diu schrift lêret. . . .
> swer mit den sünden blîbet
> und von im niht entrîbet
> unrehte gelust
> unde ander ârkust
> unz an sînen tôt,
> der muoz lîden dise nôt.[8]

While Alber shies from an abstract consideration of *reht*, he readily gives concrete examples of the practice of *unreht*, even where his source is more reticent or general. Marcus, for example, had devoted a chapter of his *Visio* to the evil of Satan and the torments he must suffer. With Satan are the worst sinners: "Such . . . as those who completely deny Christ or who do the works of those who deny him, like adulterers," etc.[9] The very worst sinners, according to Marcus, are however the "potentes" who misuse their God-given power by oppressing their "subjects." This mentioning of the concept of "potentia" gives Marcus an opportunity to discuss power and the duties of the powerful toward their subjects in a manner similar to his comments on mercy and justice.[10]

In his version of this passage, Alber again ignores the chance to rise to even a moderate level of abstraction and instead describes the *unreht* of the "potentes" in a long passage, for which there is no parallel in the Latin original:

hie sint die begênt den gewalt,
sî sîn junc oder alt,
die sich niht kunnen erbarmen
und die ruobent die armen.
ze allen ir vreisen
verstôzent witwen unde weisen,
und unrehte rihtent,
und die sich phlihtent
ze aller ungüete:
die sint in der glüete.
die sich selbe rihtent,
ir untertâne beswichent
mit ungefüeger stiure,
die sint in dem fiure.
die velschlîchez reht sprehent,
die den armen abe brechent
ir lützelen gewin;
die dar an wendent ir sin,
die des alles blîbent âne riuwen
die müezen hie entriuwen
immer alsô brinnen.
wæren sî in rehten sinnen,
sî liezen die gewinne
und ledegten sich von hinne.[11]

Alber's *Tnugdalus* is a late work and with its strong interest in knights and their conduct already shares much in common with high courtly literature. But in his eschewal of any theoretical explanation of *reht* and in his concentration on the practice of *reht*, Alber is typical of all the Early Middle High German poets. Equally typical is his clear denunciation of *unreht*, which offers a succinct distillation of the Early Middle High German poets' strictures on the duties of the rich and the powerful.

Since Early Middle High German authors offer no formal discussion or definition of *reht*, one might hope that its meaning could be inferred from their usage. This is, however, no simple matter. We have seen how both Schützeichel and Gentry had interpreted *reht* in the "Memento mori" as *iustitia*, while at the same time understanding quite different things by it. Middle High German usage of *reht* is often profoundly ambiguous. Consider for example, the anonymous poem "Vom Rechte" (ca. 1150), from which, as its title implies, one would expect the clearest understanding of what Early Middle High German *reht* means.[12]

"Vom Rechte" begins with a paean to *reht*, which has been the source of not a little confusion:

Nieman ist so here
so daz reht zware.
wan got ist ze ware

ein rehtir rihtære.
von diu hiez er den sinen chneht
vil starke minnen daz reht,
daz er nach im vienge
unde sin reht begienge.
wan mit im nemach nieman gestan,
er newelle daz reht han.
wan er scheidet die unrehten
von sin selbes chnehten.[13]

Every commentator has remarked on the lack of clarity in the poet's use of *reht*. In the first and most important detailed analysis of "Vom Rechte," Carl Kraus wrote with frustration of the poet's ambiguity: "The poet uses the word *reht* in the most varied meanings without being aware of their differences . . . already in line three he relates the *duty* of line two to God's *justice*."[14] For Kraus, *reht* thus means either duty or justice.

The prominent literary historian Gustav Ehrismann, on the other hand, wrote that "To understand the poem it is first necessary to determine the meaning of the concept of *reht*. Middle High German *reht* means both right [*Recht*] as well as duty, the right that comes to me from others and the duty I have towards others. According to the teachings of the Church, right is established by God. Here [in "Vom Rechte"] almost exclusively duties are meant . . . ."[15] Ehrismann, however, also equates some of the instances of *reht* in the poem with *iustitia*, and thus for him *reht* has at least three meanings: right, duty, and *iustitia*.[16]

Ingeborg Schröbler translated *reht*, like most recent commentators, simply as New High German *Recht*. *Recht* can mean either the totality of laws regulating a community (English, "the law"), which German jurists refer to as "objective *Recht*," or an individual's rights, which the jurists call "subjective *Recht*." But she also refers to *reht* as "duty" as well as "order" and, in its "narrow sense," as "justice."[17]

Stephan Speicher, in the most recent full commentary on the poem, also uses New High German *Recht* to translate *reht*, but he is highly critical of Ehrismann's differentiation of *reht* into "right" and "duty." Instead, Speicher relies solely on the legal historian Fritz Kern's well-known conception of early medieval *Recht*, according to which *Recht* is an indivisible combination of subjective rights that together constitute the legal order, the "law."[18] Speicher paraphrases Kern's views, showing how *reht* also means what is "right" or "just": "If one keeps in mind that what was *reht* was at the same time always right and just and that it not only required respect for the rights of others but in fact was constituted by these rights, then Kraus and Ehrismann's differentiation [between subjective right and objective law] becomes obsolete."[19]

Early Middle High German *reht*, according to these different scholars, can thus mean "right," as well as "duty," "law" as well as "order," and "the Right" as well as "the Just," and sometimes simply *iustitia*.

The standard lexicons of Middle High German cannot help resolve these difficulties, for their definitions of *reht* are similarly diffuse. Thus BMZ divide the meanings of *reht* into subjective right, "a general norm," objective law, "Standesrecht" (the Law of Estates), which includes both rights and duties, as well as "the Right," "the Just," a court, a judicial sentence, and a legally imposed fine.[20] Since BMZ and Lexer generally base their definitions on post-1170 works, one might turn to Ulrich Pretzel's *Nachträge* to Lexer's *Mittelhochdeutsches Handwörterbuch*, which often cover the Early Middle High German period. Unfortunately, however, the *Nachträge* offer little to clarify the meaning of *reht* in "Vom Rechte."[21] Beate Hennig, finally, in her completely revised version of Lexer offers a similarly wide range of meanings, including some specialized uses such as "extreme unction."[22]

The contradictions and ambiguities of literary historians' and lexicographers' understanding of *reht* lead one to the conclusion that an immanent interpretation of the "Vom Rechte" poet's use of *reht* is difficult, if not impossible. In a sense, therefore, usage alone does not determine meaning.[23] While most of the commentators blame the author of "Vom Rechte" for the obscurity of the concept of *reht* in the poem, one might do better to ask if the source of these difficulties lies rather in the sometimes confused conceptual understanding we moderns have of *reht*.[24] We are too often ignorant of the assumptions on which medieval writers based their usage.

An alternative approach to the immanent understanding of Early Middle High German *reht* is suggested by Speicher's reliance on an historical/legal approach to the concept. One would naturally expect legal historians to be especially interested in what *reht* means and that they could perhaps bring some clarity to the concept. Speicher's reference to Fritz Kern's seminal study, "Recht und Verfassung im Mittelalter" (1919), is surely the best starting point for such an approach.[25] For Kern, the opening lines of "Vom Rechte," "**N**ieman ist so here,/ wie daz reht zware," are a *locus classicus* for an understanding of medieval law, which Kern sees as a conflation of ecclesiastical, canonical, and especially ancient Germanic concepts. The poet's lines, in Kern's view, show the sublimity[26] of the concept in the Middle Ages: "The law stands over all men, even over the monarchs."[27]

Medieval law, according to Kern is always old; "new law is a contradiction in terms."[28] Law is not legislated or decreed, it must rather be discovered. The ultimate source of law is God, and "the law being sacred, both ruler and subject, State and citizen, are equally authorized to preserve it."[29] The content of law is always good, for there was no differentiation in the Middle Ages between morality, equity, and law. Law in the Middle Ages was indivisible:

> For the Middle Ages, there was no distinction between objective and subjective law; every stone of the legal edifice, of the objective law as the sum-total of all subjective rights, was equally sacred and valuable, according to the lofty theories of the period.[30]

The medieval unity of objective law and subjective rights together with the moral character of law are still expressed in modern German, which "relies on orthography alone to distinguish what is 'right' (*recht*) from what is 'law' (*Recht*)."[31]

Kern's understanding of *Recht* is not without difficulties. To appreciate them, however, it is necessary to have some grasp of where Kern's theories fit in the acrimonious disputes among German historians and legal scholars.[32] Kern's essay has been influential not only because he brought such clarity to the concept of *Recht*, but even more importantly because his understanding of *Recht* could be readily appropriated by those German constitutional historians who hoped to overthrow the traditional legal historians' picture of early medieval *Recht*.[33] There is another reason to sketch some of the issues that divide legal and constitutional scholars. Literary historians often refer to such scholars' works as if they represented some kind of objective, uncontroversial scheme into which their own less reliable literary documents can be safely placed. But the documents and evidence over which legal and constitutional scholars argue are often ambiguous; one ought best to confront the documents themselves—not to ignore the expert mediation of others, of course, but in order to examine the evidence such mediators provide.

Some nineteenth- and early twentieth-century German exponents of the legal and social history of the Middle Ages achieved such authoritative status in their nation's scholarship that the synthesis of their work is generally still referred to as "die herrschende Lehre" (the dominant teaching), or sometimes simply the "HL." Georg Waitz (1813–1886), generally considered the originator and inspiration of this synthesis, argued for a strong continuity between the Germanic period, as first described by Tacitus, and medieval German history. According to this view, there was no substantial break between Germanic conceptions of law and justice and those of the Carolingians, who merely imposed a veneer of Christianity onto the Germanic concepts. The Germanic notion of law was the foundation for the freedom of the full members ("die Gemeinfreien") of the Germanic tribes, who while accepting the concept of kingship, knew of no hereditary nobility under the king. The "principes," of whom Tacitus wrote, were merely elected servants of the king. The Germanic conception of kingship was thus in Waitz's view a kind of primitive constitutional monarchy, in which *Recht* guaranteed the freedom and rights of the "liberi" or "franci" of the Germanic law books or *Leges*. The height of Germanic kingship, in this view, was the reign of Charlemagne upon whose death the traditional Germanic ideal began a process of degeneration that ended with the demise of the Staufen dynasty in the 13th century.[34]

Waitz's views, obviously colored by a liberal constitutional monarchism, dominated German legal history until the early 1920's and 1930's when a new school of constitutional historians, connected with the names of Theodor Meyer, Walter Schlesinger, Otto Brunner, Karl Bosl, and Heinrich Dannebauer arose. This new generation of scholars, while accepting the continuity of Germanic and German history, rejected the notion of Germanic freemen and the importance of law in guaranteeing their legal rights. The new constitutional historians, who favored non-legal sources as evidence for their theories, placed "Herrschaft" (lordship or domination) in the center of their reinterpretation of medieval history and law.[35]

The juristic niceties of traditional legal historians and the importance of normative law were swept aside in this new picture, which emphasized the continuity
not of the *liberi* or *franci*, but of a noble ruling class. Aristocratic violence and force
replaced constitutional consent, or as Graus once commented, law was replaced by
domination.[36]

Kern's view of medieval *Recht* was so readily accepted by these constitutional
historians in part because it had diminished the role of normative law.[37] In Kern's
own words, "We are not . . . to infer from the impressive sublimity of the medieval
idea of law that in practice the law was particularly sacred . . . ." On the contrary,
"power was decisive."[38]

Starting in the 1960s the views of these constitutional historians have in turn
come under a gradually increasing attack from a new generation of historians and
legal historians. The continuity of Germanic and German history and ideas has
been seriously questioned. Most recent legal historians instead emphasize the legal
and conceptual continuity between Late Antiquity and the rise of the
Christian/Germanic kingdoms. Many of the leading concepts of constitutional
historians, such as "Herrschaft" and "Adel" have been questioned and found either
inadequate or simply not justified by the sources.[39]

It is difficult for literary historians to orient themselves in the face of these con-
troversies between legal and constitutional historians. Often one has the impression that their differences are sometimes reducible to their interests in normative
law on the one hand, and political and social "reality" on the other, differences
which in turn might be traceable to their preferred sources: legal texts versus char-
ters and chronicles.[40] It should also be obvious that all of these issues were influenced by contemporary development in German politics. This is not to say that
arguments about fascism underlay scholarly debates, but it is doubtless the case that
they played a role.

In view of these disagreements among specialists about the continuity of
Germanic concepts of law, historians can no longer argue that the meaning of
medieval legal terms can be uncritically explained by reference to their Germanic
cognates. Rather, one must now approach all such claims with skepticism.
Skepticism is especially called for in an investigation of the concept of *reht*.
Constitutional historians' reliance on Kern's good and old law to buttress their
theories of "Herrschaft" has been the particular target of many attacks, especially
from the so-called "Göttingen School" of legal historians under the inspiration of
Karl Kroeschell. Kroeschell himself has written:

> The usual argument about the alteriety of medieval law as compared with the
> modern age, the well-known doctrine, most successfully formulated by Fritz
> Kern, of old, unchangeable, good, divine law, is no longer acceptable. It is orient-
> ed to a conception of law that has long since been superseded by a more com-
> plicated and differentiated picture. . . .[41]

Rather than hypothesizing a Germanic concept of *Recht* that underlies
medieval ideas about law, as Kern had done, Kroeschell proposed an empirical
investigation of the Latin terminology of the early Middle Ages, specifically the

words "ius" and "lex," and its evolution from Classical and Late Antiquity. The formative Latin usage should then be contrasted with the first attempts at translation of these Latin concepts into Old High German (starting roughly in 700).

In Classical Latin, according to Kroeschell, *ius* usually meant objective law, but on occasion it had the same double meaning as modern German *Recht*, namely objective law and subjective right.[42] In Vulgar West Roman Law, however, *ius* became more restricted to subjective right or privilege.[43] *Lex*, on the other hand, which in Classical Latin usually referred to a specific and enacted "law," came in the Early Middle Ages to mean "objective law," not as an abstract norm, but as a "judgement rendered in concreto."[44]

The Old High German glosses and translations of these Latin concepts are fairly consistent, according to Kroeschell: *ius* in its ablative form *iure* is initially translated by "piuualti" or "kiwaltidu," but these soon give way to the typical translations of the eighth through tenth centuries, "pirehte" or "mitrehte."[45] The ablative usage of *ius*, however, should not tempt one to the conclusion that *ius* (subjective right) was always translated by *reht*: "to assume *ius* and *Recht* were equivalent would be an . . . oversimplification. . . . both concepts only gradually approached one another and came to have similar meanings.[46] The word *reht* is used to translate not only *ius*, but *iustitia* as well. While *iustitia* often has the meaning *ius* or subjective right, its Classical meaning "justice," no doubt highly influenced by biblical usage, significantly colors the vernacular *reht*. Kroeschell concludes: "That the concept of *iustitia* is the source of meaning and the German *reht* the recipient, that there was no Germanic conception equivalent to *iustitia* can be seen from the fact that the German word "Gerechtigkeit" [justice] is a loan formation, modeled on Latin.[47]

According to Kroeschell, medieval German *reht* is thus a combination of *ius*, or subjective right, and *iustitia*, while the regular Old High German translation for objective law is usually *êwa* or *ê*. This consistent distinction between *reht* and *êwa* makes Kern's concept of an indivisible *Recht*, uniting objective law and subjective rights and always good or just, highly questionable.[48] Kroeschell concludes on the basis of his investigation of *ius*, *iustitia*, and *lex* and their Old High German equivalents *reht* and *êwa*, that "A traditional Germanic-German conception of an unchangeable, good, old *Recht* is not to be found."[49] Kern's concept of *Recht* is thus inadequate for the early Middle Ages.

In the course of the twelfth century, Kroeschell argues, the concepts begin to change. *Ius* regains its primary classical meaning of objective law and begins in turn to influence the meaning of *reht*, but this is a slow and sometimes confusing process:

> Naturally *ius* and *reht* do not cease meaning subjective right, and there are numerous instances where the apparently objective meaning is still to be understood in its subjective sense. . . . In general, the previous meanings do not simply disappear in the twelfth century, rather they continue to be used. At the same time, the words have new contents, which had previously been unknown and in which the understanding of *Recht* of that time is expressed.[50]

Thus, in the High Middle Ages, *reht* slowly came to its modern double meaning of subjective right and objective law. Equally important, however, is the development of a new high medieval conception of *reht* as the basis of the divine order whose first vernacular expression, Kroeschell claims, is none other than the opening lines of "Vom Rechte," which to Kroeschell appears as "a rhymed tract on the theological doctrine of *Recht*."[51]

Kroeschell's conclusions thus far are not so much a total rejection of Kern's work as an introduction of a more carefully used terminology and a radical revision of Kern's chronology. Kroeschell seems to believe that Kern's concept of *Recht* is perhaps appropriate to the High Middle Ages. His comments would appear to confirm Speicher's reliance on Kern to explain the prologue of "Vom Rechte," but run counter to Speicher's contention, based on Kern, that the poem is a succinct expression of Germanic-German *Recht*.[52]

Parallels between the use of *reht* in "Vom Rechte" and in other, much older Early Middle High German poems should, however, make one wary of accepting Kroeschell's understanding of the "Vom Rechte" poet's use of *reht* in a new sense of divinely established objective law guaranteeing subjective rights. Kroeschell's conclusions, moreover, have been seriously modified in an extended study by his student Gerhard Köbler on the meaning *Recht* in the early Middle Ages. While Köbler follows Kroeschell's method of first determining the Latin concepts and then comparing them with their Old High German vernacular translations, his investigation is based on far more material and his explanations of the Latin and vernacular terms are both more differentiated and convincing.[53]

Köbler generally confirms Kroeschell's sketch of the Classical meanings or *ius* and *lex*, but he also shows the degree to which *ius* was not confined to "objective law," but could also refer to a subjective right, while *lex* showed a gradual development even in Late Antiquity from its original meaning of a concrete "law" to the general concept of objective law, whereby the biblical usage of the *lex vetus* of Moses and the *lex nova* of Christ played an important role.[54]

In the early Middle Ages, *ius*, as Kroeschell had claimed, generally refers to a subjective right and is used synonymously with *potestas*.[55] The ablative form, *iure*, however, reveals important distinctions that had been overlooked by Kroeschell. *Iure* has less a concrete legal meaning than a more general sense of *legitime* or *rationabiliter*, with which it is frequently exchanged. *Iure* is thus not "according to one's rights," as Kroeschell had suggested, but "legitimately, rightly, or justly."[56] Finally, Köbler claims *ius* can also preserve its dominant Classical meaning, objective law.[57] *Lex* is used less frequently than *ius* in the early Middle Ages and often has a religious connotation, but it gradually regains its Classical meaning of an individual law beginning already in the ninth century.[58]

In the case of the Old High German translations of *ius* and *lex*, Köbler comes to very different conclusions from Kroeschell. Although *ius* is sometimes translated by *reht*, they are not usually synonyms. Köbler's more careful differentiation between *ius* and its ablative form *iure* shows that in most of the cases where *ius* is translated by *reht*, it is the ablative usage which is equated: *iure* (which, as noted had a non-legal meaning, "rightly" or "justly") = *mit rehte* or *bi rehte*.[59] In its non-ablative form and especially when connected with *potestas, ius* is translated by *giwalt* (as are *potestas* itself, *dominatio, potentia, imperium*, etc.).[60]

The noun *reht* alone is overwhelmingly a translation of *iustitia*,[61] and alternative translations of *iustitia* are almost non-existent.[62] *Reht* is also used to translate *iustificatio, aequitas, rectitudo*, and *aequum*, while *unreht* is used for *iniuria, iniquitas, nefas*, and *pravitas*. The adjective *reht*, finally, is given for *iustus, rectus, aequus*, and its adverbial negation, *unrehto*, for *iniuste, improbe, indigne*, and *corrupte*.[63] *Lex*, on the other hand, as Kroeschell had claimed, was usually translated in Old High German as *êwa*, which was also used to translate *ius* in its less common meaning of objective law.[64] Köbler's evidence that *iure* (justly or rightly) = *mit rehte, ius* or *potestas* (subjective right) = *giwalt*, and that *iustitia* = *reht* vitiates Kroeschell's claim that *iustitia* is often used synonymously with *ius* and that both mean subjective right. *Iustitia* means "justice."

Köbler also attempts to disprove Kroeschell's contention that there was no Germanic concept of justice. To do this he turns to the etymological roots of *reht*. *Reht* is cognate with Gothic *raihts*, Anglo-Saxon *riht* (modern English "right"), Old Norse *rettr*, as well as Latin *rectus* and Greek *orektos*, from all of which an Indo-European adjectival root **reg* has been hypothesized. The primary meaning of **reg* has been postulated as "straight," but the written tradition already shows that the extended meanings "just," "justified," "true," "proper," and "flawless" began to prevail early on.[65] According to Köbler, then, *reht* was used in the sense of "justice," etc. even before the influence of Classical and Medieval Latin *iustitia* and is therefore Germanic in origin, which explains why *iustus* and *iustitia* were so consistently translated by the adjectival and substantive forms of *reht*.

Köbler's claim that there was a Germanic concept of *iustitia*, which he describes as "that which is correct," is controversial but need not affect the study of the meaning of *reht* in the Early Middle High German period. The works of this time are products of Christians, whether monks, priests, pious laymen or, as in the case of Frau Ava, laywomen, who are clearly not recent converts from some pagan Germanic world-view. Their concept of *reht*, therefore, is undoubtedly influenced by Latin tradition, either directly or indirectly.

Köbler concludes that *reht* in the sense of "the Right" or *iustitia* gradually changed to take on its common high medieval and modern double meaning of subjective right and objective law:

> The connection between *ius* and *reht* is still rarer in Notker's works [who died in 1022] than that between *iustitia* and *reht*, which from the beginning of vernacular translations was very stable. Therefore *reht* should not be understood to mean law [*das Recht*] but that which is correct or proper [*das Richtige*] . . . . The more frequently *iure* and *reht* were connected—perhaps the more frequently 'correct' judgement was judicially determined—the easier it became to render other uses of *ius* with *reht* and thereby expand the content of *reht*.[66]

It is important to note that Köbler's detailed study has a chronological limit of 1100 and that for the vernacular translations of legal terms he limits himself to the Old High German period, that is up to around 1050. Köbler's work thus can provide extraordinarily useful material and suggestions for the historian of Early Middle High German literature, but it cannot be used conclusively to determine the meaning of *reht* in the years following 1050. Rather, as Köbler himself has argued, these years were a period of fluctuation and change during which the original meaning of *reht* as *iustitia* is slowly widened to include the high medieval ambiguity of *ius*, first "subjective right" and finally "objective law."

Köbler sees this process of change in the meaning of *reht* as having been completed by the time of Eike's *Sachsenspiegel* (1224/25). Nowhere does he draw any firm conclusions about the Early Middle High German period. But when Speicher claims that because it deals with an earlier period, Köbler's book is irrelevant to understanding the concept of *reht* in "Vom Rechte," he is begging the question.[67]

Köbler's study clearly shows that Old High German *reht* means *iustitia* and that this *iustitia* is thoroughly infused with Christian overtones. As a working hypothesis for an understanding of *reht* in the Early Middle High German period, one might reasonably assume that Early Middle High German *reht* also means *iustitia* unless it can be shown that the poets' use of the concept has already been influenced by the changed meaning of *ius* as "right" and "law."

It might be argued, however, that my working hypothesis that *recht* means *iustitia* is too slavishly dependent on the Göttingen School's leading contention that Latin concepts determine vernacular usage, a reversal of the traditional legal and constitutional historians' method of giving primacy to the Germanic vernacular languages. Early Middle High German literature is so thoroughly imbued with Christian concepts that this objection, which might have some validity for so-called secular texts, seems to carry little force. For the sake of argument, however, let us ask if there is any solid evidence of a Germanic substratum to the Old High German concept of *reht*, which in turn might have influenced Early Middle High German *reht*.

A useful approach to this question is through the work of Ruth Schmidt-Wiegand who has steered a middle course in her studies on Old High German *reht*. She acknowledges many of the conclusions of Kroeschell and Köbler, yet still approaches the content of *reht* first from the vernacular. She begins, therefore, with the derived etymological meaning of the adjective *reht* and claims that this original Germanic meaning, "straight," is still prevalent in, for example, Otfrid's *Evangelienbuch* (between 863 and 871).[68] She claims further that this primary meaning expands to include "appropriate, correct", and "true."[69] From this she concludes that the noun *reht* "accordingly refers to that which is *reht*, in Otfried an unequivocally subjective stance."[70]

Her examples are not especially convincing. When Otfrid writes of Zacharias and Elizabeth that:

> Wárun siu béthu   góte filu drúdu
>   joh íogiwar sínaz   gibot fúllentaz,
> Wízzod sínan   ío wírkendan
>   joh reht minnonti   ana méin0dati.[71]

it would seem that *reht minnon*, perhaps suggested by the words "iusti" or "iustificationes," in the biblical text, is simply a translation of the biblical phrase "iustitiam diligere."[72] It is in any case unclear how this use of *reht* is an example of a "subjective stance."

Schmidt-Wiegand also points to Otfrid's description of the prophetess Anna, who serves God with praying and fasting:

> Si állo stunta bétota   joh filu ouch fásteta,
>   gótes willen húatta   joh thíonost sinaz úabta.
> Dáges inti náhtes   fleíz si thar thes réhtes . . . .[73]

She then compares this passage with Jesus' command to his disciples:

> Bi thíu sit io wákar   állaz iuer líb hiar,
>   dáges inti náhtes   so thénket io thes réhtes.[74]

and concludes "Praying, fasting, keeping vigils: all this indicates that *reht* in Otfrid is a way of acting."[75] This is surely not so clear in the last cited example, and one might well question whether Anna's praying and fasting are truly equivalent to "reht flîzan."[76] Schmidt-Wiegand's examples are simply too isolated to serve as the basis of any firm conclusion.

Otfrid in fact seems most clearly to use the noun *reht* to translate or suggest *iustitia*. He writes, for example:

> "Theist gibót minaz zi íu: ir iuih mínnot untar íu,
>   joh íagilih thes thénke,   thero mínnono ni wénke."
> In tho druhtin zélita,   want ér se selbo wélita,
>   mánota sie thes náhtes   managfaltes réhtes.[77]

And in III, 7, 68, he uses the phrase "widar rehte," which can only mean "contra iustitiam" or perhaps "contra legem" (in its objective sense!). It surely cannot refer to a "subjective" attitude.

Otfrid's adjectival use of *reht*, furthermore, often translates or seems to suggest *iustus*:

> In hímil farent thánana   thie gotes drútthegana,
>   thie rehte joh thie guate   blídlichemo múate.[78]

and especially:

> Nirdeilet únrehto,   thaz iamen ádal ahto;
>   duet rehtaz úrdeili   úns zuein hiar giméini![79]

Schmidt-Wiegand, following Kroeschell, says of Otfrid's use of *bí rehte* that the phrase is probably used "with the simple idea that one is acting *mit Recht* when one ... fully utilizes a given power (*giwalt*)."[80] Again, a close examination of Otfrid's usage does not substantiate this claim, but rather supports Köbler's view that *bí rehte* means *iuste*, whereby this contains no legal sense, but simply means "rightly," "properly," or "justly."[81]

As a final example of Otfrid's use of *reht*, Schmidt-Wiegand refers to the poet's depiction of Annas' interrogation of Jesus. A servant of Annas' strikes Jesus after reproving Him for an ambiguous answer. Otfrid writes of Jesus:

> Mit wángon tho bifilten   bigán er ántwurten,
> mánota sie thes náhtes   thes wízzodes réhtes,
> "Ob íh hiar úbilo gispráh,   zéli thu thaz úngimáh;
> spráh ih avur alawár,   ziu fíllist thu mih thanne sár?"[82]

Schmidt-Wiegand comments: "In this context, *reht* means the requirement or regulation of law."[83] But what "requirement of the law" can He have in mind? It seems far more likely that the phrase "thes wizzodes rehtes" is meant in a vaguer sense, namely "legis iustitia," the justice of the law. Contrary to Schmidt-Wiegand, Otfrid's use of *reht* seems therefore to offer no hint of any Germanic sense of the word.[84] Instead, it offers another confirmation of Köbler's conclusion that Old High German *reht* means *iustitia*.

Schmidt-Wiegand returned to a consideration of Old High German *reht* from the vernacular standpoint in an essay contrasting the development of the early medieval notions of *reht* and *êwa*.[85] In this second, modified study, Schmidt-Wiegand speaks of the "central importance" of *reht* in the Old High German period and defines it as "the law, justice, a legal matter, a law, commandment, duty, right belief, truth, the just."[86] Her purpose is again to see how the primitive Germanic meanings of the adjective *reht* came to be transformed into the "broad spectrum of meanings" contained in the high medieval notion of the noun *reht*. She contends that: "It is a question of a type of word formation that is grounded in the system of the language itself; for its development there is no need for impulses from outside [the system?], such as the language of educated Latin," an implicit criticism of both Kroeschell's and Köbler's views.[87]

To prove the initial absence of the conceptual influence of Latin on Old High German *reht*, Schmidt-Wiegand first claims that the Old High German phrase *mit rehto* refers to one's "duty," but again her evidence is not compelling.[88] As shown, Köbler has asserted—more correctly in my opinion—that *mit* or *bî reht* was usually a translation of *iure* or "justly," or "rightly," and in the examples Schmidt-Wiegand offers, this latter rendering seems more appropriate than "according to one's duty." One might infer that if a person does something *iuste*, it is indeed his duty to do so, but from this inference it does not follow that *reht* is equivalent to duty.

Schmidt-Wiegand also sees the meaning "subjective right" already inherent in Old High German *reht* as it is used in the Old High German alliterative poems.[89] Her example, from the "Hildebrandslied," is somewhat misleading. Hildebrand says to his son Hadubrand:

> doh maht du nu aodlihho, ibu dir din ellen taoc,
> in sus heremo man hrusti giwinnan,
> rauba birahanen, ibu du dar enic reht habes.[90]

Schmidt-Wiegand says that this *reht* is the ancient legal (subjective) right of the victor in a judicial duel to the vanquished opponent's armor. If one grants, however, that the Christian influence on the "Hildebrandslied" is stronger than scholars had once admitted and that the duel between father and son is perhaps an example of an early medieval, ecclesiastically influenced *iudicium Dei*, then *reht* could also mean *iustitia* here, and the last half-line could then be understood as "if you have any *iustitia* (justice or right) on your side." The passage is at best ambiguous and an unfortunate choice for proving anything about the meaning of *reht*.[91]

Schmidt-Wiegand more willingly concedes the influence of Latin on some of the other Old High German works, and she admits that in the "Muspilli" *reht* can mean "justice." She ascribes this "new" meaning to the influence of Christianity, an influence she also sees—as well one must—in many of the Old High German translations.[92]

In her discussion of Otfrid, Schmidt-Wiegand is more reticent than in her earlier analysis, and she revises her previous contention that the phrase "thes wizzodes rehtes" (*Evangelienbuch*, IV, 19, 18) refers to "a single requirement of the law." Instead, she now thinks that Otfrid meant "that which results from divine law as an objective norm for the subjective position of the individual."[93] More simply stated, one might again contend that *reht* here means *iustitia*.

To summarize Schmidt-Wiegand's revised view of the development of the meaning of *reht*, the word previous to the influence of Latin/Christian terminology, meant "subjective right" or "duty" and under the influence of Christian notions slowly acquired the meaning "justice." There is no need, she claims, to posit the influence on *reht* of *ius* meaning "right" (and eventually "objective law") to explain the high medieval meaning of *reht*. Old German *reht* already had these meanings. The evidence for this contention, however, is either ambiguous or simply wrong. *Reht* as a Germanic concept no doubt meant something subtly or perhaps radically different from *iustitia*, but it appears a fruitless endeavor to expect more than a highly equivocal hint of these primitive meanings from any Old High German text. There is no Old High German work untainted by Latin/Christian usage, which should surprise no one who remembers the status of the authors, translators, or scribes of these texts, namely clerics or monks.[94]

I see no compelling reason, therefore, to reject Köbler's conclusion that Old High German *reht* almost always means *iustitia* or to revise my working hypothesis that Early Middle High German *reht* also means *iustitia*, unless one can detect the gradually increasing influence of *ius* in the sense of "subjective right" or "objective law."

As a first test of this hypothesis, we can now finally return to the problematic opening lines of "Vom Recht" and ask if the poet's meaning is not best apprehended by translating the noun *reht* as *iustitia* and its adjectival form as *iustus*. Lines 1–12, quoted above, would then mean: "No one is as venerable as justice truly is, for God is truly a just judge. Therefore He commands His servant to love justice greatly and to imitate Him and to practice His justice. No one can rest with God unless he desires justice, for God will divide the unjust from His own servants."

The ambiguity and inconsistency of these lines, of which previous scholars had all complained, disappear in this reading and one can more readily appreciate the biblical allusions in the poet's language. Lines 3-4, for example, "wan got ist ze ware/ ein rehtir rihtære," are a clear translation of the biblical commonplace that God is a "iudex iustus."[95] Lines 5-6, "von diu hiez er den sinen chneht/ vil starke minnen daz reht," echo the biblical phrase "iustitiam diligere."[96] While lines 9-12, finally, on the Last Judgement, recall such biblical passages as II Timothy, 4, 8: "reposita est mihi iustitiae corona, quam reddet mihi Dominus in illa die, iustus iudex . . ." or Matthew, 25, 46: "Et ibunt hi in supplicium aeternum, iusti autem in vitam aeternam."

In rendering *reht* as *iustitia* or "justice" in these lines, one has scarcely determined what *reht* meant to the Early Middle High German poets, for to show that the concepts are equivalent is, in part, merely to place the burden of proof on *iustitia*. It will be recalled, for example, that both Schützeichel and Gentry had interpreted *reht* in Noker's "Momento mori" to mean *iustitia*. But each had understood something quite different, Schützeichel arguing that *iustitia* meant "sacraments," while Gentry, citing Saint Augustine, took it to mean "love of God and one's neighbor." If the historical resonance and importance of Early Middle High German *reht* are to be adequately apprehended, one must first try to understand *iustitia*.

NOTES

1 Maria Mackensen, "Soziale Forderungen und Anschauungen der frühmittel-hochdeutschen Dichter," *Neue Heidelberger Jahrbücher, Neue Folge* (1925), 146.

2 Rupp says, e. g., of Noker: "Es geht ihm darum, den Menschen . . . zur Bewahrung des 'rehtes,' der richtigen Ordnung im Dasein, aufzufordern," (17) and further: "Nicht der Dualismus ist das Entscheidende, nicht Weltflucht an sich, sondern, wie in so vielen Dichtungen dieser Zeit, das richtiger In-der-Welt-Sein 'sub specie aeterni,' der 'ordo,' das 'reht'" (28). Rupp also speaks of the "rechtlich eingestellte Theologie" of the poet of the "Ezzolied" (43) and of his "rechtliche Auffassung der Erlösung" (79). The relation between God and man in the poem is, according to Rupp, "weitgehend rechtlicher Art" (79). In the case of the "Summa Theologiae," Rupp comments on the poem's "knappe, fast juristische Diktion" (93), and the goal of the Arme Hartmann's "Rede vom Glauben," Rupp says, is the "Ringen um die richtige Ordnung, um das richtige Verhältnis von Gott und Mensch, um die rechte Ordnung der Werte und des menschlichen Lebens" (190). Rupp writes of all the poets he treats that "ihr Ziel ist Aufruf zur richtigen Lebensführung, zur rechten Weltgestaltung; sie wollen mit ihren Dichtungen die richtige Ordnung der Werte lehren" (271).

3 Linguistically, Alber's poem, with its reduced vowels, already belongs to the classical Middle High German period.

4 See the authoritative study by Nigel F. Palmer, *"Visio Tnugdali." The German and Dutch Translations and Their Circulation in the Later Middle Ages* (Munich: Artemis, 1982), 10–15, 35–41, as well as Wiebike Freytag's entry in the *VL*.

5   *Visio Tnugdali. Lateinisch und Altdeutsch*, ed. Albrecht Wagner (Erlangen, 1882), 25, 20–22.

6   Ibid., 26, 6–11. See Jaroslav Pelikan, *The Growth of Medieval Theology (600–1300)*, vol. 3 of *The Christian Tradition* (Chicago: University of Chicago, 1978), 106–157 and Harold J. Berman, *Law and Revolution: The Formation of the Western Legal Tradition* (Cambridge: Harvard, 1983), 179–180 on the traditional harmonization of God's justice and mercy.

7   See Anselm's "Proslogion," 9–4.

8   *Visio*, 937–944; 949–954. "God grants great mercy, yet it is granted to none except him who is found to be penitent for what he has done *zunrehte* and who makes it good again, as scripture tells us . . . . Whoever persists in his sin and to his death does not expel *unrehte* desire and other deceit must suffer this misery.

9   *Visio*, 38, 4–7.

10   *Visio*, 38, 7–39, 7.

11   *Visio*, 1407–1429. "Here are those who have power—young or old—but know no mercy for the poor and rob them to their own danger. Those who oppress widows and orphans and judge *unrehte* and pledge themselves to every sin are in the hot flames. They judge themselves who oppress their subjects with unreasonable (feudal) dues. They are now in the fire. Those who speak false *reht* and who steal from the poor their meager gain, those who plan such things and remain unrepentant: truly they all shall burn like these here. If they had had *reht* sense, they would have left their gain and freed themselves from this."

12   The title, as is the case for almost all Early Middle High German works, is an addition from a modern editor, in this case Theodor von Karajan, who first edited the poem in 1846.

13   Werner Schröder, ed., *Kleinere deutsche Gedichte des 11. und 12. Jahrhunderts*, II, (Tübingen: Niemeyer, 1972), ll. 1–12. "No one is so venerable as *reht* truly is, for God is truly a *rehtir rihtære*. Therefore He commands His servant to love *reht* greatly, to imitate Him, and to carry out His (or his?) *reht*. For no one can abide with God unless he desires *reht*, for God will divide the *unrehten* from His own servants." S. B. Chimes's translation of lines 1–2, "No one is so much lord that he may coerce the law," is confused (Chimes, trs., Fritz Kern, *Kingship and Law in the Middle Ages* [New York: Harper and Row, 1970], 182). I have used Schröder's short-line edition of the poem (Schröder, II, 112–131) rather than Maurer's long-line version (Maurer, *RD*, II, 153–177) for reasons which will be noted in the more extended discussion of "Vom Rechte" in Chapter III, below.

14   Carl Kraus, "'Vom Rechte' und 'Die Hochzeit,'" *SB WAW* 123 (1891), 8–9.

15   Gustav Ehrismann, *Geschichte der deutschen Literatur*, II/i: *Frühmittelhochdeutsche Literatur* (Munich: Beck, 1922), 196.

16   Ehrismann, ibid.

17   Ingeborg Schröbler, "Das mittelhochdeutsche Gedicht vom 'Recht,'" *PBB* 80 (1958), 219 ff. Schröbler's unacknowledged debt to Ehrismann's differentiation of *reht* into "right" and "duty" becomes clear in her second article on "Von Rechte," "Von den Grenzen des Verstehens mittelalterlicher Dichtung," *GRM NF* 13 (1963), 10.

18   Stephan Speicher, "*Vom Rechte.*" *Ein Kommentar im Rahmen der zeitgenössischen Literaturtradition,* (Göppingen: Kümmerle, 1986), 24–27. The most recent translator of "Vom Rechte," Gisela Vollmann-Profe, ed. and trs., *Frühmittelhochdeutsche Literatur* (Stuttgart: Reclam, 1996) similarly renders *reht* as *Recht* although in her notes, which follow Speicher very closely, she states: "Das Wort [Recht] deckt ein weites Bedeutungsfeld ab: 'Recht,' 'Pflicht,' 'Stand,' 'Gericht,' 'Gesetzgebung;' es kann alles bezeichnen, was recht und beziemend ist, also auch die 'rechte Ordnung' im Großen wie im Kleinen." (269).

19   Speicher, 27. In fact, Kraus differentiates not between objective and subjective "Recht," but between "duty" and "justice," while Ehrismann, as shown, does not so much distinguish between two separate meanings of *reht* as claim that Middle High German *reht* subsumes different meanings, a position no different from Speicher's. Speicher seems also to confuse Kern's remarks on the differences between objective law and positive law, i.e., the law which is enacted by a ruler or a state. See Speicher, 26–27.

20   BMZ, II, 618–623. Lexer, II, 377-378 basically repeats BMZ.

21   For a possible exception, see *Nachträge,* 438 where Pretzel writes that "sîn reht begân" (cf. "Vom Rechte, l. 8) means "seine Pflicht tun." Unfortunately, Pretzel gives no references, and it is thus unclear if his translation applies to "Vom Rechte" or not.

      In his *Mittelhochdeutsche Bedeutungskunde* ([Heidelberg: Winter, 1982], 33), Pretzel writes of *reht:* "Das Wort hat neben dem Begriff der rechtmäßigen Ordnung oft den der inneren 'Pflicht' mit einbegriffen. . . ." None of the examples cited stems from the Early Middle High German period.

22   Beate Hennig, *Kleines Mittelhochdeutsches Wörterbuch,* 3rd. ed. (Tübingen: Niemeyer, 1998), 258.

23   See John R. Searle, *The Construction of Social Reality* (New York: The Free Press, 1995) 54–55 for a discussion of some of these semantic issues.

24   A point forcefully made by Schröbler, "Grenzen," 120.

25   Fritz Kern, "Recht und Verfassung im Mittelalter," (1919), translated by S. B. Chimes as "Law and Constitution in the Middle Ages," in Chimes, trs., 147–205. Chimes consistently translates New High German *Recht* as "law" which is possible if one remembers the double meaning of the modern German word described above, namely subjective right as well as objective law. Where there is any ambiguity I will use *Recht.*

26   One meaning of "hêr," "sublime," is retained to a certain degree in modern German "herrlich." Speicher makes much of the fact the "hêr" in Old High German also means "old," which he relates to Kern's concept of law as old and good (Speicher, 24–25: Vollmann-Profe, 268, is a paraphrase of Speicher). In my translation of *her* in line 1 of "Vom Rechte," I used the word "venerable" (Vollmann-Profe writes "erhaben," 155; see also her comment, 268–69), but perhaps the best translation would be "senior," in its technical feudal sense of Latin *senior* or "lord" (see F. L. Ganshof, *Feudalism,* trs. Philip Grierson [New York: Harper and Row, 1961], 29 and Chapter III, below.

27   Kern, 181–182.

28   Kern, 151.

29   Kern, 151. From this last claim, Kern derives his famous theory of the medieval right of resistance; see Chimes, 1-146, for a translation of Kern's book *Gottesgnadentum und Widerstandsrecht im früheren Mittelalter* (1914).

30   Kern, 163.

31   Kern, 155.

32   The publication of an English translation of Otto Brunner's landmark contribution to these debates indicates that they are not without interest to contemporary English-speaking scholars. See Brunner, *Land and Lordship: Structures of Governance in Mediaeval Austria*, trs. Howard Kaminsky and James van Horn Melton (Philadelphia: University of Pennsylvania Press, 1992).

33   To avoid confusion, it should be noted that "constitution" or "Verfassung" has a much wider meaning for German medievalists than the English "constitution." As well as political "constitution," it embraces the social order as a whole.

34   This sketch is mostly based on Frantisek Graus ("Verfassungsgeschichte des Mittelalters," *HZ* 243 [1986], 547) who gives a good, if sometimes inordinately polemical overview of modern German scholarship on the "constitutional history" of the Middle Ages.

35   See Graus, 552–573.

36   F. Graus, "Die Gewalt bei den Anfängen des Feudalismus und die 'Gefangenbefreiung' der merowingischen Hagiographie," *Jahrbuch für Wirtschaftsgeschichte* I (1961), 63, ft. 11, quoted in Karl Kroeschell, "Verfassungsgeschichte und Rechtsgeschichte," *Der Staat, Beiheft* 6 (1983), 57.

37   Karl Bosl, for example, accepted Kern's picture of medieval *Recht* without the slightest modification. See: Karl Bosl, "Herrscher und Beherrschte im deutschen Reich des 10. - 12. Jahrhunderts," *SB BAW*, Phil-Hist., Heft 2 (1963), 7–9.

38   Kern, 155 and 194. Cf. Kroeschell's comments: "Als unveränderliche, ewige Größe kann das 'gute, alte Recht' zwar Widerstand und Fehde legitimieren, aber nicht die soziale Realität gestalten. Hier waltet nur Herrschaft" (Kroeschell, "Verfassungsgeschichte," 57).

39   See, e.g., Herbert Grundmann, "Freiheit als religiöses, politisches und persönliches Postulat im Mittelalter," *HZ* 183 (1957), 23-53; F. Graus, "Über die sogenannte germanische Treue," *Historica* 1 (1959), 71-121, and "Herrschaft und Treue. Betrachtungen zur Lehre von der germanischen Kontinuität," *Historica* 12 (1966), 5-44; Karl Kroeschell, *Haus und Herrschaft im frühen deutschen Recht* (Göttingen: Otto Schwartz, 1968); Hans K. Schulze, "Rodungsfreiheit und Königsfreiheit," *HZ* 219 (1974), 529-550; and Hanna Vollrath, "Herrschaft und Genossenschaft im Kontext frühmittelalterlicher Rechtsbeziehungen," *HJ* 102 (1982), 33-71, as well as the pertinent entries in the *HdR*.

40   This, however, has been vigorously denied by Hans K. Schulze, "Reichsaristokratie, Stammesadel und fränkische Freiheit," *HZ* 227 (1978), 363–364.

41   Karl Kroeschell, "Recht und Rechtsbegriff im 12. Jahrhundert," *Probleme des 12. Jahrhunderts*, vol. XII of *Reichenauer Vorträge und Forschungen* (Konstanz:Thorbecke, 1968), 314. More succinctly, Kroeschell wrote in 1983 of Kern's views: "Viele von

uns halten davon allerdings nichts mehr" (Kroeschell, "Verfassungsgeschichte," 57).

42   Kroeschell, "Rechtsbegriff," 314.

43   Kroeschell, "Rechtsbegriff," 314–315.

44   Kroeschell, "Rechtsbegriff," 322, ft. 135. Whether the *lex* comes of custom or state legislation is irrelevant in the early Middle Ages, according to Kroeschell: "*Lex* heißt also das Recht, das wirklich in Gebrauch ist, das man tatsächlich befolgt oder übt" (321).

45   Kroeschell, "Rechtsbegriff," 317. Old High German "kiuualt" usually has the sense of "power" and should not be confused with modern German "Gewalt" or "violence."

46   Kroeschell, "Rechtsbegriff," 318. Kroeschell's occasional use of modern German *Recht* to render medieval *reht* is unfortunate and confusing.

47   Kroeschell, "Rechtsbegriff," 319.

48   Kroeschell, "Rechtsbegriff," 322.

49   Kroeschell, "Rechtsbegriff," 326.

50   Kroeschell, "Rechtsbegriff," 327, ft. 161.

51   Kroeschell, "Rechtsbegriff," 330, ft. 195.

52   See Speicher, 28 for his dependence on Kroeschell.

53   Köbler's chief objective is to show how little the early medieval sources confirm Kern's view of medieval "Recht," and thus he is especially attentive to whether *ius, lex, mos,* and *consuetudo* are described as either old or good or as capable of modification or even creation.

54   Gerhard Köbler, *Das Recht im frühen Mittelalter* (Cologne: Böhlau, 1971), 140-143, 153–160, 159.

55   Köbler, 43–52.

56   Köbler, 52–54.

57   Köbler, 56–58.

58   Köbler, 91–92.

59   Köbler (176) is far more skeptical of the interpretation of the *iure* = *piuualti* or *kiwaltidu* passages to which Kroeschell had confidently referred for his understanding of *iure.*

60   Köbler, 176.

61   Two exceptions to this general rule should be noted since they have evoked generalizations that appear to be unjustified by the vast majority of the sources. Notker on occasion translated *ius* in its objective sense as *reht*, but in these instances, Köbler argues, he has been influenced by Ciceronian concepts and not by any inherent meaning of *ius* in *reht.*

The second example of *reht=ius* is from the Old-Saxon *Heliand* where the concept *landreht* occurs. Köbler suggests that this example is too isolated to form the basis of more general speculations, and that the *Heliand* poet might even have used *reht* simply to fit an alliterative context. Köbler, 179–181.

62   Köbler, 177.

63   Köbler, 177-178.

64   Köbler, 182-183. An important exception is Otfrid of Weißenburg who general-
        ly avoided *êwa* and usually translated *lex* as *wizzod* (Köbler, 186).

65   Köbler, 178. Köbler writes that the Germanic derivations of **reg* only seldom
        appear with the original meaning "straight."

66   Köbler, 220.

67   Speicher writes of Köbler: "Seine Ergebnisse betreffen die hier zu diskutierenden
        Probleme allerdings weniger, da es ja um einen Text geht, der in rechts-
        gechichtlicher Betrachtung bereits dem christlichen Hochmittelalter angehört
        . . ." (Speicher, 25). But it is this claim which must first be determined. Speicher
        was perhaps influenced in this conclusion by Kroeschell's comments quoted
        above, according to which "Vom Rechte" was the first vernacular expression of
        the high medieval concept of law. Since Kroeschell's understanding of *reht* is dif-
        ferent from Köbler's, a combination of the two authors' conclusions should be
        carefully avoided.

        One might also note further that Köbler's chronology of the gradual shifts in
        meaning of *reht* do not therefore justify Speicher in relying on Kern. While
        Köbler convincingly shows, at the least, that Kern's view of *Recht* is inadequate
        for the early medieval period, it by no means follows that Kern is still relevant for
        the High Middle Ages, as Speicher argues (Speicher, 25). Perhaps Speicher is here
        again following Kroeschell, who, as mentioned, seems to grant the validity of
        Kern's view of *Recht* for the High Middle Ages. Köbler, however, is more cau-
        tious (Köbler, 232).

        Finally, Speicher's general skepticism regarding Köbler's conclusions is scarce-
        ly justified by the review of Köbler's book to which he refers. (See Gerhard
        Dilcher's review of Köbler in the *ZRG* [*GA*] 90 [1973], 267–273). Dilcher is
        indeed highly critical of what he call Köbler's "positivistic" method and many of
        the details of Köbler's book, yet he concludes: "Es ist zumindest deutlicher
        geworden, daß das so klare und einheitliche Bild vom Rechtsverständnis des
        Mittelalters, das Fritz Kern gezeichnet hat, in dieser Form nicht zu halten ist
        . . ." (273).

        Cf. also the review in *DAEM* 28 (1972), unmentioned by Speicher, in which
        the reviewer concludes a somewhat critical appraisal of Köbler's book with the
        words: "Diese Einwände könnten zu Differenzierungen zwingen, doch dürften
        sie das Ergebnis der vorliegenden Untersuchung kaum erschüttern" (297).

68   Ruth Schmidt-Wiegand, "Rechtswort und Rechtszeichen in der deutschen
        Dichtung," *FMS* 5 (1971), 279. She gives no references for this assertion, howev-
        er, and a careful study of Otfrid's use of the adjective *reht* reveals no clear and
        unequivocal instances of *reht* meaning "gerade gerichtet."

69   Schmidt-Wiegand, "Rechtswort," 279. These are good approximations of Otfrid's
        most typical use of adverbial *reht*. See, for example, *Otfrids Evangelienbuch*, ed.
        Oskar Erdmann, 6th ed., Ludwig Wolff, ed., (Tübingen: Niemeyer, 1973), IV, 11,
        46 where adverbial *rehto* is a translation of the Latin *bene* or IV, 18, 14, where *rehto*
        translates *vere*. These meanings, however, are so colorless and vague that one
        should hesitate to infer the content of the noun *reht* from them. Etymologically,

the noun *reht* is indeed derived from the adjectival root, but this appears to have occurred long before the written record.

70 Schmidt-Wiegand, "Rechtswort," 279.

71 Otfrid, I, 4, 5–8. "They were both much beloved of God and they always observed His commandments, doing His law and loving *reht.*" Cf. Luke, 1, 6: "Erant autem iusti ambo ante Deum, incedentes in omnibus mandatis et iustificationibus Domini, irreprehensibiles."

72 Cf., for example, Psalms 10, 8 and 44, 8, Wisdom 1,1, (quoted in Hebrews 1,9), or Wisdom 8, 7. Cf. also "Vom Recht," ll. 5–6: "von diu hiez er den sinen chneht/ vil starke *minnen daz reht.*"

73 Otfrid, I, 16, 11–13. "She constantly prayed and fasted much. She obeyed God's will and practiced His service. Day and night she attended to *reht.*" Cf., Luke 2, 37: "Et haec vidua . . . quae non discedebat de templo, ieiuniis et obsecrationibus serviens nocte et die."

74 Otfrid, IV, 7, 83–84. "Therefore be ever vigilant your entire life here. Day and night, be mindful of *reht.*" Cf. Luke 21, 36: "Vigilate itaque omni tempore orantes."

75 Aside from the inconsequential repetition of the phrase "dages inti nahtes" and the word "orantes" in the Latin text, there is nothing in this second example from *Das Evangelienbuch*, which contains Otfrid's account of Jesus' apocalyptic discourse (cf. Matthew 24 and Luke 21), to justify Schmidt-Wiegand's claim that the above lines are somehow related to the description of Anna or refer to "Beten und Fasten" (Schmidt-Wiegand, "Rechtswort," 279).

76 Could Otfrid have perhaps been influenced by such biblical passages as "lingua mea tota die meditabitur iustitiam tuam" (Psalm 70, 25) or "Beatus vir qui . . . in iustitia sua meditabitur" (Ecclesiasticus, 14, 22)? Praying and fasting might well be considered a part of justice and as such they would be its subjective fulfillment, but surely they do not exhaust the meaning of *reht.*

77 Otfrid, IV, 15, 51–54. "'This is my command to you: you shall love one another. Let everyone remember this and waver not in love.' This the Lord told them for He Himself had chosen them. He admonished them that night [to practice] many kinds of *reht.*" Cf. also Otfrid, IV, 15, 19 and V, 23, 126.

78 Otfrid, V, 22, 1–2. "God's dear followers shall go to heaven, the *rehte* and the good, with cheerful countenance" Cf. Matthew 25, 46: "Ibunt . . . *iusti* in vitam aeternam."

79 Otfrid, III, 16, 45–46. "Do not judge *unrehto*, let no one consider anyone's nobility; give *rehtaz* judgement to us two together." Cf. John 7, 24: "Nolite iudicare secundum faciem, sed iustum iudicium iudicate."

80 Schmidt-Wiegand, "Rechtswort," 280.

81 See Otfrid, I, 1, 52; II, 9, 40; III, 2, 13.

82 Otfrid, IV, 19, 17–20. "His cheek having been wounded, He began to answer. He admonished them that night of the *reht* of the law. 'If I have spoken evil, tell me the wrong; but if I spoke the truth, why do you strike me so?'" Cf. John, 18, 23: "Respondit ei Iusus: 'Si male locutus sum, testimonium perhibe de malo; si autem bene, quid me caedis?'"

83   Schmidt-Wiegand, "Rechtswort, "282.

84   Otfrid is in any case an odd source for investigating putatively Germanic concepts. His *Evangelienbuch* is sufficiently long and varied as a data base and is not merely a translation of the biblical text. But at the same time, it is the theologically most sophisticated vernacular religious work of its era (Otfrid's teacher was Rabanus Maurus) and as such, very much influenced by Latin usage.

85   Schmidt-Wiegand, "*Reht* und *ewa*. Die Epoche des Althochdeutschen in ihrer Bedeutung für die Geschichte der deutschen Rechtssprache," in *Althochdeutsch*, ed. Rolf Bergmann et al., II (Heidelberg: Winter, 1987), 937–958.

86   Schmidt-Wiegand, "*Recht*," 938.

87   Schmidt-Wiegand, "*Recht*," 939. One may note that in purely linguistic terms, Schmidt-Wiegand's formulation is scarcely tenable.

88   Schmidt-Wiegand, "*Recht*," 939-941. Without comment, Schmidt-Wiegand's former dependence on Kroeschell's understanding of the phrase as the fulfillment of one's "gewalt" or "right" has disappeared.

89   Schmidt-Wiegand, "*Recht*," 941-42.

90   "Hildebrandslied," 55-57, *Althochdeutsches Lesebuch*, ed. Wilhelm Braune, 16th ed. Ernst A. Ebbinghaus, ed. (Tübingen: Niemeyer, 1979). "But you can easily win the armor from such an old man if your strength is sufficient and if you have any *reht*."

91   See Klaus Düwel's entry on the "Hildebrandslied" in the *VL* (esp. col. 1246) for a succinct review of the problems caused by this text and a short review of the various scholarly positions.

92   Schmidt-Wiegand, "*Recht*," 949-951.

93   Schmidt-Wiegand, "*Recht*," 951.

94   Cf. the careful study of such putatively Germanic concepts as Old High German *truhtîn* or *hûshhêrro* in Karl Kroeschell's *Haus und Herrschaft im frühen deutschen Recht*, op. cit. Kroeschell argues that these concepts had lost any primitive Germanic meaning by the Old High German period.

95   Cf. Psalm 7, 12: "Deus iudex iustus;" See also Tobias 3, 2; Psalms 118, 137-138 and 144, 17; John 5, 30; and 2 Timothy 4, 8. The biblical source of lines 4-5 of "Vom Rechte" has long been acknowledged by most commentators, despite their uncertainty about the meaning of *reht*. The phrase "rehtir rihtære" is a commonplace in Early Middle High German literature (see the references in Speicher, 27–28).

      Speicher questions whether *rihtære* means simply "judge" or whether it retains its older Old High German sense of "rex" or "rector" (Speicher, 28; cf. Vollmann-Profe, 269 who again accepts Speicher's arguments). He cites Köbler's article ("Richten—Richter—Gericht," *ZRG* [*GA*] 87 [1970], 56–113, esp. 102-107) to support this view. Köbler, however, nowhere claims that *rihtære* still had this older non-judicial meaning as late as 1150. On the contrary, Köbler plainly shows that the word had changed its "Inhalt gegenüber der früheren Zeit" (102) already in Notker's works. Indeed, Kroeschell, too, had argued that the poet's use of *rihtære* as *iudex* is a clear indication that "Vom Rechte" is obviously distant from the Carolingian understanding of *rihtære* (Kroeschell, "Recht," 330). In addition to these chronological difficulties, it is in any case unlikely in view of the threat of God's final *judgement* contained in lines 11–12, that the author of "Vom Rechte" meant by *rihtære* anything other than "judge."

96   As was mentioned in the discussion of Otfrid's use of the same phrase.

CHAPTER II
Iustitia and *Ordo*

1. *IUSTITIA*

A. The Medieval Concept of *iustitia*

Immediately following the prologue on *reht* or *iustitia*, the author of the poem "Vom Rechte" gives three particular instances of *reht*:

> **D**er reht sint vil manigiu
> unde besliezzent alliu samet driu,
> (15)   unde begiengen wir diu,
> wir mohten immer genuoch haben
> unde mohten mit allen eren leben.
> **E**in reht daz sint diu trewe,
> da wir mit schulen bouwen.
> (20)   **E**in andir reht daz ist also getan,
> daz wir uns selben wellen haben,
> daz solten wir ein andir geben,
> wolden wir christlichen leben.
> **W**ir solten sin gewære,
> (25)   daz wære michel ere.
> der diu driu reht behabet,
> die wile daz er nu lebet,
> unz an sinen tot,
> dem *hu*lfe got von der not.
> (30)   ez wære man odir wip,
> er gæbe im den ewigen lib,
> der da nimmer zergat
> unde immer ewich stat.[1]

The poet's three forms of *reht* seem fairly clear: *triuwe* or *fides*, the Golden Rule,[2] and "gewære sîn" or *veritas*. It is easy to see why commentators on "Vom Rechte" often claim that *reht* here must refer to "duty," for what else could the poet mean by these three definitions of *reht* or when he says "Der reht sint vil manigiu"? Can there be more than one *iustitia* or are these lines in "Vom Rechte" indeed an instance of the new high medieval understanding of *reht* as *ius*, a right which implies as well a duty, as Kroeschell had claimed? To answer these questions we must first try to grasp what the early Middle Ages understood by *iustitia*.

Iustitia is, of course, a key, if not *the* central ethical category in both the Old and the New Testaments as well as in the works of the most influential Christian theologian in the early Middle Ages, Saint Augustine. But while both biblical usage and Augustinian concepts were certainly the most formative influences on the meaning of *iustitia* in the early Middle Ages, neither was appropriated directly. Both were rather understood through the mediation of tradition.

Throughout the Middle Ages, *iustitia* was considered the royal virtue *par excellence*,[3] and perhaps the best approach to its early medieval meaning is through the literature directed to kings and other rulers. In a German royal consecration ceremony from the end of the tenth century, the king is incessantly admonished to *iustitia* by the officiating archbishop. "Vis sanctam fidem a catholicis viris tibi traditam tenere et operibus iustis observare?" he first asks the king-to-be.[4] And in language replete with biblical imagery, the archbishop continually prays for the king, that "in diebus eius oriatur iusticia" and that the king's reign "cum iocunditate et iusticia aeterno glorietur in regno."[5] The bishop hopes that the king's servants will always speak justice and asks God to grant the king a "corona iusticiae et pietatis."[6] The officiant prays that the king rule justly and that "nullus insidiantibus malis eum in iniusticiam vertat,"[7] and that the king be "iusticiam diligens, per tramitem similiter iusticiae populum ducens."[8] Finally, when the bishops invest the king with staff and sword, they admonish him to be a "gloriosus iusticiae ... cultor egregius."[9]

Behind this ceremony lies the sometimes confusing development of the royal virtue of justice. In the Merovingian era, *iustitia* usually had a narrow judicial meaning of strictly, sometimes even harshly applied justice. In an admonitory letter probably addressed to Chlodwig II from the middle of the seventh century, an anonymous bishop writes that the king should be "in iudicio rectus" and that "omnes gentes tibi adversantes de tuo recto et iusto regimine pavebunt."[10] Yet this severe justice should be tempered by mercy (*pietas*), especially to the weak and the poor: "in vindicata pius, in pauperibus misericors."[11] The king's subjects, especially the powerless, shall rejoice:

> ubi veritas non abnegatur, sed iustitia pronunciatur, ut . . . aequitatis radiante lumine, sic iustitia procedat, ut cum laude clarificetur Deus iustoque iudicio in cauto sancto palatio iudicato laetificentur et exultent pauperes, viduae defensionem habeant, orfani tutelam suscipiant.[12]

The king should know that he is a servant of God from whom he derives his power. He should be a merciful listener, but a strong master. Corrupt judges, especially, should be severely corrected:

> Sic te, Deo adiuvante, tempera in omnibus, ut qui [scl. the iudices] mali sunt in
> omni gradu regalem timeant auctoritatem, legem et rationem; boni vero ament
> fidem et misericordiam; singuli iudicent iustum iudicium.[13]

In Visigothic Spain, *iustitia* also meant strictly applied judicial justice. Isidore of
Seville, for example, writes in a passage which seems to turn Christian principles
on their head that:

> Reddere malum pro malo vicissitudo justitiae est: sed qui clementiam addit justi-
> tiae, non malum pro malo culpatis reddit, sed bonum pro malo offensis impertit.
> . . . Populi enim peccantes judicem metuunt, et a malo suo legibus coercentur.[14]

Isidore, however, softens this advice in his admonition to judges:

> Omnis qui recte judicat stateram [i.e. scales] in manu gestat, ut in utroque penso
> justitiam et misericordiam portat. Sed per justitiam reddit peccati sententiam, per
> misericordiam peccantis temperat poenam, ut justo libramine quaedam per
> aequitatem corrigat, quaedam vero per miserationem indulgeat.[15]

Like the Merovingians, the Visogothic king should thus render strictly applied
justice and show mercy. He should be both "iustus" and "pius," as the Visigothic
royal coins proclaimed, with the emphasis usually on mercy.[16] Isidore, for example,
writes: "Virtutes Regiae praecipue duae, iustitia et pietas; plus autem in regibus
laudatur pietas; nam iustitia per se servera est."[17]

Iustitia was not always confined to this judicial sense of strictly applied justice.
Isidore, for example, also gives an Augustinian definition in which justice includes,
above all, the love of God and the veneration of religion and consists in honoring
one's parents, benefiting all and harming none, embracing the bonds of fraternal
charity, and showing mercy to the poor.[18]

A combination of these two different meanings of *iustitia*, severe justice to the
evil and mercy toward the poor, and a virtual compendium of Christian virtues as
well, is given in an Irish tract from the seventh century "De duodecim abusionibus saeculi," which was extraordinarily influential in the Carolingian period and
beyond:[19]

> Justitiae vero regis est neminem injuste per potentiam opprimere, sine person-
> arum acceptione inter virum et proximum suum juste judicare, advenis et pupil-
> lis et viduis defensorem esse, furta cohibere, adulteria punire, iniquos non exaltare,
> impudicos et histriones non nutrire, impios de terra perdere, paricidas et perjantes
> vivere non sinere, ecclesias defendere, pauperes eleemosynis alere, justos super
> regni negotia constituere . . . per omnia in Deo confidere . . . cuncta adversa
> patienter tolerare, fidem catholicam in Deum habere . . . certis horis orationibus
> insistere, ante horas congruas cibum non gustare.[20]

In the Carolingian period, *iustitia* in its many different forms continues to be
demanded of kings and other rulers. Hincmar of Rheims, for example, liberally
quotes from the "Duodecim abusionibus" in his own tractate "De regis persona et
regio ministerio," which is addressed to Charles the Bald. His second chapter,
"Quod populi felicitas sit rex bonus, infelicitas rex malus," mostly consists in an
exact repetition of the passage quoted immediately above.[21] Hincmar, however,

tends to emphasize the practice of strict judicial justice and warns against the abuse of a too freely bestowed *misericordia*.[22]

Alcuin, on the other hand, is more cautious in advocating strict justice, which he sometimes simply calls "disciplina." In his admonition to Count Wido, "De virtutibus et vitiis liber," he writes: "In judice misericordia et disciplina debent esse: quia una sine altera bene esse non possit."[23] In the twentieth chapter, "De judicibus," Alcuin excerpts most of his advice from Isidore's *Sententiae*, admonishing the judge carefully to weigh justice and mercy, to give preference to no one, and above all, never to accept bribes: "Acceptio munerum in judiciis, praevaricatio est veritatis." Alcuin then concludes: "Qui Deum timentes juste judicant, aeterna a Domino accepturi sunt praemia."[24] Alcuin again treats the venality of judges in Chapter XXX, "De avaritia," where he writes that avarice in its different forms leads to unjust judgement and is "contraria misericordiae, eleemosynis in pauperes, et toti pietati in miseros."[25]

Iustitia is not confined in "De virtutibus et vitiis" to judicial justice and the care of the poor. In the penultimate chapter on the four cardinal virtues, Alcuin writes:

> Justitia est animi nobilitas, unicuique rei propriam tribuens dignitatem. In hac divinitatis cultus, et humanitatis jura, et justa judicia, et aequitas totius vitae conservatur.[26]

One can explain these different conceptions of justice only in part by biblical usage. *Iustitia* in the Bible often seems to refer to virtue in general. The *via* or *semita iustitiae* is a frequent image of the moral life,[27] and God Himself is equated with justice: "Nosse enim te [Deum] consummata iustitia est et scire iustitiam et virtutem tuam, radix est immortalitatis."[28] And in another passage interpreted as a prophecy of Christ, one reads "Et orietur vobis timentibus nomen meum, sol iustitiae."[29]

Biblical *iustitia* is also frequently a judicial virtue and thus is commonly used in the context of judgement, especially by the Prophets.[30] Judicial justice is sometimes explicitly contrasted with mercy, as in the influential passage from Psalm 84, 11: "Misericordia et veritas obviaverunt, iustitia et pax osculatae sunt." Judical *iustitia* is thus frequently associated, if not equated with *veritas*.[31] That judicial justice must be impartial is a biblical commonplace,[32] as is the castigation of venial judges.[33]

Biblical judicial justice tends to favor the poor and powerless, especially strangers, orphans, and widows.[34] Justice thus can be equated with the care of the poor later known as the *opus misericordiae*:

> Frange esurienti panem tuum et egenos vagosque induc in domum tuam. Cum videris nudum operi eum et carnem tuam ne despexeris. Tunc erumpet quasi mane lumen tuum et sanitas tua citius orietur, et anteibit faciem tuam iustitia tua et gloria Domini colliget te.[35]

Almost equal in influence to that of the Bible was Saint Augustine's conception of *iustitia*. Isidore's non-judicial conception of *iustitia* as the love of God and the veneration of religion and Alcuin's definition of the cardinal virtue of justice as the nobility of the soul, granting each thing its own dignity, for example, are more Augustinian than biblical in origin.

Augustine's understanding of *iustitia* initially seems inconsistent.[36] On the one hand, he appears to comprehend justice as the source of all other virtues and equivalent to charity, usually the greatest of all Christian virtues. In an isolated, but influential comment in which he explains the different numbers of people in the biblical accounts of the miracle of the loaves and the fishes, Augustine uses the classical scheme of the cardinal virtues to show the prominence and Christian content of *iustitia*:

> Neque in ipsa turba quinque millia hominum fuerunt, sicut illic, ubi carnales legem accipientes, id est, quinque sensibus carnis detiti significantur; sed quatuor millia potius, quo numero significantur spirituales, propter quatuor animi virtutes, quibus in hac vita spiritualiter vivitur prudentiam, temperantiam, fortitudinem, et iustitiam. Quarum prima est cognitio rerum appetendarum et fugiendarum: secunda, refrenatio cupiditatis ab iis quae temporaliter delectant; tertia, firmitas animi adversus ea quae temporaliter molesta sunt: quarta, quae per ceteras omnes diffunditur, dilectio Dei et proximi.[37]

But, more typically, Augustine defines *iustitia* in non-biblical, Ciceronian terms as distributive justice: "to each his due." Classical in heritage and apodictic in authority, this definition pervades St. Augustine's work: "Iam iustitiam quid dicamus esse nisi virtutem, qua sua cuique tribuuntur?" asks Augustine the teacher. His dutiful pupil responds: "Nulla mihi alia justitiae notio est."[38] It is also his most consistently precise definition of justice. It appears in his earliest works such as *De ordine*,[39] as well as in his later works, notably in the famous discussion of the relation between justice and the *res publica* in Book XIX of *De civitate Dei*: "Iustitia ... ea virtus est, quae sua cuique distribuit."[40]

Augustine's view of distributive justice can serve as an implicit, though usually tacit, link between the varying early medieval definitions of *iustitia*. In Augustine's hands, distributive justice entails a universal scheme of order on the basis of which justice must be rendered. But to understand how Augustine can link the different meanings of justice, one must first turn to the classical origin of distributive justice.

Socrates rightly called distributive justice "a riddling definition" of the virtue of justice, for its apparent simplicity is filled with far-reaching implications.[41] The first to delineate some of these implications was Aristotle in his seminal discussion of justice in Book V of the *Nicomachean Ethics*. Aristotle begins with a negative definition of justice, which shows that the word as it is commonly used has a twofold meaning, namely "law-abiding" and "fair:"

> Now the term 'unjust' [adikos] is held to apply both to the man who breaks the law and the man who takes more than his due, the unfair man. Hence it is clear that the law-abiding man and the fair man will both be just. 'The just' therefore means that which is lawful and that which is equal or fair. . . .[42]

The first form of justice, that which is lawful, Aristotle calls "universal justice." Law has as its aim "the common interest of all ... so that in one of its senses [lawful] the term 'just' is applied to anything that produces and preserves the happiness, or the component parts of the happiness of the political community" (V, i).

The object of law is social, preserving the well-being of the community. Therefore, he who obeys the law, the just man, strives to uphold the happiness of the community. This sense of justice is the sum of all other virtues for it "involves relationship with someone else," which "accounts for the view that Justice alone of virtues is the 'good of others'. . ." (V, i). As the only unequivocal social virtue, "being the practice of virtue in general towards someone else," this sense of justice is the "whole of virtue" and therefore universal (V, ii).

The second form of justice, that which concerns the equal or fair, Aristotle calls "particular justice." It is separate from and subordinate to universal justice "since the unfair is not the same as the unlawful, but different from it, and related to as part to the whole" (V, ii). Particular justice, in turn, can be divided into two forms:

> One kind (traditionally called distributive justice) is exercised in the distribution of honor, wealth, and the other divisible assets of the community, which may be allotted among its members in equal or unequal shares. The other kind (traditionally called corrective or commutative justice) is that which applies a corrective principle in private transactions" (V, ii).[43]

Aristotle's initial description of distributive justice is, of course, open-ended. How are "honor, wealth, and the other divisible assets of the community" to be defined and allotted, and more importantly, according to what measure are they to be distributed in unequal as well as equal shares? Without some kind of standard of allocation and a clear definition of each one's due, distributive justice often seems vacuous.[44] Aristotle concedes this problem: "All are agreed that justice in distributions must be based on desert . . . ." But not all agree on the definition of desert: "democrats make the criterion free birth; those of oligarchical sympathies wealth, or in other cases birth; upholders of aristocracy make it virtue" (V, iii).

Each person's due, then, is based on his worth, value, or desert, which in turn, according to Aristotle, depends on one's view of the ideal social order and each person's place within that society. The concept of distributive justice, therefore, implies and demands some system of order according to which the just measure of each person can be determined. The formula "to each his own or due" presumes a clear view of social order because the exercise of justice is impossible without it.

Saint Augustine, as shown, begins with the distributive sense of justice, and he arrives at a conclusion remarkably similar to Aristotle's: "Iustum. . . deum omnes fatemur: totum igitur ordine includitur" (*De ordine*, I, xix). Justice, which Augustine anchors in the divinity, is inconceivable without order. Augustine's journey to this conclusion, however, is far removed from the paths of Aristotelian discursive logic. How does Augustine's understanding of *ordo* determine his view of justice?[45]

De ordine, one of Augustine's earliest works, is the natural starting point for an examination of his concept of order.[46] The dialogue is of interest not only because it presents the earliest version of Augustine's ideas of order and justice, but also because it is so explicit. Its view of the relation between order and justice is stated with an unencumbered clarity and simplicity, free of the finer philosophical distinctions and hesitations of Augustine's mature thought. At the same time, those later works do not appear fundamentally to diverge from the tenets of *De ordine*; in fact, they seem to suppose them. What is implicitly assumed in *De civitate Dei* is often explicitly formulated in *De ordine*.

The purpose of the dialogue is to perceive and to grasp "ordinem rerum . . . quo cohaeretur hic mundus et regitur" (*De ordine*, I, i), admittedly a "most difficult and rare" endeavor for all humans. Augustine appears to conceive of order in two different ways, first as a physical order of causes and effects, and second, as an ethical order of merits.[47] In fact, the metaphysical or cosmic order, which Augustine later defined in *De civitate Dei* as the "parium dispariumque rerum sua cuique loca tribuens dispositio" (XIX, xiii), is intimately related to the ethical definition of order given in *De ordine*: "Ordo est, quem si tenuerimus in uita, perducet ad deum, et quem nisi tenuerimus in uita, non perueniemus ad deum" (IX, xxvii). The link between the two views of order is provided by the concept of justice.

No one, begins Augustine, is so blinded in his reasoning as to doubt the order "in the physical world" that is, the order of the visible world, for "Nothing can become without a cause" (I, ii). *Ordo* seems then primarily to refer to causal order. Cause and effect are not merely facts. They are also anchored in a hierarchy of values, the "naturae ordo" (*De civitate Dei*, XIX, xvi), Neo-Platonic in origin[48] and fundamental to all of Augustine's thought: the spiritual is superior to the corporal, the incorruptible to the corruptible, the rational to the irrational, the creator excels the created, cause is greater than effect. This hierarchy is simply a self-evident, *a priori* dogma, as Augustine on occasion admits.[49]

Existence without a hierarchy is inconceivable, as an isolated and succinct comment shows: "Cum omnia Deus fecerit, quare non aequaliter fecit? Quia non essent omnia, si essent aqualia." All things would not be, if they were equal. Augustine's justification clearly begs the question: "Non enim essent multa genera, quibus conficitur universitas, primas et secundas et deinceps usque ad ultimas ordinatas habens creaturas. Et hoc est quod dicitur omnia."[50] All things are included in a hierarchy by degrees. If all things were equal, that which is unequal, namely everything, would not be.

While everyone recognizes the physical *ordo* of the world, there are yet many who refuse to see or are incapable of perceiving any order in human relations, that is in the moral sphere. Others deny the goodness of the *ordo* of the visible world. In a seminal passage for the understanding of the connection between order and justice, Augustine refutes them by reference to the justice of God:

> Si autem, ut nobis traditur nosque ipsius ordinis necessitate sentimus, iustus est deus, sua cuique distribuendo utique iustus est. Quae autem distinctio, si bona sunt omnia? Quidue praeter ordinem reperiri potest, si dei iustitia bonorum malorumque meritis sua cuique redduntur? (*De ordine*, I, vii)

Justice and order are so conflated in this passage as to render the argument circular: We know by the very fact of the existence of order, says Augustine, that God is just, that He assigns each his own. But can there be distribution without distinctions, without a hierarchical order? Augustine denies this with the words quoted above: "Iustum autem deum omnes fatemur: totum igitur ordine includitur" (I, xix). If order implies a just God, divine justice, which gives each his own, implies order.

Augustine is consequential in his view of the inseparability of order and justice. In a later section of *De ordine*, the question arises whether divine justice and order existed before the origin of evil, for God is just precisely "because He judges between the evil and the good," and the good are distinguished from the evil by order (II, vii). Augustine answers that of course God was always just, but before the existence of evil he was just only in an absolute sense. Justice, "which He always possessed," was, rather, only put into practice after the origin of evil. Similarly, "there is always order with God, but it did not come to be used until after evil had arisen" (II, vii).

Augustine in his later works held fast to the view of justice and order as presented in *De ordine*, although the relation between the two was rarely so explicitly formulated. Consider first, however, another early dialogue, *De libero arbitrio*, a work in which Sergio Cotta claims Augustine "s'occupe avec plus d'ampleur de problèmes juridiques."[51] Augustine writes that:

> ordinem creaturarum a summa usque ad infimam *gradibus iustis* ita decurrere ut ille inuideat qui dixerit: 'Ista non esset,' inuideat etiam ille qui dixerit: 'Ista talis esset.' . . . nec tibi occurrit perfecta uniuersitas, nisi ubi maiora sic praesto sunt, ut minora non desint" (*De libero arbitrio*, III, ix, emphasis added).

Not only is hierarchical order just and ontologically necessary, but the most just law, the *lex aeterna*, is defined in terms of order:

> Ut igitur breviter aeternae legis notionem, quae inpressa nobis est, quantum ualeo, uerbis explicem, ea est, qua iustum est, ut omnia sint ordinatissima (I, vi).

Augustine's most profound reflections on justice and order are found in Book XIX of *De civitate Dei*.[52] Book XIX has a two-fold aim: First, to describe and delineate the goal of the members of the heavenly city, namely Jerusalem or the *visio pacis* and second, finally to give an answer to the question posed in Book II, xxi, whether the Roman *res publica* ever corresponded to Scipio's definition of a just commonwealth.

The *visio pacis* is the ideal of perfect order, a graded vision, which in terrestrial terms begins with the well-ordered body and culminates in the ordered tranquility of the universe or cosmos:

> Pax itaque corporis est ordinata temperatura partium, pax animae inrationalis ordinata requies appetitionum, pax animae rationalis ordinata cognitionis action-isque consensio, pax corporis et animae ordinata uita et salus animantis, pax hominis mortalis et Dei ordinata in fide sub aeterna lege oboedientia, pax hominum ordinata concordia, pax domus ordinata imperandi atque oboediendi concordia cohabitantium, pax ciuitatis ordinata imperandi atque oboediendi concordia ciuium, pax caelestis ciuitatis ordinatissima et concordissima societas fruendi Deo et inuicem in Deo, pax omnium rerum tranquillitas ordinis. (XIX, xiii)

The well-ordered cosmos, in which the irrational is subordinate to the rational, the body to the soul, man to God, in short, the lesser to the greater, is justly ordered for "Deus . . . naturarum omnium sapientissimus conditor et iustissimus

ordinator [est]. . ." (XIX, xiii). Therefore, the moral imperative follows that if justice is "to give each his own" (XIX, iv), then on the basis of God's just order "in
unoquoque iustitia est, ut oboedienti Deus homini, animus corpori, ratio autem
uitiis etiam repugnantibus imperet, uel subigendo uel resistendo. . ." (XIX, xxvii).
It is the duty of everyone who would be just to conform himself in obedience to
the just order of God.

Augustine's moral ideal clearly betrays its Stoic pedigree.[53] But as Anton-
Hermann Chroust, among many others, rightly remarks, Augustine's "most fundamental and far-reaching contribution. . . to the history of legal philosophy" is in
his personalization of the Stoic cosmos.[54] The Stoics' ethical ideal commanded one
to act in accordance with an impersonal nature or cosmic reason; Augustine, in
contrast, subordinates man to the Christian God.

By the same logic, Augustine claims that the pre-Christian Roman commonwealth never corresponded to Scipio's definition of the *res publica*, for the concord
of the *res publica* "sine iustitia nullo pacto esse potest" (II, xxi)[55] and "procul dubio
colligitur, ubi iustitia non est, non esse rem publicam" (XIX, xxi). "Justice,"
Augustine yet again affirms "is that virtue which grants to each his own." But as
he has repeatedly shown, the Romans consistently violated this principle: "Quis
enim ad hunc librum [sc. XIX] per superiores huius operis libros peruenit, qui
dubitare adhuc possit malis et inpuris daemonibus servisse Romanos. . . ?" (XIX,
xxi) By serving evil and impure demons, the Romans denied to God His due:

> quae igitur iustitia est hominis, quae ipsum hominem Deo vero tollit et inmundis
> daemonibus subdit? Hocine est sua cuique distribuere? . . . ubi homo Deo non
> seruit, quid in eo putandum est esse iustitiae. . . ? Et si in homine tali non est ulla
> iustitia, procul dubio nec in hominum coetu, qui ex hominibus talis constat"
> (XIX, xxi).

Not that God needs our worship and love. Rather, it is for our own well-being
that we should give God his due.[56]

Augustine's view of distributive justice can be summarized as follows. Justice is
that virtue which renders to each what is his own or due. One's due is defined
according to one's *locus* in the divine order of the cosmos, which is by necessity
hierarchical and, as a product of the divine will, just. As was clearly stated in *De
ordine*, justice therefore cannot be exercised without the existence and knowledge
of divinely-inspired order. For this reason, Augustine can assert in *De doctrina christiana* that to be just, one must perceive the divine order that assigns all things their
place and renders to all their due or what conforms to their place:

> Ille autem iuste et sancte uiuit, qui rerum integer aestimator est, ipse est autem
> qui ordinatam habet dilectionem, ne aut diligat, quod non est diligendum, aut
> non diligat quod diligendum est.[57]

Note that Augustine does not limit the "suum" of the formula "cuique suum
tribuens" to the "divisible assets of the community," whether tangible or intangi-
ble, as did Aristotle and the Roman jurists. What is owed or due to God and one's
neighbor is love, not wealth or honor. It is for this reason that Augustine can also
describe justice in terms of the Golden Rule, "Quod tibi fieri non uis, alii ne

feceris," and claim "Quae sententia cum refertur ad dilectionem dei, omnia flagitia moriuntur, cum ad proximi, omnia facinora" (*De doctrina christiana*, III, xiv). If one bears in mind that in Augustine's understanding distributive justice encompasses all things and not simply the "divisible assets of the community," then there seems no reason to assert that distributive justice is opposed to the Golden Rule.[58] Rather, the Golden Rule is simply another instance of rendering unto others what is their due according to the divine commandment. Similarly, mercy or strictly-applied judicial justice are due to certain people in certain instances, strict justice to the powerful and reprobate, mercy to widows, orphans, and the poor.

As we have seen, one should not expect from the Early Middle High German poets even a remotely similar degree of conceptual clarity and consistency to that of Augustine. *Reht* or *iustitia* is used by the poets sometimes as virtue in general, sometimes as the prime virtue of kings and rulers, sometimes as the *opus misericordiae*, and sometimes in its strict judicial sense as the opposite of mercy.[59] That Early Middle High German *reht* can have such different meanings is hardly surprising in view of the development of the concept of *iustitia*.

Interesting parallels to this conceptual diversity in the understanding of *reht* can also be found in Latin theological texts of the twelfth century. D. O. Lottin writes of Stephen Langton, for example, that "Le mot iustitia, note-t-il, revêt au moins trois sens."[60] Lottin quotes Langton from an unpublished manuscript:

> Dicimus quod ad minus hoc nomen iustitia tripliciter accipitur. In una significatione est generale nomen cuiuslibet uirtutis et quelibet uirtus est iustitia; et secundum hoc Christus dicitur sol iustitie, et secundum hoc qualibet uirtute est aliquis iustus. In alia significatione summittur strictissime, secundum quod iustitia tantum ad iudicium refertur et attenditur tantum modo in iudicando, et secundum hoc dicitur una cardinalium. Item prout dicitur una cardinalium largius summittur quandoque, secundum quod dicitur quod iustitie est unicuique suum reddere, et non solum homini, sed unicuique rei.[61]

Lottin writes of William of Auxerre that he too distinguishes a general justice embracing all virtue and a special, distributive justice according to which God, one's parents, inferiors, and superiors must be rendered their due. The cardinal virtue of justice, finally, can be understood in a broader or a stricter sense. In its broad sense, this form of justice includes one's duties to God and neighbor and especially the practice of mercy. In its stricter, judicial sense, justice is opposed to mercy.[62]

B. The Variety of *reht*

No one would wish to claim that the author of "Vom Rechte" or any of the other Early Middle High German poets were in any way acquainted with such theological tracts as those from which Lottin quotes. The Latin theologians were merely selectively summarizing the varying meanings of *iustitia* as they had evolved from the Bible and Augustine through the early Middle Ages and as they seem to have been familiar to the Early Middle High German writers. But with these different definitions of *iustitia* in mind, we can now return to the "Vom Rechte" poet's puzzling statement that there are three *reht* and try to understand them as three species of the all-embracing virtue of *iustitia*.

The poet's third *reht*, "gewære sîn, " in line 24 of "Vom Rechte" is obviously derived from the frequent fusion of *iustitia* and *veritas*.[63] That the poet did not only simply mean that one should be honest, but had, in part, a more specific and judicial context in mind, becomes clear when the opposite of "gewære sîn" is given in lines 42-43:

> bi des iegelicher sinen muotwillen gechosot,
> so stat daz reht verbosot.[64]

The poet later gives a practical example of what he intended and the judicial context of "gewære sîn" is revealed beyond any doubt:

> Nieman ist so here
> so daz reht zware.
> des megen wir uns wol enstan,
> swa wir ze rehte schulen gan.[65]

"Ze rehte gan" here means to go to trial. The poet, of course, has medieval judicial procedure in mind. The medieval court was convened by a *iudex* who was not a professional judge in the modern sense, but the presider of the court. The *iudex* would have been the count or his assistant (the *vicarius* or viscount), or the hundredman or *centenarius* (the popularly elected presider over a *centenarium* or hundred court), or a bishop, abbot, or the advocate of an ecclesiastic immunity, or even a local lord who presided over his seigniorial court.[66] Judgement, at least in theory, was rendered not by the *iudex*, but by the judgement-finders, who, again in theory, were peers of the accused.[67]

Initially there was almost no public prosecution. A person usually had to go to trial only if he was privately accused. After having been accused, the plaintiff, usually with the assistance of seven other compurgators (Eideshelfer), would declare in a carefully-worded traditional formula his innocence or admit his guilt. If this oath was censured by the judgement-finders as containing even a minor deviation from the accepted formula or if the (private) prosecutor gave a similar, flawless oath of accusation, the plaintiff might be forced to undergo a *judicium Dei*, which consisted in a judicial duel,[68] an ordeal by water, or, as in the case of "Vom Rechte," an ordeal by fire.[69]

A priest or some ecclesiastical representative was usually present at such an ordeal, for the ordeal itself presumed that God would give final judgement.[70] In the ordeal by fire, the plaintiff or his or her representative would usually carry a red-hot iron in his hand for about nine paces. His hand would then be bandaged, and after a few days, the dressing would be removed. If the wound had healed, the accused was innocent, if not, guilty.[71] In "Vom Rechte," the process is described in a simplified manner as follows:

> swie harte sich der muoet,
> der daz isen gluoet

> unde ez danne hin treit,
> einem an die hant leit,
> ist er rehte dar chomen
> (daz han wir diche wol vernomen),
> daz viur in nine brennet.
> wie wol in got erchennet,
> wie verre er da gelobet stat,
> der daz reht da begat![72]

From this short sketch it should be obvious that medieval procedure with its absence of material proof "presumed the utter *bona fides* of litigants."[73] This fundamental fact, and not merely the biblical injunctions, is surely the reason for the frequent connection between *veritas* and *iustitia*, for the goal of *iustitia* in medieval procedure presumes and is based on the *veritas* of the litigants. The "Vom Rechte" poet underlines this when he concludes his description of the ordeal by fire with a warning to perjurers:

> so sint si alle betrogen,
> die in an habent gelogen.
> swie er daz nach gevare,
> so ist ir iegelichem gare
> ein isen also heiz,
> daz ir neheiner weiz,
> reht an die hant;
> daz brennet als ein brant.
> hei wie ez dem gluot,
> der in unschuligen muoet,
> der in des bedwinget,
> an daz reht bringet.
> von diu sint die lugenære
> got vil unmære.[74]

The second *reht*, which the poet defines as the Golden Rule, is, as shown, a typically religious definition of justice.[75] In "Vom Rechte" it too has a judicial content as will become apparent in the discussion of the poem in the next chapter.

Finally, there is the first *reht* of the poem, *triuwe*, which I characterized above as *fides*. The connection between *triuwe* and *iustitia* is initially less clear than in the case of *veritas* and the Golden Rule. *Triuwe* is, of course, one of the central virtues of feudalism and of the high courtly poets. Ulrich Pretzel describes it as follows:

> In Middle High German the word has a number of meanings, beginning with
> the concrete sense (pactum, foedus); it became a general word for virtue. In a
> reciprocal sense, it designates the most various ethical behaviors.[76]

The reciprocal nature of *triuwe* seems to be indicated in the "Vom Rechte" poet's description of its reversal:

mannechlich sinem friunde *niht* gestat,
als er in geminnet hat.[77]

But while these lines might appear to use *triuwe* in the same sense as it is usu-ally used by the high courtly poets as the reciprocal *fides* between lord and vassal, the detailed example of *triuwe* in lines 191–238 of "Vom Rechte" shows that the poet intended something different. In these latter lines the poet first describes God's creation of Lucifer who, infected by "ubirmuot" or "superbia," rebels against his lord:

> der *herre* an daz reht
> hiez do werden einen chneht.
> er worhte in uzzir nihte,
> er worhte in zeinem erlichem liehte,
> daz er vor im wære
> unde im leiht bære.
> do greif er an die ubirmuot,
> daz was ze niht guot.
> der herre behielt daz reht,
> do verstiez er den chneht
> in ein ellende, hin in daz apgrunde.[78]

Satan's fall thus seems to be initially described in feudal terms. These lines merit comparison with a similar description of Satan's rebellion in "Die Hochzeit" (1150), which is usually assumed to have been substantially revised, if not authored by the "Vom Rechte" poet:[79]

> **D**ar zoch *sich* bi alten ziten
> ein herre mit sinen louten.
> der herre lebete rehte,
> der habete vil chnehte;
> (160)   er lech in allen den rat,
> des er vil guot stat hat.
> sumelich sine heriste chnehte,
> die wurben niht rehte,
> die rieten an sin ere:
> (165)   des enkulten si vil sere.
>
> **D**o was undir dem gebirge
> ein vil michil sorge,
> (168)   ein tieffir charchære
>   . . .
> (172)   dar undir swief der herre
> sine ungetriuwe chnehte verre.[80]

Here the feudal imagery is especially apparent. Lines 164–165, in particular, emphasize the concept of *êre* or *honos* of which R. W. Southern wrote:

The fundamental crime against a lord and against the social order was to attempt to diminish the lord's honor. The seriousness of the crime was quite independent of the rebel's power to give effect to his evil intentions: it was his disloyalty, the loosening of the social bond, which outlawed him.[81]

Southern, speaking of France, adds that in the late eleventh century, "the word honour was at the height of its development as a term of social importance."[82] Allowing for the time lag in the development of feudalism in the Empire, one might suppose that the same could be said of the concept of honor in the German-speaking lands in the mid-twelfth century, hence its importance in "Die Hochzeit." In "Die Hochzeit," *triuwe* therefore seems to refer to the feudal, reciprocal *fides* between lord and vassal.

In "Vom Rechte," however, the conclusion that is drawn from its somewhat similar description of Satan's fall emphasizes less *triuwe* in this reciprocal sense of *fides* between lord and vassal than the need simply to maintain the "social bond," to use Southern's phrase, between lord and servant and lady and servant-girl that is the basis of the social order:

> von diu so nesol dehein vrouwe
> gestatten ir diwe,
> daz si sie vor lazze gan,
> swie schone ir varwe si getan,
> noch der herre sinem chnehte.
> daz chom von dem rehte,
> daz der allir herist chneht
> geviel an daz unreht.[83]

Triuwe in "Vom Rechte" thus only partly refers to reciprocal fidelity. More important, according to the poet, is not mutual loyalty but the *obedience* that a servant owes to his lord or master.[84] The connection between *triuwe,* in the sense of obedience, and *iustitia* is revealed by the poet in the lines immediately following those just quoted. *Triuwe* and *reht* are subtly interchanged, and *triuwe* initially seems to be simply the feminine equivalent of the *reht* between lord and servant:

> **W**il der herre unde der chneht
> bede minnen daz reht,
> so sagent diu buoch zware,
> si werdent ebenhere.
> wil diu vrouwe und diu diwe
> minnen die triuwe,
> so sagent diu buoch zware,
> si werdent ebenhere.
> swie wol der man si geborn,
> wil er unrehte varn,
> vert er unrehte,
> er hat daz reht der chnehte.
> ist diu vrouwe ungetriwe,

> si hat daz reht der diwe.
> die schalche unde die *diuwe,*
> minnent si die triwe,
> ir armuot sint nie so groz,
> die werdent der heristen genoz.
> swer da minnet daz reht,
> ez si herre odir chneht,
> der muoz ie hin fur gan,
> der andir hindir im gestan.[85]

Triuwe in the special sense of obedience and as well with the more typical meaning of responsibility for one's inferiors is a species of *reht* because the practice of *reht* or *iustitia* is impossible without the maintenance of order. The centrality of such an Augustinian conception of *ordo* to the practice of *reht*, however, is not confined to the poem "Vom Rechte," rather it is a tacit assumption in all those Early Middle High German works that deal with *reht*. To appreciate how the Early Middle High German poets anchor *reht* in their conception of order, one must therefore see how they conceive of the social order.

2. ORDO

The Early Middle High German poets and prose writers use many different categories to describe the social *ordo*.[86] Heinrich von Melk, for example, speaks of and to bishops, ecclesiastical judges, priests, princes, lords, secular judges, knights, ladies, merchants, day laborers, and farmers.[87] In their admonishments to *reht*, however, the Early Middle High German poets tend to restrict themselves to three conceptual pairs: *frîe* (freeman) and the *scalc* (slave), *rîch* (rich) and *arm* (poor), and *hêrre* (lord) and *kneht* (servant). Before considering how the Early Middle High German poets link *reht* to these three groups, we must first see how the concepts are used and what they mean.

A. *Frîe* and *scalc*

The categories *frîe* and *scalc* play an especially conspicuous role in the Early Middle High German biblical epics based on the Book of Genesis. Consider first the *Vienna Genesis*, an epic poem of about 6,000 lines, based primarily on the biblical book of Genesis, with frequent interruptions in the form of sermonic admonitions. The poem has been variously dated from 1060 to 1080. A *terminus ante quem* of 1122 is perhaps likely since royal selection and investiture of bishops, forbidden by the Concordat of Worms in that year, are mentioned in passing as a standard and unobjectionable practice.[88]

The poet's, or perhaps the poets', concern with order is immediately evident in the first 100 lines, in which God's creation of the ten choirs of angels and Satan's fall are described. Satan justifies his rebellion in terms that are quite similar to those used in "Vom Rechte" and "Die Hochzeit":

er sprach "min maister ist gewaltich
hie in himele,
er wanet ime mege iuweht sin widere.
ich pin alsame hêre,
ich newil unter ime wesen nie mere.
ich pin also schone,
ich wil mit minem chore
ebengewaltich ime wesen.
ich wil den stuol min
setzen norderen halp sin
ûf dem himele.
ich wil iz ime haben ebene."[89]

Satan's disruption of the harmony of creation consists in his desire to reject his God-given place in the order of things. With the fall of Satan, God restores the balance of hierarchical order by creating man to replace the lost choir.[90]

The *Vienna Genesis* poet's conception of the order of human society is articulated in his account of the flood and its aftermath, when the poet pauses to gloss the story of Noah and his three sons. After the waters of the flood had receded, Noah planted a vineyard and drunk with the fruit of his labor, he fell asleep naked in his tent. His second son Ham finds him and derisively reveals his discovery to his two brothers, Shem and Japheth, who dutifully cover their father. In the biblical account, Noah awakens and upon learning of Ham's mockery, he curses Ham's son.[91] The German poet writes:

Do Noe er wachete
und uil rehte urescete
wie Cham hete getan,
do er in sach plekchen,
ich weiz er in ueruluochete
mit aller siner afterchunfte.
er hiez si scalche sin,
dienen sinen bruoderen.
Die anderen zwene er wichte
zuo urîeme lîbe:
si waren in gezelten
so herren scolten.[92]

The poet's gloss reads:

*V*one Chames sculde
wurden allerist scalche.
ê waren si alle
ebenfrî unde edele.
Châmes huohes unde spottes
uile manige inkulten des.[93]

"Freeman" and "slave" are strictly legal descriptions of the order of society. The *Genesis* poet delivers the lines in passing; the amplification, in good monastic fashion, seems only to serve to show off the author's knowledge. As such, the lines perhaps seem to have little importance for Early Middle High German views of social order or the practice of *reht*, but their possible genealogy and later use are curious. The Latin biblical commentaries, a seemingly likely source for the *Vienna Genesis* poet, all follow Augustine in their interpretation of Noah's curse.[94] Isidore of Seville, for example, writes of Shem, Japheth, and Ham:

> Proinde in duobus fillis, maximo [Shem] et minimo [Japheth], duo populi figurantur, scilicet circumcisio et praeputium, unam vestem fidei a tergo portantes, sacramentum scilicet jam praeteritae dominicae passionis, neque nuditatem patris intuentur, quia in Christi necem non consentiunt, et tamen honorant velamento, tanquam scientes unde sint nati.

> Quam nuditatem, id est passionem Christi, videns Cham derisit, et Judaei Christi mortem videntes subsannaverunt. Sem vero et Japheth, tanquam duo populi ex circumcisione et praeputio credentes, cognita nuditate patris, qua significabatur passio Salvatoris, sumentes vestimentum posuerunt super dorsa sua, et intuentes aversi operuerunt nuditatem patris, nec viderunt quod verendo texerunt.[95]

Isidore interprets the significance of Ham in more detail:

> Cham porro, qui interpretatur *calidus*, medius filius, tanquam ab utroque discretus, nec in primitiis Israelitarum, nec in plenitudine gentium permanens, significat non solum Judaeorum, sed etiam haereticorum genus calidum, non spiritu sapientiae, sed impatientiae, quo solent haereticorum fervere praecordia, et pacem perturbare sanctorum.[96]

All later commentaries, such as those of Rabanus and his school, offer the same interpretation.[97] The story of Noah and his sons is interpreted by the biblical commentators as an allegory and is nowhere used to explain the historical origin of servitude.

The *Vienna Genesis* poet, therefore, ignored the tradition of the Bible commentaries and, instead drew on another source, possibly Avitus' biblical epic *De spiritalis historiae gestis* from the early sixth century.[98] Avitus writes:

> Nam servos nondum dederat natura vocari
> Nec dominos famulis discernere noverat ordo.
> Primus enim maculam servili nomine sensit
> Huius natorum medius. . . .
> Quod postquam sanctus potuit cognoscere Noe
> Natum germanis famulum dedit. inde repertum
> Tale iugum; cuncti nam semine nascimur uno.
> Servitii certe causam fecisse reatus
> Cernitur et liber peccans fit crimine servus.[99]

Avitus, in turn, was most likely inspired by a passage in Augustine's *De civitate Dei* that offers not an allegorical, but an historical interpretation of Noah's curse:

Rationalem factum ad imaginem suam noluit nisi inrationabilibus dominari; non hominem homini, sed hominem pecori. . . . Condicio quippe seruitutis iure intellegitur inposita peccatori. Proinde nusquam scripturarum legimus seruum, antequam hoc uocabulo Noe iustus peccatum filii uindicaret. Nomen itaque istud culpa meruit, non natura.[100]

This Augustinian notion enjoyed widespread popularity in the early Middle Ages, as is evidenced by its inclusion in a monastic book of questions and answers from the ninth century: "Quo ordine vel pro qua re servi facti sunt? De Cham, qui de verecundia patris sui risit."[101]

That the *Vienna Genesis* poet's gloss might be understood as more than a monastic truism is shown by another vernacular biblical epic, the *Vorauer Bücher Moses*, quite variously dated by scholars between 1130 and 1180, for which the *Vienna Genesis* or its prototype was a major source. After mentioning Noah's curse of Ham and his progeny, the *Vorauer* poet comments:

> **D**az sin dev drev geslahte,
> dev gestent mit durnahte:
> einez daz ist edele,
> di hant daz hantgemahele;[102]
> di andere frige luote,
> di tragent sich mit guote;
> di driten daz sint dinestmann,
> also ich uirnomen han,
> darunder wurden chnehte;
> daz sint dev geslahte.
> svvi wir ez chêren
> ir nist niht mêre;
> dev zale nimmer zerget
> di wile so dev werlt stet.[103]

The legal background of this passage is even more explicit than in the *Vienna Genesis*. The poet carefully uses the terminology familiar from the early medieval *Leges* and the Carolingian capitularies, namely *nobiles*, *liberi*, and *servi*, and he adds to them the newer category of *ministeriales*. With the important exception of *nobiles*, these categories do not necessarily determine social or economic status, although they certainly have such connotations. The social standing of a *liber* was naturally usually higher than that of a *servus*. Nonetheless, a *ministerialis* or *dienstman*, rightly placed by the poet as a legal sub-category of the unfree or *servi*, could in the twelfth century gain great power and standing. Eventually the knightly portion of this group would constitute the lower nobility of the late medieval Holy Roman Empire.[104]

It is by no means clear what the source of the *Vorauer* poet's amplification of the *Vienna Genesis* passage is.[105] The only prior example of a similarly tripartite interpretation of Noah's curse (nobles, free, and servants) that I could find is from a somewhat obscure Anglo-Saxon manuscript dated to the mid-eleventh century, which contains an isolated gloss on the biblical passage.[106]

A similar scheme, from about the first third of the twelfth century, that is, perhaps contemporary with the Vorauer poem, can be found in Honorius Augustodunensis' *Imago mundi*: "Huius [Shem's] tempore divisum est genus humanum in tria: in liberos, milites, servos. Liberi de Sem, milites de Japhet, servi de Cham."[107] Note, however, that Honorius has shifted the position of the freemen to first place, thus eliminating the nobles, and that he has placed knights in the second position.

Honorius' scheme, which was also translated in the German *Lucidarius* at the end of the twelfth century,[108] is close to the familiar categories of the three orders, priests, warriors, and laborers, the first explicit medieval formulation of which is found in the ninth century in Alfred the Great's translation of Boethius. Georges Duby claimed that Honorius' scheme is in fact a picture of the three orders and that therefore the "liberi" really refers to the priesthood.[109] Is the idea of the three orders also the background to the Vorauer poet's comments? Does Early Middle High German *frî* refer then to the priesthood? This interpretation seems questionable. In order to view the scheme of the *liberi, milites,* and *servi* in Honorius' *Imago mundi* as an instance of the three orders, Duby had to graft onto it another text by Honorius. In the *Summa Gloria*, Honorius does indeed identify Shem with the priesthood and Japheth with the Roman Empire. Ham has a twofold signification, "tertius filius, qui duorum fratrum servitio addicitur, populus sacerdotio et regno subiectus accipitur, vel Iudaicus populus utrique serviens intelligitur."[110] As the people subject to the priesthood and the kingdom, this is doubtless a modified instance of the classical three orders. But Ham's also prefiguring the unbelieving Jews indicates that Honorius is equally indebted to the tradition of the Latin biblical commentaries.

There seems no reason to conflate Honorius' two accounts of the outcome of Noah's curse, freemen, knights, servants in the *Imago mundi* and priesthood, empire, subject people or the Jews in the *Summa gloria*.[111] Augustine, as mentioned, used two quite distinct interpretations of Noah's curse, both in the *De civitate Dei*, to explain, on the one hand, the historical origin of the word and institution servitude, and on the other, the prefiguration of Christ's passion and his rejection by the Jews and heretics. He nowhere tries to harmonize the two interpretations. Even in the same text, let alone the same author, symbols and biblical figures could have a wide range of sometimes contradictory or mutually exclusive meanings, which stand in no need of reconciliation.[112]

The *liberi, milites,* and *servi* of Honorius' *Imago mundi* seem, therefore, not to be an example of the three orders, as Duby claimed, but a straightforward description of legal status and, in the case of the knights, social function. As such, they are a possible inspiration for the Vorauer poet's division "edelfrî," "frî," "chnehte" and "dienstman," but the uncertain dating of both the Vorauer text and Honorius' *Imago mundi* precludes any certainty.

Another possible source of the *Vorauer Genesis* is the Eddic poem "Rígsthula," in which an otherwise unknown god, Rígr, visits three households and fathers the races of the jarls, carls, and thralls, or nobles, freemen, and unfree.[113] Georges Dumézil's interpretation of the "Rígsthula" as a Germanic instance of the concept of the three orders of priests, warriors, and laborers again raises the question of whether the *Vorauer Genesis* scheme represent the three orders.[114] But while it is true that the jarl or noble figure in the "Rígsthula" is taught to interpret runes and thus perhaps has an implied religious function, he is otherwise clearly a warrior/king figure and not a priest.[115] The Eddic poem, therefore, seems not to correspond to the scheme of the three orders, but instead appears to use, like the *Vorauer* poet and Honorius in the *Imago mundi*, legalistic categories.[116]

A recent interpretation of the "Rígsthula" claims that the social view of the poem is "brutally aristocratic" and therefore opposed to the Christian view of equality. For this reason it must represent a Germanic or at least pre-Christian view.[117] Would this imply that Honorius and the *Vorauer* poet had introduced Germanic, non-Christian elements into their social schemes? Again, this seems unlikely. First, as the examples cited above from Augustine show, Christianity can sway between an assertion of equality and a justification of servitude on the basis of sin, usually Adam's, but sometimes Ham's. The tension is Pauline in origin and pervades the entire Middle Ages.[118] Gregory the Great, to take only one example among many, writes in the *Moralia in Job*:"Nam, ut praefati sumus, omnes homines natura aequales genuit, sed variante meritorum ordine, alios aliis dispensatio occulta postponit."[119] To call the "Rígsthula" Germanic on the basis of its inegalitarian social view alone, therefore, would be unwarrantable. In any case, despite similarities, the "Rígsthula," whether Germanic or not, is an unlikely source of either Honorius or the *Vorauer Genesis*, for the date of the Eddic poem is highly uncertain; opinion varies from the mid-eleventh to the mid-thirteenth century.[120]

Without more evidence, then, one must rule out an Indo-European or Germanic origin of the *Vorauer* poet's interpretation of Noah's curse. Rather, the poet, or his unknown source, has taken one strand of the interpretation of the Genesis text as the historical explanation of the origin of servitude and expanded its binary classification, free/unfree, which we saw in the *Vienna Genesis*, into a threefold scheme whose terms are primarily legal in origin. It is unnecessary to search for Indo-European or Germanic roots for this expansion. On the contrary, the tale of Noah's *three* sons seems to demand a tripartite division of some sort, as the different examples from Honorius show.[121] The question, then, is why the *Vorauer* poet chose legal concepts, especially as social historians have claimed that in the German Empire of the eleventh and twelfth centuries, the older legal division of society into free and unfree was rapidly losing its traditional importance. The unfree serfs were rising economically and many of the free farmer-warriors were sinking, with the result that the two groups were becoming subsumed under the category of the "rustici" or peasants.[122]

One can scarcely deny that the legal distinction free/unfree had completely lost its relevance in the late eleventh and twelfth centuries. Consider, for example, the Peace of God proclamation of 1083 from Cologne. Unlike the earlier French Peace of God documents, the Cologne version envisions not only ecclesiastical punishments, but also secular fines for those who violated it:"Si *liber* vel *nobilis* eam [the peace] violaverit," he will be banished and deprived of his allods or fiefs. But "Si *servus* occiderit hominem, decolletur." The Cologne peace further states:"Non ledit pacem, si quis delinquentem *servum* suum vel discipulum vel quolibet modo sibi subditum scopis vel fustibus cedi iusserit."[123] Another Peace of God, probably Bavarian from the end of the eleventh century, gives varying fines for the "nobilis, the liber aut ministerialis," and the "lito aut servus."[124]

These Peace of God documents are not merely ideological proclamations. They are also pragmatic ordinances and, as such, are meant to be effective in the real world. They cannot be accused of a nostalgic yearning for antiquated legal categories. Similar lists using legalistic categories can also be found in the vernacular literature of the late twelfth and early thirteenth centuries: "grâven unde herzogen . . . frîhêren unde dienstmann," or "grâven, vrîen, dienstman," or "fúrsten, heeren, dienstman."[125]

Of course, I do not wish to assert that a legal structure identical to that of the *Leges* or the Carolingian capitularies was still valid in the twelfth-century Empire. What does seem clear, however, is that the *Vorauer* poet uses precisely legal terminology to order society into the nobles, the free, and the servants or ministerials. He places these legal concepts in a religious context whose background is best traced to the Augustinian view of servitude and domination. The *Vorauer* poet thus weaves many different strands of tradition into one, for the Augustinian distinctions themselves are probably as much indebted to the Roman legal concepts of free and unfree[126] as they are to the biblical concepts *dominus* and *servus*. As for the distinctions of the *Leges* — noble, free, and servant — most modern legal historians no longer see them as purely Germanic or pre-Christian. Rather, they represent a conflation of Germanic and Roman/Christian terms.[127] Thus, the *Vorauer* poet presents a view of society which is perhaps best described as religious/legal. Like the *Vienna Genesis*, which he follows and amplifies, his fundamental social category is freedom in the sense of freedom from servitude, a servitude that is, indirectly, divinely sanctioned.

Although the biblical epic poets are unusual in providing an historical explanation for the rise of servitude and freedom, they are not alone in employing such concepts. Sometimes the Early Middle High German poets merely use them in passing, such as the author of "Von der Siebenzahl" in his description of the biblical jubilee: "der gechoufte scalc gie friliche heim, do newas ubiral getwanc nihein."[128] Often the terms *frîe* and *scalc* have a purely religious meaning, based on biblical usage, as when the author of the "Auslegung des Paternoster" writes of Christ's redemptive act: "verscelket het uns der alte man; gevrien muoz uns der niwe man."[129] In her vision of the resurrection, Frau Ava uses *frî* in a similar fashion, but she adds to it the non-biblical "noble:"

> So vernemet alle da bi: da sit ir edele unde fri,
> da netwinget iuch sunde noch leit,   daz ist diu ganze
> friheit.[130]

Heinrich von Melk, like Ava, also combines "freedom" and "force," but he uses *frî* in a negative sense. He writes, for example, of those priests who revel in the pleasures of this world:

> wie tiwer si danne getet
> dirre wertliche richtuom
> unt der unsælige frituom,
> daz si lebent ane twanhsal.[131]

In his castigation of ecclesiastical judges, Heinrich blends this morally conceived "unsæliger frituom" with real social and legal freedom:

> geistliche richtære,
> die mugen richsnære
> baz denne meister geheizzen.
> mugen si der scilde vil geleisten
> helme unt brunne,
> daz ist elliu ir wunne,
> daz si mit menige riten
> unt heizzen in die gegende witen
> dienen swes so si.
> ir untertanen wellent wesen fri
> ze tuonen allez, daz in gevalle.[132]

Heinrich similarly criticizes knights and ladies whose irresponsible behavior makes their subjects unruly:

> frowen unt riter
> di nedurfen niemmer gestriten,
> weder ir leben bezzer si.
> ir untertanen wellent wesen fri.[133]

In the "Linzer Antichrist," *frîe* and *scalc* are clearly used in their secular and legal sense in the poet's description of the reign of the Antichrist:

> ez si kunicriche odir bisctum,
> daz hat er danne in siner hant.
> betwungin hat er elliu diu lant:
> er gebiutet swa dehein gotis holdi si,
> er si scalc oder vri,
> lege odir phaffe,
> daz man daz scaffe
> mit guote odir mit leide
> daz er von Criste sceide.[134]

Equally explicit in his use of "freedom" in a secular, legal sense is the author of *König Rother.* Count Arnold, for example, says:

> "Mich hant mine viande
> vir triven dur iren over mut,
> nu is mir thure daz got.
> swe arme so ich si,
> ich bin von minen magen vri."[135]

This purely secular use of *frî* and *scalc* is, however, an exception in Early Middle High German literature. Even the religiously-colored use of the terms, as for example in the biblical epics, is rare compared with the almost universal division of society into *rîch* and *arm* and *hêrre* and *kneht*.

B. *Arm* and *rîch*

The conceptual pair *arme und rîche*, unlike the *frîe* and *scalce* of the biblical epics, was not derived through a complex reception and reinterpretation of Latin theological tracts, biblical commentaries, and legal definitions, but the exact meaning of the terms is by no means always clear. The combination *arme und rîche* is ubiquitous in Early Middle High German as well as in classical Middle High German, usually simply as a formula meaning "everyone."[136] It would surely be mistaken to interpret each occurrence of such a formula as an indication of an author's view of the social *ordo*, much less as a basis for determining the practice of justice. Thus when the author of "Die jüngere Judith" says:

> Si reiten al geliche, arme unde riche
> beidiu chint unde wip . . . .[137]

or when Frau Ava writes of Jesus:

> . . .   do chom got gegangen
> unt lerte alle geliche arme und riche.[138]

or when Heinrich von Melk describes the uncertainty of life:

> doch mugen wir iu manige not niht verdagen
> die den armen unt den richen
> gescent mislichen.[139]

these lines reveal absolutely nothing about their authors' conception of society.[140]

But in some Early Middle High German passages *die armen* is a substantive social category. Noker, for example writes:

> tes rehten bedarf ter armo man.[141]

Der Wilde Mann has the avaricious man ("der gire") confess:

> di armen dwanc ich under mich.[142]

And Der arme Hartmann has a sinner say:

> ich begunde dicke neisen widwen unde weisen
> und andre arme liute . . .[143]

Similarly *die rîchen* seems to refer to a real social group when Heinrich von Melk bitterly complains of the papal curia:

> man vindet da dehein zuversicht
> rehtes noch genaden,
> wan wie man dem scazze muge gelagen.
> der riche man ist edele
> unt ist der fursten gesedele
> . . .
> allenthalben ist verworfen der armman.[144]

Or when he writes of priests' venality:

> si refsent niwan die armen
> die solden in erbarmen.
> swaz der riche man getuot,
> daz dunchet sie suoz unt guot.[145]

This substantive usage of *arme* and *ríche*, however vague, seems simple enough to comprehend. The poets are using biblical categories, "rich" and "poor," as the basis for their strictures on justice, and in this they seem merely to be following one strand of the early medieval conception of *iustitia* as was described at the beginning of this chapter, namely the need for justice toward the poor. But not all scholars would agree with this interpretation. Stephan Speicher, for example, writes of the meanings of "der riche" and "der arme" in the poem "Vom Rechte" that:

> The chief meaning of *riche* is "powerful," "noble," primarily as a class description [ständische Qualifikation] when contrasted with the *arme man*, the lower-placed one (usually simple peasants). To be powerful and noble one needs property; hence one should add the sense "rich" to *riche*. Nonetheless, this material definition, "propertied," is acquired by *riche* only with the emancipation of the urban burghers.[146]

To justify this assertion, Speicher refers to Roland Ris' book *Das Adjektiv reich im mittelalterlichen Deutsch* and, somewhat more cautiously, to Karl Bosl's study on the terms *potens* and *pauper*.[147]

If Speicher intends "ständische Qualifikation" in a legal sense, then his characterization of *rích* as such a qualification can be quickly dismissed as a conceptual confusion. No one would seriously maintain the word *rích* in the twelfth century contained an explicit reference to a legal estate. At best, *rích* can be described as an estate in the sense of a *conditio*.[148]

Speicher's dependence on Ris' lengthy study is more complicated, however, and deserves to be discussed in detail. Old High German *ríhhi*, the ancestor of Early Middle High German *rích*, usually did mean powerful. According to Ris, however, this was only the case in those Old High German works whose language was based on a "purely Germanic tradition," and as an example he gives Otfrid von Weißenburg. In the Old High German translations of Latin, on the other hand, which according to Ris are characterized by an "ascetic" Christianity, *ríhhi* has purely negative connotations and is used to translate "tyrannis."[149] Ris attributes this difference in meaning to the Christian translators' hostility toward the unchristian connotations of the Germanic description of status ("germanisches Standesepitheton") *rîhhi*. *Rîhhi* in its Germanic sense of "potens," therefore, had to lead its life in the linguistic underground,

> in the heroic poetry that we can no longer directly grasp. It again comes into view for us in Early Middle High German religious and secular literature, where-by in the religious literature the tradition of Otfrid continues, while the native popular poems contributed much from their traditional collection of formulas.[150]

In the course of the development of the Old High German Christian transla-tions, Ris says, the purely Germanic connotations of *rîhhi* had been so successful-ly suppressed that by the ninth century the word could again be freely used, but this time to translate *dives*. The later Old High German translators readily seized at *rîhhi* because a standard vernacular translation of *dives* had earlier evaded them and because *rîhhi* was more susceptible to various word formations than were the ear-lier attempts at a translation of *dives* such as "êhtig" or "ôtag."[151] *Rîhhi* thus even-tually came to have a double meaning of "rich" and "powerful" that correspond-ed well to the reality of the ninth century, during which "the conception of wealth was nearly identical to that of political power."[152] Middle High German *rîch* con-tinued to have the double meaning *dives* and *potens* and only became restricted to its New High German meaning "rich," as Speicher agreed, with the emancipation of the urban burghers.[153]

In the Early Middle High German period, Ris claims, *rîch* was used especially as a divine epithet, meaning *potens*, at least in the Middle-Franconian and Rhenish dialects, while in the Upper German dialects, in particular Alemannic, this usage was far less common. Ris explains this Upper German hesitance to use *rîch* as an attribute of God:

> The more intensive missionary work, while not able completely to suppress the traces of the old native literature, was yet capable of making them disappear from the literary surface. Among these traces was the old status designation *rîche*, which could not be abandoned, but which in its epic meaning 'potens' was too remi-niscent of heathen concepts.[154]

Instead, Alemannic writers such as Notker tried to continue to emphasize the ungermanic meaning *dives*.

Ris' complex and detailed explanation of the evolution in meaning of *rîch* is largely speculative. His characterizations "Germanic" and "ascetic/Christian" are unfortunately vague; hence his division of Old High German literature into these two categories is not always enlightening. Ris' interpretation of Early Middle High German *rîch* is similarly flawed, and his account of Early Middle High German usage is neither complete nor accurate. He claims, for example, that *rîch* is used exactly six times in the *Vienna Genesis* and that it always means *potens*.[155] This is indeed true in four of his examples,[156] but in his fifth instance (as well as in line 1,836, which Ris overlooked), *rîch* is part of the formula *rîch und arm* and to assert that it here means *potens* is to beg the question:

> **D**ie got furhtent
> und nach im gerne wurchent,
> riche oder arme,
> die choment alle zuo sinem barme.[157]

While in Ris' sixth instance, *rîch* clearly means "rich:"

> **E**sau was ein rich man
> in vihe iouch in hiwen,
> daz er aller herscefte
> nehête gebresten.[158]

Ris overlooked two more instances of *rîch* in the *Vienna Genesis*, which seem to mean "rich" and not *potens*, namely line 4,177[159] and especially lines 5,176-5,183, in which the Egyptian famine is described:

> **V**one tage ze tage
> merot sich des hungeres chlage.
> suaz taz lîut scatzes hête
> ze Ioseph iz in prahte
> . . .
> des wart des chuniges chamere vil riche.[160]

In yet another example of *rîch* in the poem that Ris overlooked, the meaning is ambiguous. It could mean *potens* or it is simply a part of the formula *rîch und arm*. Yet it could also be interpreted as meaning "rich:"

> **I**oseph hiez das chorn dresken,
> lutzil machin zuo eschin.
> er hiez ez guarlichen hantelon,
> diez scolten ewantilon,
> den armen dirmite helfein,
> den richen firchouffin.[161]

Contrary to Speicher, Ris' study is therefore an unsuitable basis for determining the meaning of Early Middle High German *rîch*.

Speicher's second authority for the meaning of *rîch*, the eminent historian Karl Bosl's influential study of the concepts *potens* and *pauper*, also merits discussion.[162] Bosl's comments on the pair *potens* and *pauper* should be placed in their proper context. As was noted in Chapter I, German constitutional historians like Bosl rejected nineteenth-century legal historians' interpretation of the *liberi* of early medieval law codes as referring to the old Germanic *Gemeinfreie*. In place of this category, the constitutional historians argued that the freedom of the early medieval *liberi* was, in Bosl's words, "an unfree freedom," characterized by a strong dependence on authority, especially royal authority.[163] In an attempt to find evidence in early medieval sources of the *liberi* being characterized in this sense as "unfree freemen" or "the king's freemen" (*Königsfreie*), Bosl seized on the ubiquitous categories *potens* and *pauper*, contending that these words had a special "tech-

nical sense" and should be understood as describing the power-wielding aristo-
crats (*potentes*) and the subject "king's freemen" (*pauperes*). Bosl insists that "What
is important [about the terms *potens* and *pauper*] is not the economic and status criteria, but the legal and social ones."[164]

The existence of this class "king's freemen," as Bosl understood the term, is
today generally questioned; hence the primary sense of Bosl's technical definition
of *pauperes* is equally debatable.[165] Is it possible, nonetheless, to accept Bosl's contention that *potens* and *pauper* had some kind of technical meaning? To evaluate
Bosl's claim, one must consider in detail the sources that form the basis of his argument. Bosl's chief witness is the "Capitularia missorum specialia" from 802, which
contains injunctions to the *missi dominici* to uphold *iustitia* and to render judgment
to certain unprivileged groups. The twelfth chapter of the capitulary reads: "De
oppressionibus liberorum hominum pauperum, qui in exercitu ire debent et a
iudicibus sunt obpressi."[166] Bosl asserts that "These are the (king's) freemen, liable
for military service, who are called *pauperes* and who are to be protected from the
judges' oppression."[167] This is a characterization with which, aside from the paren-
thetic reference to the "king's freeman," no one would disagree.

But Bosl then compares Chapter 12 of the capitulary with Chapter 18:

> De banno domini imperatoris et regis, quod per semetipsum consuetus est ban-
> nire, id est de mundeburde ecclesiarum, viduarum, orfanorum et de minus poten-
> tium atque rapto et de exercitali placito instituto: ut hi qui ista inrumperint ban-
> num dominicum omnimodis conponant.[168]

Bosl states that the "minus potentes" of this chapter are identical to the "pauperes"
of Chapter 12, and he comments: "If we understand 'minus' here as a weakened
negation, then it is the corresponding negative definition of *pauper*: someone who
is not *potens*."[169] But there are no *pauperes* in Chapter 12, only "liberi homines"
who are qualified by the adjective *pauperes*. There is nothing in these two chapters
to justify equating the *liberi* homines with the *minus potentes*.

The phrase "liberi homines" (without the modifying adjective *pauperes*) appears
again in Chapter 13b along with the categories "liti," or the half-free, and "servi."
The chapter deals with the duties of these three groups in the defense of the coast-
lines and the fines imposed for neglecting them:

> De liberis hominibus qui circa maritima loca habitant: si nuntius venerit ut ad
> succurrendum debeant venire et hoc neglexerint, unusquisque solidos viginti
> conponat, medietatem in dominico, medietatem ad populum. Si litus fuerit, soli-
> dos quindecim conponat ad populum et fredo dominico in dorso accipiat. Si
> servus fuerit, solidos X ad populum et fredo dorsum.[170]

This passage, says Bosl, expresses "the social proximity of these *liberi* to the *liti*
and serfs [Leibeigene]" and it also describes "the differentiated circle of the *pauperes*."[171] It clearly does nothing of the sort, for the word *pauperes* is never used. As
for the social proximity of the three groups, which Bosl derives from their being
treated together in one chapter, this is again doubtful. Chapter 13b simply gives
the usual tripartite classification of legal groups common to all Frankish law.[172]

Bosl then refers to the conclusion of the capitulary:

> Insuper totum, undecumque necesse fuerit, tam de iustitiis nostris quacumque et iustitias ecclesiarum, viduarum, orfanorum, pupillorum et ceterorum hominum inquirant et perficiant.[173]

Bosl claims that "ceteri homines" refers to the "liberi homines" of Chapter 12, which may or may not be true, for there is nothing in this chapter to suggest or deny that.

Bosl finally argues that a passage from the *Lorsch Annals* provides "somewhat more clarity" about the meaning of *pauperes* in Carolingian sources. Charlemagne, after having been proclaimed emperor, remembers the *pauperes* in his care:

> Recordatus misericordiae suae de pauperibus, qui in regno suo erant et iustitias suas pleniter [h]abere non poterant, noluit de infra palatio pauperiores vassos suos transmittere ad iustitias faciendum propter munera, sed elegit in regno suo archiepiscopos et reliquos episcopos et abbates cum ducibus et comitibus, qui iam opus non [h]abebant super innocentes munera accipere, et ipsos misit per universum regnum suum, et ecclesiis, viduis et orfanis et pauperibus et cuncto populo iustitiam facerent.[174]

Bosl comments: *Pauper* has the sense here not of "poor, without any means" but refers rather to the underclass of those vassals who were perhaps without any fief; it is used here in a technical sense.[175] Again, there is nothing in the passage that proves this.

Bosl found the origin of the putatively technical concepts *pauper* and *potentes* in the social categories of Late Antiquity, the "honestiores" and "humiliores" or "plebei." He summarized his views as follows

> In the course of the decline of the old municipal social order, the conceptual pair *honestiores* and *humiliores* was transformed into the opposition *potentes-humiles (pauperes)*. This penetrated into the official language of the Frankish empire and became especially widespread in the ninth century. The urban culture of Antiquity had disappeared, and the old opposition *liber-servus* had become illusory in an agrarian, feudalized society dominated by the exercise of power. Opposed to a sword-carrying ruling class of *potentes* in the empire were the *liberi* (king's freemen) and *servi* who needed to be protected . . . they were subsumed under the name *pauperes*, which referred primarily to their need to be defended.[176]

Criticized for ignoring the biblical background of the concepts *potens* and *pauper*,[177] Bosl later slightly modified this position:

> With the decline of the old municipal social order of the Roman Empire, which had opposed the *honestiores* and the *humiliores*, this old conceptual pairing was transformed into an opposition of *potentes* and *pauperes*, presumably under the influence of Christianity and compelled by the dissolution of the old order.[178]

Bosl's description of the origin of the conceptual pair *potens* and *pauper* is uncertain, for he provides no evidence for his versions of the origin of the terms, although their origin is clearly a key to understanding their meaning in Carolingian literature.

Far from being technical terms echoing Late Roman municipal categories, it seems more likely that *potens* and *pauper* were simply vague descriptions derived primarily from the Bible.[179] The *minus potentes* of Chapter 18 of the "Capitularia missorum specialia," the *ceteri homines* of Chapter 19, and the *pauperes* of the *Lorsch Annals* probably are synonymous, as Bosl claims. But their meaning in the sources cited by Bosl seems scarcely different from that of the traditional objects of royal justice in the early medieval Latin literature on *iustitia* discussed above, namely the widows, orphans, and the poor. The Carolingian documents are thus repeating in a more systematic and institutionalized fashion the ideals of justice found throughout early medieval sources. This is not to deny that the *pauperes* were a real social category and that they stood in real need of protection. As Schulze, for example, has rightly remarked "The capitularies are . . . a reflection of real socio-economic processes."[180] But there seems to be no reason to consider *potens* and *pauper* as having any technical sense; rather, they simply mean "powerful" and "poor." Bosl, of course, was dealing exclusively with Latin terminology. If his interpretation of this terminology is uncertain, then there is all the more reason to avoid applying it to Early Middle High German usage, as Speicher, only one among many, has suggested.

In interpreting the Early Middle High German pair *rîche* and *arme* one would do better to consider first the influence of the traditional Christian concepts *dives* and *pauper* or *mendicus* as they are used, for example, in the parable of Lazarus and Dives in Luke 16, 19-31. In his version of the parable, for example, Der arme Hartmann speaks of "ein rich man" and "ein arm man," by which he clearly means simply "a rich man" and "a poor man" and surely not a privileged aristocrat and a putative "king's freeman" or any other technical sense of the words: There are no legal connotations in Hartmann's use of the terms.[181]

In their admonitions to *reht*, the Early Middle High German poets understand by *die armen* "die durftigen" or "needy," in Heinrich von Melk's phrase.[182] The *arme* certainly are politically powerless as Bosl had argued, but it is their poverty with which the Early Middle High German poets were primarily concerned. Similarly, Early Middle High German *rîch* can certainly mean "powerful," but in explicit or implicit combination with the *die armen*, the Early Middle High German poets usually intend it to mean simply "rich" or "wealthy."

C. *Hêrre* and *kneht*

The categories *hêrre* and *kneht* are as frequently used in the Early Middle High German poems as a basis for their description of the practice of *reht* as are *rîch* and *arm*. *Hêrre* and *kneht* are similarly biblically-colored terms, but their meaning was at least equally affected by feudal concepts. This is particularly clear in the case of *hêrre,* which in its Old High German form *hêriro* is a loan translation from the Latin "senior."[183] In Old High German, *hêriro* is used both for the religious "senior" in a monastery[184] as well as for the secular lord or "senior" as opposed to his vassals.[185] In the Old High German period, it was rarely used for God, who is typically addressed as *trûhtin*, which word, in turn, is as good as always restricted to God. Only in the course of the eleventh century does *hêrro* begin to replace *trûhtin*.[186]

In the Old High German period, *hêrro,* meaning secular "lord" or biblical *dominus,* is often paired with *scalc* or *eigenscalc,* both of which are usually used to translate *servus.*[187] *Scalc* should not, however, be confused with vassal ("homo") for which the typical German translation is "man"; it refers rather, as noted above, to a slave, a serf, or sometimes an unspecified servant.

In the Early Middle High German era, this usage continues and is fairly consistent: *hêrre* means "dominus," *scalc* "servus," and *man* "homo."[188]

According to Bumke, *hêrre,*

> remains for a long time the mark of the nobility, but already when used in an address it begins to become merely a polite form and in these cases shows no sign of being a class designation. The same is true of its Latin counterpart *dominus.*[189]

Thus, although *hêrre* in Early Middle High German often means a highly-placed lord, one should remember that its reference is becoming wider and including a broader, more loosely defined social group. Not every Middle High German *hêrre* must be a great lord; even a local, and far less powerful lord can be so characterized. *Hêrre* means the king and emperor as well as the rural seignior.

The second element of the pair *hêrre* and *kneht* is less easily explained.[190] Old High German *kneht* typically meant "boy" or "child." It rapidly expanded this meaning, however, and Notker uses it to mean "warrior" and translates "fortitudo" as "chnehtheit."[191] In Early Middle High German, *kneht,* usually modified by "guot" or "tiure" (worthy) can and usually does mean "knight." Only in the late twelfth century does the word "ritter" begin consistently to replace this use.[192] *Kneht* without the adjective "guot" can mean a warrior without heavy armor who fights on foot or a knight's page, but by 1200 it can also refer to a young aristocrat who has not yet been knighted.[193]

Kneht, however, is sometimes associated with *scalc,* which clearly has the legal meaning of unfree, however one wishes to define that.[194] Thus, as we saw above, the *scalce* of the *Vienna* and *Millstätter Genesis* epics become *chnehte* in the *Vorauer Bücher Moses.* In *Das Anegenge,* on the other hand, which is perhaps 40 years younger than the *Vorauer Bücher Moses* and completely independent of the other Early Middle High German biblical epics, the author uses *scalc* and *eigen* to describe the status of Ham's descendants. Noah says:

> . . . 'mîn sun Cham,
> der muoz sîner bruoder eigen sîn,
> die da bedahten die scham mîn!'
> (von de*m* wurden die schalche geborn,
> wan *er* hete() wol gearnet sînen zorn!)[195]

And in the poem "Vom Rechte," *scalc* is once given as a synonym for *kneht,* which is otherwise used exclusively in the poem:

> swie wol der man si geborn,
> wil er unrehte varn,
> vert er unrehte,
> er hat daz reht der chnehte.
> ist diu vrouwe ungetriuwe,
> si hat das reht der diuwe.
> die schalche unde diu *diuwe*
> minnent si die triwe. . . .[196]

Perhaps it is not insignificant that the "Vom Rechte" poet is here speaking of the *ius* of the *knehte,* for it appears that when the Early Middle High German poets are thinking in purely legal terms, *kneht* yields to *scalc* or is modified by *eigen* (*proprius*) to clarify its meaning. Thus Der arme Hartmann describes in quasi-legal terms ("holt," "dienest," and "eigen kneht") the ideal servant of God who brings his offering to the church:

> Daz opfer daz ist bequeme, gote anneme,
> iz si silbe oder golt, got macheter im holt.
> iz si daz brot oder daz ei, er gibit gote ein oblei.
> sinen zins er gote bringit, ze dieniste er sich im bekinnit
> zeigeneme knehte daz er von rehte
> sule ime ze liebe eigenliche dienen.[197]

And Hartmann uses similar terms in his description of Petrus Thelonearius, who renounces his wealth and sells himself into bondage as penance for his sins:

> er hiez in allen teile(n) den durftigen gemeine
> unde dienete mit eren sineme herren.
> alse soln tuon mit rehte eigene gecoufte knehte.[198]

The sometime confusing relation between *scalc* as a legal term meaning *servus* and *kneht* as a military term is doubtless traceable to the unfree status of the German knights or *ministeriales*. The thirteenth-century poet Reinmar von Zweter, for example, blends legal designations with descriptions of status in an interesting passage:

> Ein herre von gebürte vrî
> ob er rittr und kneht, dienstmann unt eigen sî,
> wie daz geschehen müge, des sol niht wunder nemen man noch wîp.
> Ein vrî geburt niht irren kan,
> ein hêrre ensî wol vrî unt doch der eren dienstmann,
> ein ritter sîner tât, der milde ein kneht, der zühte ein eigen lîb.
> Swelch hêrre alsus undersniten wære,
> der duhte mich ein hübscher wunderære:
> hie vrî, dort dienstmann, hie eigen,
> ûf jenez ein rittr, ûf diz ein kneht,
> wære er ze disen vünven reht,
> ein künigîn solt im ir houbet nîgen.[199]

Here the proximity of the terms *ritter, kneht, dienstman,* and *eigen* shows their connections, but the careful differentiation also indicates the legal or social gaps between them. *Dienstman* and *eigen* are legal concepts, while *ritter* and *kneht* are descriptions of function.

Early Middle High German *kneht* thus can be fairly ambiguous when not modified by *guot* or *tiure* , which give it a military sense, or by *eigen* or *gekouft,* which give it a legal sense. In connection with *hêrre,* it is almost never qualified and, therefore, seems to have simply a vague sense of "servant," which might mean a free or unfree vassal or *ministerialis,* but more likely means any servant, in a legal or non-legal sense, of a lord, and thus refers even to a peasant or serf.

Having completed this review of the social categories most typically used by the Early Middle High German poets, *frîe* and *scalc, rîch* and *arm,* and *hêrre* and *kneht,* we can now turn to how the poets use these terms indicating their conception of *ordo* to describe the practice of *reht.*

NOTES

1 "Vom Rechte," 13–29. "There are many kinds of *reht,* but together they all include three. If we would practice them, we would always have enough and would live with honor. One *reht* is the fidelity according to which we should live. The second *reht* has the following form: that which we would have for ourselves, we should give to one another, if we would live as Christians. We should be truthful, for that would be great honor. Whoever possesses the three *reht* while he lives and until he dies, God will help in his need. Man or woman, He will give them the eternal life that never will end, but lasts forever."

  The verb "bouwen" in line 19, here translated as "to live," also means to till the soil. Cf. ll. 400–403 of "Vom Rechte:" "also hiez got sinen chneht/ den wuochir bringen . . . bouwen dise wuostin." The author of "Vom Rechte" delights in agricultural images.

2 Cf. Matthew 7, 12: "Omnia ergo, quaecumque vultis, ut faciant vobis homines, ita et vos facite eis; haec est enim Lex et Prophetae."

3 See, for example, J. M. Wallace-Hadrill's comments: "justice . . . the characteristic and all-enveloping royal virtue" ("The *via regia* of the Carolingian Age," in B. Smalley, ed., *Trends in Medieval Political Thought* [Oxford: Blackwell, 1965], 34).

4 "Ordo der Königskrönung," ed. Eduard Eichmann, *Kirche und Staat,* vol I, *Von 750–1122* (1925; rpt.: Munich: Schöningh, 1968), 70.

5 Ibid., 70.

6 Ibid., 71 and 72.

7 Ibid., 70.

8 Ibid., 72.

9 Ibid., 74.

10 *MGH* Epistulae, III, 458.

11 Ibid., 458.

12 Ibid., 460.

13 Ibid., 460.

14   Isidore, *Sententiae*, III, 50, *PL 83*, col. 721–22.

15   Ibid., III, 52, col. 724.

16   Eugen Ewig, "Zum christlichen Königsgedanken im Frühmittelalter," in *Spätantikes und fränkisches Gallien*, ed. Hartmut Atsma (Munich: Artemis, 1976), 22.

17   Isidore, *Etymologicae*, 3, 5, quoted in Ewig, 29, ft. 119.

18   See Isidore, *Differentiae*, II, 58 quoted in Ewig, 30, ft. 122.

19   See Ewig, 34–39, Wallace-Hadrill, 30, and R. W. Carlyle and A. J. Carlyle, *A History of Mediaeval Political Theory in the West* (New York: Barnes and Noble, 1953), I, 223 ff.

20   "De duodecim abusionibus saeculi," *PL* IV, col. 878.

21   Hincmar, "De regis persona et regio ministerio," *PL* 125, col. 835.

22   See Chapters XVIII ("Quod Christo serviat qui improbos corripit amore justitiae") and XIX ("De discretione in habenda misericordia"), cols. 845–846.

23   Alcuin, "De virtutibus et vitiis liber," *PL 101*, col. 618.

24   Alcuin, col. 629. Cf. Isidore, *Sententiae*, III, Chapters 52–54, cols. 724–726.

25   Alcuin, col. 634.

26   Alcuin, col. 637.

27   Cf., for example, Psalm 22, 3; Proverbs 2, 8; and Ecclesiasticus 4, passim.

28   Wisdom 15, 3.

29   Malachi 4, 2.

30   Cf., for example, Isaiah 5, 7; 11, 4; 56, 1; 58, 2; Jeremiah 4, 2; 22, 3 and 15; 23, 5; 33, 15; and Ezekiel 18, passim.

31   Cf., for example, I Kings 3, 6 or Baruch 4, 13.

32   E.g., I Peter 1, 17: "Et si Patrem invocatis eum, qui sine acceptione personarum iudicat secundum uniuscuiusque opus."

33   E.g., Exodus 23, 8: "Nec accipias munera quae excaecant etiam prudentes et subvertet verba iustorum."

34   E. g., Deuteronomy 24, 17: "Non pervertes iudicium advenae et pupilli, nec auferes pignoris loco viduae vestimentum."

35   Isaiah 58, 7–8. Cf. Matthew 25, 23.

36   See Mähl, *Quadriga virtutum*, 18–19.

37   Augustine, *De diversis questionibus LIII*, (*PL* 40), 61, 4, col. 51.

38   Augustine, *De libero arbitrio*, ed. W. M. Green, *CC* vol. XXIX (Turnhout: Brepols, 1970), I, xiii.

39   Augustine, *De ordine*, ed. W. M. Green, *CC* vol. XXIX (Turnhout: Brepols, 1970), II, vii: "Memini te dixisse hanc esse iustitiam dei, qua seperat inter bonos et malos et sua cuique tribuit. Nam est, quantum sentio, manifestior iustitiae definitio."

40   Augustine, *De civitate Dei*, eds. B Dombart and A. Kalb, *CC* vol. XLVIII (Turnhout: Brepols, 1955), XIX, xxi.

41   Plato, *The Republic*, vol. I, trs. Paul Shorey, *LCL* (Cambridge, MA: Harvard, 1930), 331E. Plato claimed that Simonides (*c.* 556–468 B.C.) was the source of the concept and definition of distributive justice.

42   Aristotle, *Nichomachean Ethics*, trs. H. Rackham, *LCL* (Cambridge, MA: Harvard, 1934), V, iii.

43   While Aristotle does not use the familiar form of the definition of distributive justice, "cuique suum tribuere," in this particular section of the *Nichomachean Ethics*, it is clear from the context that that is what is meant. Cf. V, v as well as *The Art of Rhetoric*: "Justice is a virtue which assigns to each man his due in conformity with the law" (Aristotle, *"Art" of Rhetoric*, trs. John Henry Freese, *LCL* [Cambridge, MA: Harvard, 1926], I, ix) or the Pseudo-Aristotelian *On Virtues and Vices*: "Righteous is goodness of the spirit shown in distributing what is according to desert" (Aristotle, *Athenian Constitution, Eudemian Ethics, On Virtues and Vices*, trs. H. Rackham, *LCL* [Cambridge, MA: Harvard, 1952], ii, 6).

44   Cf. Hans Kelsen: "a doctrine of justice based on the empty tautology of the formula 'To everyone his due' . . . [allows] the unlimited possibility of using this formula to any purpose whatsoever" ("Aristotle's Doctrine of Justice," *Aristotle's 'Ethics:' Issues and Interpretations*, ed. James J. Walsh and Henry Shapiro [Belmont, Ca.: Wadsworth, 1967], 119).

45   The following discussion is, of course, only an attempt to synthesize Augustine's scattered remarks. As Sergio Cotta, among many others, has stated: "Il est généralement admis que ST. AUGUSTIN n'a pas formulé une doctrine systématique et complète du droit et de la justice." Sergio Cotta, "Droit et justice dans le De libero arbitrio de St. Augustin," *ARSP* 47 (1961), 159. Cf. also Gerd Tellenbach's remarks on justice and order, *Church, State and Christian Society at the Time of the Investiture Contest*, trs. by R. F. Bennett (Oxford: Blackwell, 1940), 10–25.

46   For a brilliant evocation of the circumstances in which *De ordine* was composed see Peter Brown, *Augustine of Hippo* (Berkeley: California UP, 1969), pp. 115–127. Louis Manz, *Der Ordo-Gedanke* (Stuttgart: Kohlhammer, 1937), pp. 18–24, was the first scholar, to my knowledge, to draw detailed attention to the importance of *De ordine* for the evolution of the medieval concept of *ordo*.

47   Manz, 20.

48   Cf. Arthur Lovejoy, *The Great Chain of Being* (Cambridge, Mass.: Harvard, 1936). Lovejoy, however, was more interested in genealogy than transmission with the result that Augustine is barely mentioned. For twelfth-century Platonism see M.-D. Chenu, "The Platonisms of the Twelfth Century," in *Nature, Man, and Society in the Twelfth Century*, trs. Jerome Taylor and Lester K. Little (Chicago: University of Chicago, 1968), 49–98.

49   E.g. "Nesciens, unde et quomodo, plane tamen uidebam et certus eram id quod corrumpi potest, deterius esse quam id quod non potest . . . ." Augustine, *Confessionum libri XIII*, ed. Lucas Verheijen, *CC* vol. XXVII (Turnhout: Brepols, 1981), VII, i.

50   Augustine, *De diversis questionibus LXXXIII*, ed. Almut Mutzenbecher, *CC* vol. XLIVA (Turnhout: Brepols, 1975), XLI. See Lovejoy, 67.

51   Cotta, 159.

52   The literature on this central passage is enormous. I mention only those works most apposite to my theme: Otto Schilling, "Die Rechtsphilosophie bei den Kirchenvätern," *AfRW* 16 (1922/23), 1–12; Mary T. Clark, "Augustine on Justice," *Revue des Etudes Augustiniennes* 9 (1963), 87–94; Peter Brown, "St.

Augustine," in Beryl Smalley, ed. *Trends in Medieval Political Thought* (Oxford: Blackwell, 1965), 1–21; and Johannes Christes, "Christliche und heidnisch-römische Gerechtigkeit in Augustins Werk 'De civitate Dei,'" *Rheinisches Museum für Philologie* 123 (1980), 163–177.

53 Cf. Cicero, *De inventione*, trs. H. M. Hubell *LCL* (Cambridge, Ma.: Harvard, 1949), II, liii: "virtus est animi habitus naturae modo atque rationi consentaneus." See also R. W. Carlyle and A. J. Carlyle, *A History of Mediaeval Political Theory in the West*, vol. I (New York: Barnes and Noble, 1953), 1–44.

54 Chroust, 311.

55 Cf. Cicero, *De re publica*, trs. Clinton Walker Keyes *LCL* (Cambridge, Ma.: Harvard, 1928), II, xlii.

56 "Nam Deus quidem, utpote omnium Pater, nullius indeget. Nobis est bene, cum eum per iustitiam et castitatem aliasque uirtutes adoramus," *De civitate Dei*, XIX, xxiii.

57 Augustine, *De doctrina christiana*, ed. Joseph Martin *CC* XXXII (Turnhout: Brepols, 1962), I, xxvii. A similar argument is also given in a laconic statement at the beginning of Justinian's *Institutions*. Justice is first defined as distributive: "Iustitia est constans et perpetua voluntas ius suum tribuens." To render everyone his right, one must understand the human and divine order: "Iuris prudentia est divinarum atque humanarum rerum notitia, iusti atque iniusti scientia" (*Justinian's Institutes*, trs. Peter Birks and Grant McLeod with the Latin text of Paul Krueger [New York: Cornell, 1987], I.1).

58 Sergio Cotta, however, has argued precisely that. He identifies distributive justice with the *lex temporalis*, in his understanding "une justice purement sociale et temporelle elle aussi," and he equates the Golden Rule with the *lex aeterna* (Cotta, 169). To see the *lex aeterna* as opposed to the *lex temporalis* is in itself a dubious interpretation of Augustine's thought, for the latter is merely subordinate to the former. Cotta bases his argument solely on Book I of *De libero arbitrio*. Cf. however *Confessiones*, III, vii and *De doctrina christiana*, III, xii–xiv as well as Schilling's brief remarks, *op. cit.*, pp. 4–6.

59 To give only a few examples of these different meanings, cf. Christ as the "sol iustitiae:" "diu sunne des rehtes" (*Das Anegenge*, l. 1,383). *Reht* as the royal virtue: "du [God] chunige und rihtære/ unt ander ir volgære/ muozist givesten an dem rehten,/ und verdruchist die wider vehten/ christinliches glouben" (Heinrich's "Litanei," *RD* III, ll. 899–903) and "Dar rigte der gode keyser/ widewin unde weisin" (*König Rother*, ll. 3,099–3,100).

Reht as opposed to *misericordia*: "ir [St. Paul and St. Peter] sult uns nach genaden vurstellen,/ swan ir vor gotis gesihte,/ besizzit daz gerihte/ der jungisten scidunge,/ diu an barmunge/ irget, niht wan nach rehte" (Heinrich's "Litanei," ll. 548–553), "diu gnade temperet daz reht, ze sune ist worden der chneht./ vater ist, der e herro was, so begagenet in misericordia et veritas" ("Auslegung des Vaterunsers," *RD* I, 4, 6–7); and *Das Anegenge*, ll. 2,254–2,394, which contain perhaps the first vernacular version of the "querella filliarum Dei," between "reht," "erbermde," "gewalt," and "wahrheit" (see Eduard Johann Mäder, *Der Streit der Töchter Gottes* [Bern/Frankfurt: Lang, 1971], 46–52). Cf. also

Hartmann von Aue, *Iwein*, ed. Ludwig Wolf (Berlin: De Gruyter, 1968), l. 172: "gnade ist bezzer danne reht."

60   "La concept de justice chez les théologiens du moyen âge avant l'introduction d'Aristote," *Revue Thomiste* 44 (1938), 513.

61   D. O. Lottin, 513, fn. 4.

62   See Lottin, 514. The passage from William dealing with the last two definitions of *iustitia* deserves to be quoted in full: "Dicimus quod iustitia que est una cardinalium dupliciter accipitur. Uno modo secundum quod est ordinatio ad Deum et proximum: ad Deum quidem per modum subiectionis, ad proximum per modum cuiusdam equalitatis.

      . . . unde secundum hanc acceptionem non diuiditur misericordia a iustitia, sed est species eius . . . . Alio modo strictior sumitur iustitia secundum quod est ordinatio ad proximum in eis in quibus tenemur ex necessitate secundum hunc modum diuiditur misericordia et iustitia ab invicem" (William of Auxerre, *Summa aurea in quattuor libros* [unpublished manuscript], quoted in Lottin, 514, ft. 2).

63   Cf. also the arme Hartmann's "Rede vom Glauben," ll. 15, 7–8 (*RD* II), where *veritas* is even equated with *reht*: "universe vie domini misericordia et veritas also dutit unz daz:/ got wil in allen sinen wegen gnædic und reht wesen."

64   "When everyone says whatever he wishes, then justice is maligned."

65   Ll. 239–242. "No one is so venerable as justice truly is. We can see that clearly whenever we must go to justice (i. e. trial)."

66   The right of jurisdiction was constantly shifting in the Middle Ages due to social changes and pressures. The ascent to power of new groups or individuals led to their seizing jurisdictional rights from the originally popularly or royally constituted Frankish court authorities (see Hans Hirsch, *Die hohe Gerichtsbarkeit im deutschen Mittelalter* [1922; rpt.: Darmstadt: Wissenschaftliche Buchgesellschaft, 1958], 50–68). The often chaotic devolution of jurisdiction in parts of France, as decribed by Georges Duby, "The Evolution of Judicial Institutions," (*The Chivalrous Society*, trs. Cynthia Postan [Berkely: University of Calafornia, 1977], 15–58), however, should by no means be equated with events in the Empire where the older Carolingian forms of jurisdiction were more tenacious.

      For the development of the seignorial lord's jurisdiction over his free as well as unfree dependents, see Georg Meyer, "Die Gerichtsbarkeit über Unfreie und Hintersassen nach ältestem Recht," *ZRG* (*GA*) 2 (1881), 83–114 and *ZRG* (*GA*) 3 (1882), 102–126.

67   In English law, the "doomsmen," in Frankish law the "rachinburgi," later called the "scabini." For this theoretically strict separation between judgement and the presiding *iudex*, see Jürgen Weitzel, *Dinggenossenschaft und Recht*, vol. I (Cologne: Böhlau, 1985), 56–64.

68   If the plaintiff or his or her advocate was of military stature.

69   For this description of procedure, I have followed Heinrich Mitteis's account in *Deutsche Rechtsgeschichte*, rev. by Heinz Lieberich (Munich: Beck, 1966), 29–32. Mitteis gives an ideal account that ignores regional and chronological differences or abuses.

70 The "Vom Rechte" poet's complete lack of criticism of the ordeal would seem to belie Kroeschell's contention that "Vom Rechte" is the first vernacular expression of the high medieval, ecclesiastically-influenced concept of "Recht" (Kroeschell, "Rechtsbegriff," 329–330). The Church's views on the ordeal were ambiguous. In the early Middle Ages, some Church officials approved, but others were strenuously opposed (see Herbert Kolb, "Himmlisches und irdisches Gericht in karolingischer Theologie und althochdeutscher Dichtung," *FMS* 5 [1971], 284–303). Peter Brown has argued that the Church's eventually unequivocal condemnation of the ordeal in 1215 is an indication of the rejection of subjective dependence on the supernatural in favor of the acceptance of a rational, mundane ordering of society ("Society and the Supernatural: A Medieval Change," *Daedalus* 104 [1975], 133–151). There is not the remotest sign of such a change in "Vom Rechte."

71 See A. Erler's entry, "Gottesurteil," in the *HRG.*

72 "Vom Rechte," ll. 239–252. "How much he exerts himself who heats the iron and then carries it to someone and lays it on his hand. If that person [i. e. the accused] has come in justice — we have often heard this — then the fire never burns him. How well God acknowledges him, how greatly he is praised, who has done justice there!"

73 Julius Goebel, *Felony and Misdemeanor* (1937; rpt: Philadelphia: University of Pennsylvania, 1976), 72.

74 "Vom Rechte," ll. 253–266. "But those who lied about him are all deceivers. No matter what happens afterwards, an iron so hot is prepared for them that none of them can know *reht* on his hand; it burns like a hot flame. Oh, how red hot it is to him who oppressed the innocent and coerced him to go to trial! For this reason liars are not loved by God."

Speicher (*Vom Rechte*, 67–68) comments on these lines that it is unclear whether the false accusers are being threatened with divine punishment or a judicial punishment by which the accuser must undergo the same ordeal by fire —with presumably a less auspicious outcome. Speicher tends to the former interpretation, for there is no evidence that the torment of the ordeal, if successful, would be repeated against the unsuccessful accuser.

It could be, however, that the poet is not thinking of a second ordeal but of the usual punishment for perjury, namely the loss of one's hand. See, for example, Goebel (79) who, citing a capitulary to this effect from 799, explains that the loss of one's hand "brutally and automatically excludes him (the perjurer) from being a witness, for without his hand he cannot swear." Cf. also the "Capitulare missorum generale" from 802: "Et usum periurii omnino non permittant, quid hoc pessimum scelus christiano populo auferre necesse est. Si quis autem post hoc in periurio probatus fuerit, manum dexteram se perdere sciat" *MGH,* Cap I, no. 33, ch. 36.

The perjurer's hand would, of course, have been cut and not burnt off. But perhaps the author of "Vom Rechte" repeats the image of the hot iron merely for effect. This admittedly speculative interpretation has the merit of offering an explanation of the otherwise obscure lines 258–259: "daz ir neheiner weiz,/ reht an die hant." These lines would mean something like "so that none of them can again impart justice by his hand."

75   Schröbler, as mentioned, called this *reht* "Recht im engeren Sinne, Gerechtigkeit" ("Vom Rechte," 219). This might be partly true for thirteenth-century scholastic definitions of *iustitia*, but as shown above it is an inaccurate description for the twelfth-century theologians, for whom *iustitia* in its "narrow sense" ("strictissime") meant judicial justice.

76   Ulrich Pretzel, *Bedeutungskunde*, 41. For a detailed discussion of the concept of *triuwe* see: Francis G. Gentry, *Triuwe and vriunt in the Nibelungenlied*, Amsterdamer Publikationen zur Sprache und Literatur 19 (Amsterdam: Rodopi, 1975), 17–43.

77   Ll. 40–41. "Many a one does not help his friend as he has been loved by him."

78   Ll. 197–208. "The Lord commanded justice [Christ] to make a servant. He fashioned him from nothing to be an honorable light, that he would go before Him and bear Him light. He seized at pride: that was good for nothing. The Lord upheld justice. He threw the servant into banishment, down into the abyss."

79   See, e. g., Schröbler, "Vom Rechte," 228–29. Peter Ganz's comment ("Vom Rechte," *VL*, col. 76) that the parallels between the two poems are restricted to formulas and therefore inconclusive evidence for their identical authorship should not imply that "Vom Recht" and "Die Hochzeit" are not obviously closely related. Such a position would be scarcely credible in view of the many and extensive parallels, by no means all of them formulas, noted by Kraus, "'Vom Rechte' und 'Die Hochzeit,'" 42–44.

80   "Die Hochzeit," ed. Schröder, *Kleinere deutsche Gedichte*, vol. II, ll. 156–168; 172–173. "In the olden days, a lord traveled with his followers. The lord lived justly [or simply properly]: he had many servants. He gave counsel to them all that he had much wealth. Many of his most senior servants did not act justly [or rightly]. They plotted against his honor and for this they paid dearly. There under the mountain [where the lord's castle was] was a great thing to fear, a deep dungeon . . . . Far down into it the lord swept his unfaithful servants."

The word "chneht" is used with different meanings in "Vom Rechte" and "Die Hochzeit," in the one, usually as a description of social condition and in the other as a synonym for vassal (Middle High German "man") or a vassal-like follower. In my translations I have ignored these differences and simply rendered it as neutrally as possible as "servant." The meanings of *chneht* will be discussed in more detail below.

81   R. W. Southern, *Saint Anselm*, 112.

82   Ibid., 112.

83   "Vom Rechte," ll. 209–216. "Therefore no lady should allow her servant girl to go before her however pretty her color. Nor should the lord permit his servant to go before him. This comes from justice, for the most senior servant succumbed to injustice."

84   In his careful discussion of *triuwe*, Gentry (*Triuwe and vriunt*) nowhere mentions the obedience of an inferior to his superior. This sense of *triuwe* seems to be unique to the author of "Vom Rechte."

85   "Vom Rechte," ll. 217–238. "If both lord and servant love justice then the books
       truly tell us they will become equally venerable. If the lady and the servant girl
       love fidelity then, the books truly tell us, they will become equally venerable.
       However noble a man is born, if he acts unjustly he acts unjustly and he has the
       law of servants. If a lady lacks fidelity then she will have the law of servant girls.
       If the slaves and the servant girls love fidelity (obedience) then however great
       their poverty, they will become the companions of the most senior. Whoever
       loves justice, be he lord or servant, he will always go first and the other stand
       behind him."
           Lines 228 and 230 are good examples of the influence of *ius* on *reht*. The poet
       is presumably referring in these lines to the "ius servientium" (cf., for example,
       MGH DD HIV, 125).

86   For studies on the social order of the Middle Ages as well as on the concept of
       the three orders I have consulted the following works; those by Congar and
       Oexle are particularly rich in information about medieval Latin authors: Yves
       Congar, "Les laïcs et l'ecclésiologie des 'ordines' chez les théologiens des XIe et
       XIIe siècles," in *I laici nella "societas christiana" dei secoli XI et XII*, ed. Giuseppe
       Lazzati and Cosimo D. Fonseca (Milan: Sociatà editrice vita e pesiero, 1968),
       83–117; Helmuth Stahleder, "Zum Ständebegriff im Mittelalter," *Zeitschrift für
       bayerische Landesgeschichte* 35 (1972), 523–570; Jacques LeGoff, "Les trois functions
       indo-européennes, l'historien et l'Europe féodale," *Annales ESC* 34 (1979),
       1187–1215; D. E. Luscombe, "Conceptions of Hierarchy before the 13th
       Century," in *Soziale Ordnungen im Selbstverständnis des Mittelalters. Miscellanea
       Mediaevalia*, Albert Zimmermann, ed., vol. 12/1 (Berlin: De Gruyter, 1979), 1–19;
       Georges Duby, "The Origin of a System of Social Classification," *The Chivalrous
       Society* tr. Cynthia Postan (Berkeley: University of California, 1980), 53–57; Duby,
       The Three Orders, tr. Arthur Goldhammer (Chicago: University of Chicago, 1980);
       LeGoff, "A Note on the Tripartite Society, Monarchical Ideology, and Economic
       Renewal in Ninth- to Twelfth-Century Christendom," *Time, Work, and Culture in
       the Middle Ages*, tr. Arthur Goldhammer (Chicago: University of Chicago, 1980),
       53–57; Otto Gerhard Oexle, "Die funktionale Dreiteilung der 'Gesellschaft' bei
       Adalbero von Laon. Deutungsschemata der sozialen Wirklichkeit im frühen
       Mittelalter," *FMS* 12 (1978), 1–54; Oexle, "Die 'Wirklichkeit' und das 'Wissen.'
       Ein Blick auf das sozialgeschichtliche Œuvre von Georges Duby," *HZ* 232
       (1981), 61–91; Oexle, "Tria genera hominum. Zur Geschichte eines
       Deutungschemas der sozialen Wirchlichkeit in der Antike und im Mittelalter,"
       Institutionen, Kultur und Gesellschaft im Mittelalter. Josef Fleckenstein Festschrift, ed.
       Lutz Fenske et al. (Sigmaringen: Thorbecke, 1984), 483–550; Oexle,
       "Deutungschemata der sozialen Wirchlichkeit im frühen und hohen Mittelalter,
       in *Mentalitäten, Vorträge und Forschungen XXXV*, ed. Frantisek Graus (Sigmaringen:
       Thorbecke, 1987), 65–117.

87   Cf. J. Batany, "Le vocabulaire des catégories sociales chez quelques moralistes
       français vers 1200," in *Ordres et classes*, ed D. Roche and C. E. Labrousse (Paris:
       Mouton, 1968), 59–92. Batany writes of a similarly broad — and vague — use of
       social categories in vernacular French didactic literature: "A la fin du XIIe siècle,

la littérature française est encore dans l'enfance et la langue française encore mal structurée. Si bien que le thème des 'états du monde' et le vocabulaire social n'ont encore aucune rigueur" (59). I am skeptical, however, as to whether this vagueness of social terminology may be traced to linguistic causes. In German vernacular literature, at least, the explanation for the sometimes imprecise usage of social terms more properly lies in the history of sermonic theory and practice.

88   *Wiener Genesis.*, ed. Viktor Dollmayr (Halle: Niemeyer, 1932), ll. 287–290: "Ouch hat der chunig ze site/ daz pischtuom mahilen darmit [the ring finger]/ suelehen phaffen/ er ze herren wil machen."

89   *Wiener Genesis*, ll. 42–54. "Satan spoke: 'My master is powerful here in heaven and thinks that no one can be opposed to Him. But I am equally senior and I will no longer be under Him. I am equally splendid and with my choir I want to be as powerful as He. I want to place my throne to the north of His in heaven. I want to be on equal to Him.'"

90   The creation of man to replace the gap in the heavenly choirs of angels is a commonplace in Early Middle High German literature. Cf., for example, ll. 65–74 of the "Summa theologiae," Schröder, ed., vol. I. Freytag, in his commentary on the "Summa," gives the Latin background of the motif and numerous parallels from vernacular literature (Freytag, *Kommentar*, 62–70).

The connection between *reht* and *ordo* seems to be explicitly stated in the interpretation of Satan's and Adam's fall in the *Annolied*: "Du sich Lucifer du ze ubile gevieng, unt Adam diu godis word uberging,/ duo balch sich is got desti mer, daz her andere sini werch sach rehte gen" (*RD*, II, 3, 1–2).

91   Cf. Gen. 9, 24–27: "Evigilans autem Noe ex vino, cum didicisset quae fecerat ei filius suus minor, ait: 'Maledictus Chanaan. Servus erit fratribus suis.' Dixitque: 'Benedictus Dominus Deus Sem. Sit Chanaan servus eius. Dilatet Deus Iafeth et habitet in tabernaculis Sem. Sitque Chanaan servus eius.'"

92   *Wiener Genesis*, ll. 1,502–13. "When Noah awoke and learned what Ham had done when he had seen him naked, I know that he cursed him and all his progeny. He commanded them to be slaves and to serve Ham's brothers. The other two sons he consecrated to a free life: they lived in tents as lords should."

Whether one wishes to translate *scalc* as "slave" or "serf" will depend, in part, on one's views on the chronology of the demise of slavery. Georges Duby, for example, wrote of eleventh- to twelfth-century Germany that "the primitive notion of slavery still survived. In the documents many are called 'household slaves,' *servi salici*, and 'slaves in perpetual service'" (Duby, *Rural Economy and Country Life in the Medieval West*, trs. Cynthia Postan [Columbia, SC: University of South Carolina, 1968], 191–192). But Friedrich Lütge argued that the legal rights of the *servi* were rising in the same period: "Immer mehr wächst die Personen-Qualität des Unfreien; er kann ausschließlicher nur als Inhaber eines abhängigen Gutes betrachtet werden, nicht als Vermögensgut. Zu Fahrnisgut wird lediglich noch der fremde, d. h. heidnische Sklave betrachtet und, wie man weiß, isoliert von Boden verkauft oder verschenkt" (Lütge, *Geschichte der deutschen Agrarverfassung vom frühen Mittelalter bis zum 19. Jahrhundert* [Stuttgart: Eugen Ulmer, 1963], 34). No doubt conditions varied widely at different times and in different places. In order to distinguish *scalc* from *kneht*, I have translated the former as "slave" and the latter as "servant," without wishing to imply anything final about the question.

93   *Wiener Genesis*, ll. 1,530–1,535. "From Ham's sin, slaves first came to be. Before, all had been equally free and noble. Many a one has paid dearly for Ham's mockery and derision." Cf. also *Millstäter Genesis* (ed. Joseph Diemer [Vienna, 1849]), I, 31,10–32–9, esp. 32, 3–4: "**V**on Chamen bosen gedanchen w[u]rden alerste schalchen,/ e waren si alle uri und edele und lebeten wol und ebene." The relation between the *Vienna Genesis* and the *Millstäter Genesis* will be discussed in Chapter III.

94   Augustine, *De civitate Dei*, XVI, ii. Augustine, following Cyprian, first states that Noah's drunkenness prefigures the passion of Christ. In a reading for which I have found no clear precedent, Augustine then identifies Sem as those Jews who believed in Christ, Japheth as the converted gentiles, and Ham as the heretics or those who lead scandalous lives.

95   Isidore of Seville, *Questiones in vetus testamentum*. *PL* 82, col. 235.

96   Ibid., col. 236.

97   Cf., for example, Rabanus Maurus, *Commentarii in Genesim*, II, ix (*PL* 107, cols. 225–26). Rabanus actually presents a conflation of Augustine's and Isidore's interpretations and includes as well some remarks from Gregory the Great, based in turn on Augustine.

98   Alfred Weller, *Die frühmittelhochdeutsche Wiener Genesis nach Quellen, Übersetzungsart, Stil und Syntax*, Palaestra 123 (Berlin, 1914), 58–59.

99   Avitus, *De spiritalis historiae gestis*, ed. R. Peiper *MGH*, AA 6.2, III, ll. 404–415.

100   *De civitate Die*, XIX, xv. In Book XVI, Chapter ii, mentioned above, in which Augustine offered his allegorical interpretation of Noah's curse, he remarks in an interesting excursus on biblical exegesis that he is more interested in prophetic foresight than historical accuracy. The opposite is obviously true of Avitus and the *Vienna Genesis* poet.

101   "Ein Fragebüchlein aus dem 9. Jahrhundert," ed. W. Wilmans, *ZfdA* 15 (1872), 169.

102   The meaning of "handgemahele" is obscure. Lexer's derivation from "zeichen an der hand" is incorrect; see W. Weber, "handgemal," *HDR* and Ruth Schmidt-Wiegand, "*hantgemælde* (Parzival 6, 19): Rechtswort und Rechtssinn bei Wolfram von Eschenbach," in *Studien zu Wolfram von Eschenbach. Werner Schröder FS*, ed. Kurt Gärtner and Joachim Heinzle (Tübingen: Niemeyer, 1989), 333–342.

103   *Vorauer Bücher Mosis*, ed. Joseph Diemer, *Deutsche Gedichte des 11. und 12. Jahrhunderts* (Vienna, 1849), 15. ll. 1–9. I have arranged Diemer's uninterrupted prose form of the text into short-line verse and added modern punctuation. "These are the three orders [or genera]. They shall always exist. One is noble, they have the *handgemahele;* the second are the freemen who live from their estates, the third are the ministerials, among whom, as I have heard, servants first arose." Note that the Vorauer poet has changed the *scalce* of the *Vienna Genesis* into *chnehte*.

Cf. also Schmidt-Wiegand's paraphrase of the passage: "Freie Leute sind Grundstückseigentümer, Edelleute haben darüber hinaus ihr Handgemale und damit verbundene Herrschaftsrechte." For this interpretation of "handgemahele," she cites Friedrich Kauffmann ("Aus dem Wortschatz der Rechtssprache," *ZfdP* 46 [1918], 153–209), and she compares the lines in the *Vorauer Moses* with lines 7,141–43 of the *Kaiserchronik*: "ze Rôme was luzel dehain edel man,/ er neworht im ain hantgemæle,/ daz man iemer von im sagete ze mære." (Schmidt-Wiegand, "*handgemælde*," 340–41). While perhaps slightly speculative, Schmidt-Wiegand's interpretation seems to me to be basically correct.

104   Benjamin Arnold, *German Knighthood. 1050–1300* (Oxford: Clarendon, 1985), 53–75.

105   Cf. Klaus Grubmüller, "Nôes Fluch. Zur Begründung von Herrschaft und Unfreiheit in mittelalterlicher Literatur," In Dietrich Huschenbett et al., ed., *Medium Aevum deutsch. Kurt Ruh Festschrift* (Tübingen: Niemeyer, 1979), 99–119. Grubmüller is heavily dependent on Oexle, "Die funktionale Dreiteilung der 'Gesellschaft' bei Adalbero von Laon. Deutungsschemata der sozialen Wirklichkeit im frühen Mittelalter," *op. cit.*, and claims that the development of Noah's curse reflects an increasingly more realistic view of society. See, however, Duby's and LeGoff's works, also cited above, according to which different views of social order are only partly based on social reality, whatever that may be. Both Duby and LeGoff emphasize, instead, how social schemes are chiefly attempts to control and constrain certain social groups. In LeGoff's words, for example, the scheme of the three orders is "un croisement de réalité et d'idéologie, de description et d'interprétation" (LeGoff, "Les trois functions," 1979).

106   Cited in Thomas Hill, "Rígsthula: Some Medieval Christian Analogues," *Speculum* 61/1 (1986), 83.

107   Honorius Augustodunensis, *Imago mundi*, PL 172, col. 166.

108   "Von Sem camen die frigen, von Jafet camen die ritere, von Kam camen die eigin lûte," *Lucidarius*, ed. Felix Heidlauf (Berlin, 1915), 8.

109   Georges Duby, *The Three Orders*, 258.

110   Honorius Augustodunensis, *Summa gloria*, MGH, Libelli de lite, 3, 67.

111   LeGoff, too, seems not to consider Honorius's *liberi*, *milites*, and *servi* as an example of the trifunctionality of the three orders (LeGoff, "Les trois functions," 1,207). By the Late Middle Ages, the two schemes did indeed become conflated. LeGoff quotes an interesting passage from the *Chronica* of Johann Naucler from 1579: "Hoc tempore [scl. Noah's] divisum est genus humanum in tria: in liberos, in milites, in servos : vel ut alii volunt, in sacerdotes, in milites, et servos" (LeGoff, 1,214, ft. 44). The wording of this passage is identical to that in Honorius's *Imago mundi*.

112   See Friedrich Ohly, "Vom geistigen Sinn des Wortes im Mittelalter," *ZfdA* 89 (1958), 1–23.

113   "Rígsthula," ed. Hans Kuhn, *Edda* (Heidelberg: Winter, 1962), I, 280–287.

114   Georges Dumézil, "La Rígsthula et la structure sociale indo-européenne," *Revue de l'histoire des religions* 154 (1958), 1–9.

115   Hill, *Speculum*, 89, ft. 21.

116   LeGoff, in his discussion of the different interpretations of the "Rígsthula," similarly concludes "son principe de classification est essentiellement juridique" (LeGoff, "Les trois functions," 1,201).

117   Hill, *Speculum*, 86 and 79.

118   Cf. Oexle ("Die funktionale Dreiteilung der 'Gesellschaft,'" 9) who, citing Ernst Troeltsch, speaks of "die von der 'folgenreichen inneren Aufeinanderbeziehung konservativer und revolutionärer Elemente' geprägten Paulus-Briefe." These contradictions help explain, for example, why Noker, the author of the "Memento mori," could speak of the primal unity of humankind, while at the same time accepting social divisions. Oexle attributes the apparent contradictions in the Pauline epistles to Paul's apocalyptic convictions: "Daraus resultierte einerseits eine radikale Nivellierung aller sozialen Unterschiede, zum Beispiel der im antiken Denken unüberwindlichen Kluft zwischen Freien und Sklaven (Gal. 3, 28; Kol. 3, 11), die aber anderseits sogleich wieder aufgehoben wurde durch die völlige Bedeutungslosigkeit, der die sozialen Unterschiede angesichts des Vergehens der Gestalt dieser Welt (I Kor. 7, 31) anheimfielen" (Oexle, ibid., 9).

119   *Moralia in Job*, ed. M. Adriaen, CC vol. CXLIII (Turnhout: Brepols, 1979), XXI, xv.

120   Klaus von See, "Das Alter der Rígsthula," *Acta Philologica Scandinavia* 24 (1961), 1–12.

121   That the three sons could be identified with such different groups is not surprising, for as Sybilla Mähl has noted, medieval interpretation of biblical numbers and amounts can be fairly arbitrary (Mähl, *Quadriga virtutum*, 24).

122   See, e.g., Josef Fleckenstein, "Zur Frage der Abgrenzung von Bauer und Ritter, in *Wort und Begriff "Bauer,"* ed. Reinhard Wenskus et al. (Göttingen: Vandenhoeck und Ruprecht, 1975), 247: "Wie schon Georg Waitz gezeigt hat, haben sich die Unterschiede zwischen den Freien und den Hörigen und Unfreien, welche den Volksrechten stets zugrunde gelegt hatten, im 10. und 11. Jahrhundert mehr und mehr geschliffen." Werner Rösener gives a similar view in his essay "Bauer und Ritter im Hochmittelalter," in *Institutionen, Kultur und Gesellschaft im Mittelalter*, ed. Lutz Fenske et al. (Sigmaringen: Thorbecke, 1984), 667 ff.

       Karl Bosl, although he speaks of an "Emanzipationsprozeß," is generally more cautious and says that there was only a partial demise of the older legal categories of free and unfree ("Gesellschaftsprozeß und Gesellschaftsstrukturen im Mittelalter," Bosl and Eberhard Weis, *Die Gesellschaft in Deutschland von der fränkischen Zeit bis 1848* (Munich: Martin Lurz, 1976), 65–73, 83, 91–96 (here, 91–92). In an earlier essay, Bosl had written: "Der Gegensatz frei und unfrei innerhalb der Unterschichten in Frankreich [verblaßte] seit dem 10. Jahrhundert viel rascher als in Deutschland, wo sich die starke Differenzierung der Karolingerzeit bis in das 12. Jahrhundert erhielt" ("Freiheit und Unfreiheit," *Vierteljahrszeitschrift für Sozial- und Wirtschaftsgeschichte* 44 [1957], 196).

       Cf. also Georges Duby who likewise remarks that "in the second half of the eleventh century the words *servus* and *francus* and their equivalents fell little by little in disuse in most French provinces .... [But] in Germany and its western borders, the Low Countries and Lotharingia, the dividing line between freedom and servitude was still [in the eleventh and twelfth centuries] as clearly marked as in the Carolingian times" (*Rural Economy*, 188).

123   "Pax Sigiwini archiepiscopi coloniensis," *MGH*, Con, 1, No. 424, 604. The emphases are mine.

124   "Pax dei incerta," ibid., No. 426, 609.

125   All examples (from, Eilhart, Lichtenstein, and Rudolph von Ems) are to be found in Joachim Bumke, *Studien zum Ritterbegriff im 12. und 13. Jahrhundert* (Heidelberg: Winter, 1964), 137.

126   Cf. Gaius' proclamation in the *Institutes*: "Et quidem summa diuisio de iure personarum haec est, quod omnes homines aut liberi sunt aut serui" (*The Institutes of Gaius*, trs. by W. M. Gordon and O. F. Robinson with the Latin text of Seckel and Kuebler [Ithaca: Cornell, 1988], 1,9) which appears to have been echoed in a capitulary from 801–814: "Non est amplius nisi liber et servus" (*MGH*, Cap, No. 58, chap. i). For discussion of this famous Carolingian pronouncement, see Thomas Zotz, "Adel, Oberschicht, Freie: Zur Terminologie der frühmittelalterlichen Sozialgeschichte," *Zeitschrift für die Geschichte des Oberrheins* 125 (1977), 13.

127   Cf. Claus-Dieter Schott, "Freiheit und libertas," *ZRG* (*GA*) 104 (1987), 84–109; Gabriele von Olberg, "Zum Freiheitsbegriff im Spiegel volksspachlicher Bezeichnungen in den frühmittelalterlichen Leges," 411–426; and Karin Nehlsen-von Stryk, "Die Freien im Frankreich als ungelöstes Problem der Rechts-, Sozial- und Verfassungsgeschichte," 427–441, together with Olberg in *Ius commune*, ed. Dieter Simon (Frankfurt a. M.: Klostermann, 1987).

128   "Von der Siebenzahl," 7, 4 (*RD* I). "The bought-slave went home free. Nowhere was there any compulsion." Cf. Leviticus 25, 39–40: "Si paupertate conpulsus vendiderit se tibi frater tuus, non eum opprimes servitute famulorum, sed quasi mercennarius et colonus erit. Usque ad annum iobelorum operabitur apud te."

129   "Auslegung des Paternoster," 19, 5 (*RD* I). "The old man [Adam] enslaved us; the new man [Christ] will free us." Cf. Galatians 4, 31–5, 1: "Qua libertate nos Christus liberavit. State et nolite iterum iugo servitutis contineri."

130   "Das jüngste Gericht," 32, 1–2 (*RD* II). "Therefore listen everyone. You will be noble and free. Neither sin nor sorrow will oppress you: that is complete freedom."

131   "Von dem gemeinen Leben," ll. 138–141 (*RD* III). "How greatly worldly riches will cost them and the unholy freedom in which they live without restraint."

132   "Von dem gemeinen Leben," ll. 409–419. "Ecclesiastical judges are better called rulers than masters. They can afford many shields, helmets, and breast armor. All their pleasure consists in riding with others to far-off places and commanding them to serve others. Their subjects want to be free to do anything they please."

133   "Von dem gemeinen Leben," ll. 427–430. "Ladies and knights can scarcely argue about who leads the better life. Their subjects want to be free."

134   "Linzer Antichrist," ll. 641–652 (*RD* III). "Kingdom or bishopric, the Antichrist holds it in his hand. He has conquered all the lands. Wherever there is no one loyal to God, he commands with enticements or with threats that everyone, be he slave or freeman, layman or priest, separate himself from Christ."

135 *König Rother*, ll. 1,420–1,424. "'My enemies' pride has forced me into exile. Now I can afford nothing. But as poor as I may be, I am yet by birth free.'" Cf. the Ermlitzer Fragment version: "Mine vint vertriben mich von ere/ nv ist mir guot tivre./ Und idoch swi arm ich si,/ ich bin von rehtes edel fri," ll. 1,420.1–1,422.4.

136 Lexer, II, 416.

137 "Die jüngere Judith," 40, 1–2 (*RD* II). "They all rode together, poor and rich, both children and women. . . ."

138 "Johannes," 23, 2–3 (*RD* II). "then God came and taught everyone alike, poor and rich."

139 "Von des Todes Gehugde," ll. 544–546 (*RD* III). "We cannot hide from you the many pains that will afflict the poor and the rich in many ways."

140 Cf. but a small selection of this use of *arme und rîche* in "Linzer Antichrist," l. 2,244 (*RD* II), *Wiener Genesis*, ll. 1,836 and 2,083, *Das Anegenge*, l. 2,244, and especially *Die Kaiserchronik*, ll. 635; 1,758; 3,061; 5,078, 9,674; 10,047; 12,680; and 16,115.

141 "Memento mori," 9, 2 (*RD* I). "The poor man needs *reht*."

142 "Van der Girheit," l. 353 (*RD* III). "I oppressed the poor."

143 "Rede vom Glauben," 104, 5–6 (*RD* II). "I began often to plague widows and orphans and other poor people."

144 "Von dem gemeinen Leben," ll. 400–408. "One finds there no good faith or trust, neither justice nor mercy, nothing but how one can seek more money. The rich man is considered noble and is the table-companion of princes. . . . Everywhere the poor man is rejected."

145 "Von dem gemeinen Leben," ll. 123–126. "They never assist the poor on whom they should have mercy. But whatever the rich man does they consider sweet and good."

146 Speicher, *Kommentar*, 45.

147 Roland Ris, *Das Adjektiv reich im mittelalterlichen Deutsch*, QF NF 40 (Berlin: de Gruyter, 1971) and Karl Bosl, "Potens und pauper. Begriffsgeschichtliche Studien zu gesellschaftlichen Differenzierungen im frühen Mittelalter und zum 'Pauperismus' des Hochmittelalters," (1963) in *Frühformen der Gesellschaft im mittelalterlichen Europa* (Munich: Oldenburg, 1964), 106–134.

148 The examples are from Helmuth Stahleder, "Zum Ständebegriff im Mittelalter," 540. Stahleder notes that *rîch* as an attribute of an estate in the legal sense begins to occur in the fourteenth century (ibid., 562).

149 Ris, 135–6.

150 Ris, 136.

151 Ris, 138–139.

152 Ris, 138.

153 Ris, 155.

154 Ris, 295.

155 Ris, 297.

156 Namely *Wiener Genesis* ll. 3,177; 3,254; 4,138; and 5,143.

157 *Wiener Genesis*, ll. 2,081–2,084. "Those who fear God and do His will, *riche* or poor, they will all come to His bosom."

158 *Wiener Genesis*, ll. 3,424–3,427. "Esau was a *riche* man in cattle and in servants, so that he had no lack in all his dominion." Cf. Genesis 36, 6–7: "Tulit autem Esau uxores suas et filios et filias et omnem animam domus suae et substantiam et pecora et cuncta quae habere poterat in terra Chanaan et abiit in alteram regionem recessitque a fratre suo Iacab. *Divetes* enim erant valde et simul habitare non poterant, nec sustinebat eos terra peregrinationis eorum prae multitudine gregum" (my emphasis).

159 *Wiener Genesis*, ll. 4,176–4,178: "**D**uo tet er [Pharaoh] in [Joseph] gehît,/ er gab ime ein riche wib,/ eines piskofes tohter."

160 *Wiener Genesis*, ll. 5,176–5,183. "Day by day the cry of hunger grew. Whatever money the people had they brought to Joseph [to buy food] . . . . As a result the king's [Pharaoh's] treasure became quite *riche*." Cf. Genesis 47, 13–14: "In toto enim orbe panis deerat et oppresserat fames terram maxime Aegypti et Chanaan, e quibus omnem pecuniam congregavit pro venditione frumenti et intulit eam in aerarium regis."

161 *Wiener Genesis*, ll. 4,236–4,241. "Joseph ordered the grain to be threshed so it could be eaten. He ordered those who had to work it to handle it carefully and to use it to help the poor and to sell it to the *richen*."

162 Speicher, it should be noted, does not accept Bosl's definitions uncritically (as Vollmann-Profe seems to; see Vollmann-Profe, ed. and trs., *Frühmittelhochdeutsche Literatur* [Stuttgart: Reclam, 1996], 271). Referring to Bosl, Speicher says of "der rîche" in "Vom Rechte": "Hier ist . . . noch an die alte Bedeutung potens zu denken . . ., allerdings ist nicht klar, ob das Gegensatzpaar *rich-arm* dem mittellateinischen Gegensatz potens-pauper entspricht" (Speicher, 45). Since Speicher is convinced that "der riche" does indeed mean "potens," it is difficult to see how "der arme" cannot but mean "pauper."

163 Karl Bosl, "Freiheit und Unfreiheit," 198–199.

164 Bosl, 113.

165 See, for example, Hans K. Schulze, "Rodungsfreie und Königsfreiheit. Zur Genese und Kritik neuerer verfassungsgeschichtlicher Theorien," *HZ* 219 (1974), 529–550, and the same author's review of the literature on the "Königsfreie": "Reichsaristokratie, Stammesadel und fränkische Freiheit," *HZ* 227 (1978), 353–373.

166 "Capitularia missorum specialia," *MGH,* Cap. I, no. 34, c. 12. Cf. also Wilhelm A. Eckhardt, "Die Capitularia missorum specialia von 802," *DA* 12 (1956), 498–516. Eckhardt gives variant readings to the text, none of which, however, affects this discussion.

167 Bosl, "Potens," 107.

168 *MGH,* Cap., no. 34, c. 18.

169 Bosl, 107 and 108.

170 *MGH,* Cap., no 34, c. 13b.

171 Bosl, 108.

172 See Heinrich Brunner, *Deutsche Rechtsgeschichte* (1906; rpt. Berlin: Duncker und Humbolt, 1961), I, 332–376.

173 *MGH,* Cap., no. 34, c. 19.

174   *Annales Laureshamenses, MGH*, SS, I, xxxv.

175   Bosl, 108.

176   Bosl, "Potens und pauper," 111.

177   Cf., for example Psalm 71, 4: "[Deus] iudicabit pauperes populi, salvabit filios pauperis et confringet calumniatorem" and especially verses 11–13: "Et adorabunt eum omnes reges; universae nationes servient ei quia eruet pauperem a potente et inopem cui non est adiutor. Parcet inopi et pauperi et animas pauperum salvabit."

178   Bosl, "Herrscher und Beherrschte," 10.

179   Oexle, "Die funktionale Dreiteilung der 'Gesellschaft'," 12 and 12, fn. 58.

180   Schulze, "Reichsaristokratie," 367.

181   See also Werner Schröder's comments, "Armuot," *DVjZ* 34 (1960), 501–526, esp. 504–510.

182   "Von des Todes Gehugde," l. 762.

183   *Hêriro* is the comparative form of the Old High German *hêr,* meaning "alt, ehrwürdig; von hohem Rang" (Rudolph Schützeichel, *Althochdeutsches Wörterbuch* [Tübingen: Niemeyer, 1981]. In opposition to Speicher's view (*Kommentar*, 25), Gustav Ehrismann claimed that while *hêriro* combines both meanings ("alt" and "ehrwürdig"), "nicht die materielle (Bedeutung) von 'alt' allein ist die Zentralidee, sondern es liegt darin eingeschlossen das tiefere Ethos von 'ehrwürdig, geehrt'" ("Die Wörter für 'Herr' im Althochdeutschen," *Zeitschrift für deutsche Wortforschung* 7 [1905–06], 190).

184   Ehrismann, 174.

185   Ehrismann, 177.

186   Ehrismann, 188.

187   Ehrismann, 178 and passim.

188   "Dominus" also comes to mean the lord of a vassal. See Ganshof, *Feudalism*, 69–70 for a review of tenth- to thirteenth-century terminology.

189   Joachim Bumke, *Studien zum Ritterbegriff im 12. und im 13. Jahrhundert, Beihefte zum Euphorion* (Heidelberg: Winter, 1964), 67.

190   Cf. Eggers, *Sprachgeschichte*, 374–75: "Die Bedeutungsbreite des Wortes, die tiefe Einblicke in die Entwicklung sozialer Verhältnisse gewähren würde, ist im einzelnen nicht untersucht."

191   Eggers, *Sprachgeschichte*, 375.

192   Joachim Bumke, 36.

193   Bumke, 103, ft. 68.

194   Mackensen ("Anschauungen der frühmittelhochdeutscher Dichter," 165) denies this: "'knecht' ist nicht mehr Bezeichnung der Unfreien." *Kneht*, as noted however, originally did not mean "unfree."

195   *Das Anegenge*, ll. 2,039–2,043. "'My son Ham shall be the slave of his brothers who covered my shame.' (From Ham slaves were born, for he truly deserved his father's anger.)"

196   "Vom Rechte," ll. 225–231. The passage quoted above in its entirety is part of the discussion of *triuwe*.

197   "Von dem Glauben," 75, 1–6 (*RD* II). "The offering is suitable and pleasing to God. Be it silver or gold, he makes himself beloved of God. Be it bread or be it an egg, he thus gives to God an offering. He brings his tribute to God and he commends himself to His service as an *eigen kneht*, that he should rightly serve Him as an *eigen*."

198   "Von dem Glauben," 119, 4–6 (*RD* II). "He ordered that all his money be divided in common for the needy people and he served with honor his lord. *eigene gecoufte knehte* should rightly do the same."

199   Quoted in Bumke, 67–68.

CHAPTER III

The Practice of Justice

1. INTRODUCTION: *FRÎE* AND *SCALC*

The divinely established order of creation and one's assessment of it determine how justice is to be rendered and practiced. As Hans Eggers remarks: "*Reht* is that conduct that is in accord with *ordo*."[1] In the German vernacular religious poems of the eleventh and twelfth centuries, the social categories that are used to describe the hierarchical *ordo* of human society seem to present a series of unrelated and, in part, contradictory views. If the German poets display no unanimity in their views of the social order, however, then their conception of justice, of what is due to and from each member of this order, would also likely vary. But the religious poets in fact reveal more fundamental agreement on the nature of their society and thus on their ideal of the practice of justice than the review in the last chapter might have suggested. Despite some critics' claims to the contrary,[2] all the poets acknowledge and affirm the hierarchical nature of their society. Depending on their biblical or Patristic models, they differ on the chronology and cause of the origin of inequality, and they vary in their description of the nature of inequality, whether *frîe* and *scalc*, *rîch* and *arm*, or *hêrre* and *kneht*. Some authors, like Noker, accept the unfortunate state of inequality, while simultaneously recalling the original unity and equality of humankind; others look forward to the abolishment of inequality in the life to come. Nevertheless, the present fact of hierarchy and its justness are never seriously called into question.

The Early Middle High German poets' consensus and lack of real ambiguity on the nature of hierarchy can be seen most clearly by contrasting them with the views of a later author whose criticism of servitude and its supposed divinely-sanctioned origin is unmistakable. In his *Sachsenspiegel* (ca. 1224-25), Eike von Repgow pauses in his exposition of the Saxon *Landrecht* or territorial law to discuss the origin of "egenscap" or serfdom.[3] Eike's comments arise in the context of his treatment of the *ius ministerialum*: "Nu ne latet uch nicht wunderen, dat dit buk so luttel seget van denstlude rechte: went it is so manichvolt, dat is neman to ende komen ne kan" (III, 42, § 2).[4] What is more, Eike states, the entire concept of servitude, of which the status of the *ministeriales* is but one aspect, is suspect. He begins his argument, the form of which has rightly been called scholastic,[5] with an appeal to secular history:

> Do men ok recht erst satte, do ne was nen denstman unde (do) waren alle de lude vri, do unse vorderen here to lande quamen. An minen sinnen ne kan ek is ok nicht op genemen na der warheit, dat ieman des anderen scole sin. Ok ne hebbe we is nen orekunde. (III, 42, § 3)[6]

Eike then turns to biblical history and reports that some say "egenscap" or servitude originated with Cain's murder of Abel, while others maintain that it began with Noah's son Ham, or with Ishmael, or with Esau (II. 42, § 3). Eike first uses biblical evidence to refute these views.[7] He writes, for example, of Ham that: "Noah segende twene sine sone, an deme dridden ne gewuch he nener egenscap; Cam besatte Affricam mit sime geslechte, Sem blef in Asia, Japhet, unse vordere, besatte Europam; sus ne blef er nen des anderen" (II, 42, § 3).[8] Eike's argument is strictly speaking correct. The Bible states that Noah cursed not his son Ham, but Ham's son Canaan,[9] a discrepancy that was not lost to earlier biblical commentators.[10]

Eike next brings an argument from secular law:

> We hebben ok in unseme rechte, dat neman sek selve to egen gegeven ne mach, it ne weder legge sin erve wol; wo mochte do Noe oder Issac enen anderen to egen gegeven, sint sek selve neman to egen gegeven ne mach (it weder legge sin erve wol). (II, 42, § 3)[11]

The Bible, Eike further states, confirms secular law, for it speaks of the manumission in the Jubilee Year of those captured in war as well as of slaves; therefore the status of servitude cannot be permanent. Finally, man, the image of God, can only belong to God, not to another man (III, 42, § 4-5).[12]

Servitude is nevertheless a fact. If it is neither divinely sanctioned nor justified by sacred history or by Saxon law, whence did it arise? Eike's answer is succinct and, as will be shown, uses concepts that are crucial in understanding the Early Middle High German religious poets' concept of justice:

> Na rechter warheit so hevet egenscap begin van dwange unde van verknisse und van unrechter gewalt, de men van aldere in unrechte gewonheit getogen hevet unde nu vor recht hebben wol. (III, 42, § 6)[13]

Nothing in the German religious poems even approaches Eike's unequivocal denunciation of the justification of servitude.[14] The German poets, on the contrary, all agree on the justness of the ordered hierarchy in this world, including servitude, regardless of how they justify and explain it.

The varied conceptual pairs, *frîe* and *scalc*, *hêrre* and *kneht*, and *rîch* and *arm*, therefore, do not imply completely varied conceptions of society and its order; instead they are perhaps better conceived as emphasizing different aspects of this order. Early Middle High German authors, furthermore, tend to use some of these categories more than others. They particularly favor the combinations *hêrre* and *kneht*, and *rîch* and *arm,* and it is by means of these social categories, however vague, that the poets most frequently determine what is due from others as well as to others. No doubt because of the nature of their audiences, the poets usually concentrate on the first element of each pair, *die hêrren* and *die rîchen*. In comparison, the few passages explicitly directed to the *knehte* or *die armen* are always short and concise and tend to be more sparing in their expectations and criticisms.

The legal categories, *frîe* and *scalc* are only rarely specifically invoked by the poets in their calls to justice. An interesting and important exception to this rule is to be found in the retelling of the story of Joseph and his brothers in the complex of Early Middle High German biblical epics based on the book of Genesis. The major part of the Genesis epics is devoted to the story of Joseph, close to 2,000 out of about 6,000 lines in the *Vienna Genesis*; the manuscript evidence suggests that the Joseph story might have been circulated separately.[15] We have already seen that the authors of the biblical epics highlighted legal status in their versions of Noah's curse. It plays a central role in their explanations of Joseph's conduct during the famine in Egypt. Chapter 47, 13 ff. of the Book of Genesis relates how Joseph exploited the seven years of famine in Egypt to Pharaoh's advantage. In exchange for distributing food and seed, which he had wisely stored during the previous seven years of plenty, Joseph first demanded of his starving petitioners their livestock and other chattels. Reduced to indigence, the Egyptians then offered themselves and their lands to Joseph. To facilitate a comparison with the vernacular epics I quote the relevant biblical passage in full:

> (18) Venerunt [the Egyptians] anno secundo et dixerunt ei [Joseph]: "Non celamus dominum nostrum quod deficiente pecunia pecora simul defecerint; nec clam te est quod absque corporibus et terra nihil habemus. (19) Cur ergo moriamur te vidente; et nos et terra nostra tui erimus. Eme nos in servitutem regiam et praebe semina ne pereunte cultore redigatur terra in solitudinem." (20) Emit igitur Ioseph omnem terram Aegypti vendentibus singulis possessiones suas prae magnitudine famis, subiecitque eam Pharaoni (21) et cunctos populos eius a novissimis terminis Aegypti usque ad extremos fines eius, (22) praeter terram sacerdotum quae a rege tradita fuerat eis, quibus et statuta cibaria ex horreis publicis praebebantur et idcirco non sunt conpulsi vendere possessiones suas.

Joseph then initiates a system, in which a fifth of the Egyptians' crops should be rendered to Pharaoh in exchange for seed and the use of their former lands.

This passage must have seemed surprisingly familiar to medieval readers, for its account of both the form of land tenure and the sacerdotal privileges bears similarity to their own rural society.[16] Early medieval biblical commentators on the famine naturally emphasized what they approvingly interpreted as ecclesiastical immunity from royal taxation. On the other hand, since Joseph was universally interpreted as the typological prefiguration of Christ, his measures against the laymen were a definite cause for concern. His scheme imposes in effect involuntary servitude on the hapless free small landowners and would have run contrary to Church doctrine on slavery.[17] His actions must therefore be justified. Bede, for example, felt compelled to exonerate Joseph by drawing subtle distinctions:

> Jam de Hebraeis dicitur, quod violenter in servitutem redacti sunt. Aegyptium vero populum facile in servitutem redegit Pharao. "Per Joseph omnis terra Aeypti

Pharaoni traditur," de quo facile excusatur Joseph, vendiderunt enim semetipsos. Hoc Paulus fecit, cum illum qui indignus erat sanctorum consortio, traderet Satanae. [Cf. I Corinthians 5, 5.] Nemo itaque Paulum dixerit dure egisse, qui hominem de Ecclesia ejecerit, ut expulsus disceret non blasphemare.[18]

Bede then quickly turns to the typological interpretation of the passage, according to which the Egyptians' selling themselves and their land to Joseph signifies Christ's buying or redeeming (emere) the entire world with his teaching and his body.

Bede's discomfort with Joseph's actions was shared by the author of the *Vienna Genesis*. He begins with a fairly literal poetic adaptation of the biblical passage:

> Do daz iâr hine chom,
> Josebe si zuo sprachen
> er lieze ime irbarmin
> daz si vil armen nehaten fihi noh scatz
> er hulf in etwaz:
> in niware nieht bestanten
> in scaze noh gewante,
> sine heten nieht mere
> newan des lîbes unt der erde,
> er name dei zime,
> cherts in des chuniges frume,
> si wurten selbe sine scalche,
> gap in dei eigin zu siner gewelte
> ub er si generte
> und die erde mit samen bewarte.[19]

But the poet then emphasizes that Joseph had no desire to take advantage of their situation:

> Er lîe si selben frî bisten,
> er ni wolt ire ze scalchtuom.
> iz duht in sunte, die er frî funte
> ub er die ze scalche tate durch dehein ire nôte.[20]
> Er wolte si giwielten ire,
> so der hunger wurte fure,
> daz si denne fridelichen[21] mahten ire dinch werven,
> daz ir ieglich gnuoch giwunne,
> ub in nieman neduvnge.[22]

It certainly would appear that the *Vienna Genesis* poet is here "polemicizing against the words of the Bible."[23] The biblical account clearly says that Joseph was able to buy all of the Egyptian lands "prae magnitudine famis" and that the priests, in contrast to the lay Egyptians, were not "compelled" to sell their lands to Joseph. When the *Vienna Genesis* poet says that Joseph refused to buy the Egyptians' land "durch dehein ire nôte" he flatly contradicts the biblical account in Joseph's favor.

The immediately following lines in the *Vienna Genesis* suggest that the divergence from the Bible was perhaps inspired by the same distinction between the freely ("facile") accepted servitude of the Egyptians and the imposition ("violenter") of servitude on the Hebrews such as Bede had drawn:

> Swer im bôt daz eigen,
> den newolt er nieht werigen.
> er chouft in des chuniges gualt
> die ere[24] manichfalt,
> uon des lantes ente chouft er iz
> al ze des chuniges hente.[25]

These lines represent a faithful account of the outcome of the biblical story, but throw a better light on Joseph's actions. The *Vienna Genesis* author's former deviation from the Bible (ll. 5,210-5,221) might therefore be explained as follows. The poet wanted to make clear that Joseph did not force (*violenter*) the Egyptians to give him their lands and incur servitude; rather, they offered themselves voluntarily (*facile*). Joseph then declined to refuse them despite his original desire that they retain their freedom.

This distinction, like Bede's, must strike one as sophistry. Nonetheless, it allows the poet to uphold his portrait of Joseph as the paradigmatic just ruler. To have made slaves of free men by exploiting their need[26] would have been sinful ("sunte," l. 5212), that is, unjust.[27] If they offer themselves freely, on the other hand, their just due is upheld. Do not the Egyptians, following the biblical account (Gen. 47, 25), exclaim to Joseph "**W**ir sehen daz al unser gnist/ in diner hant ist./ nu geruoche du unsich anescouwen,/ wir dienen deme chunige mit frouden"?[28]

The *Millstätter Genesis* account of chapter 47 of Genesis substantially departs from the *Vienna/Vorauer* solution of the problem of Joseph's treatment of the Egyptians, but, unfortunately, might be corrupt at a crucial juncture. In contrast to the *Vienna/Vorauer* text, the *Millstätter* poet underlines the initially purely financial aspect of the transaction (picking up the biblical "emere" and "vendere" (Gen. 47, 19-20)). The Egyptians promise to Joseph: "sine schalche wrden si selbe, daz eigen gæben si im ze gælde."[29] In the *Millstätter* version, there is no sophistic allusion to Joseph's ostensible refusal to exploit the Egyptians' distress and impose servitude on them; servitude under any circumstances, voluntary or enforced, is flatly rejected:

> **E**r sprach einez wolde er tuon, er gert ir niht ze scha*l*chtuom,
> ez duochte in sunte, die er uri funte
> ob er die ze des chuniges gewelte wolde uerschelchen.
> **E**r sprach 'uernemet mich, iur erde undirwind ich
> dem chunige wærlichen biz daz der hungir entwiche;
> so muget ir danne furbaz genesen: war ist daz
> daz ir genuoch gewinnet, der *hunger* ivch niht bedwnget.[30]
> **S**wer im daz eige*n* bot dem half er uon hungirs not.
> die anderen muosen in daz dienst swerigen ob si den lib wolden erigen.[31]

The *Millstätter* poet omits the exculpating phrase of the *Vienna/Vorauer Genesis* that Joseph would not make the Egyptians slaves "durch dehein ire nôte," because he presents the circumstances of their contract with Joseph in a quite different fashion. There is no mention that Joseph had wanted them to retain their liberty, but that they had nevertheless freely offered to become Pharaoh's slaves and that Joseph did not refuse them. Rather, Joseph unequivocally states in the Millstätter version that he will hold their lands only until the end of the famine.

The final two lines of the passage quoted above (104, 14-15), however, are curious. The poet appears to make a distinction between the Egyptians who offer Joseph their lands and whom he, therefore, rescued from the famine, and those, on the other hand, who had to swear their service to save their lives. Whether these latter had no land to offer and thus could only render the labor of their hands or whether they merely swore manual service while retaining control of their land cannot be known.

The interpretation of the entire passage is complicated by Diemer's suggestion that there is a gap in the text immediately following the last line (104, 15). Assuming that the *Millstätter* author followed the same original as the *Vienna/Vorauer* text, Diemer noted that the *Millstätter* poet has omitted 81 lines.[32] He postulated that the *Millstätter* scribe was misled by the end rhymes in line 104,15 of the *Millstätter Genesis* "swerigen" and "nerigen" and that in the course of his copying, mistook them for the lines equivalent to lines 1,855-56 in the *Vienna/Vorauer* version: "noh ne mahtes sich irwerigen,/ erne muos imes *swerigen*" (my emphasis). This resulted in an entire page of the original being overlooked and thus excluded. Diemer filled this postulated gap with the corresponding lines contained in the *Vienna/Vorauer Genesis.*[33] Line 104, 15 in the *Millstätter* version would thus be followed by the *Vienna/Vorauer Genesis* lines discusse above: "er chouft in des chuniges gewalt die ere manecfalt/ uon des landes ende choufte erz allez ze des chuniges hende," etc. Diemer accused the *Millstätter* poet of contradicting himself, claiming that line 104, 15 ("die anderen muozen in daz dienst swerigen ob si den lib wolden nerigen") cannot be reconciled with Joseph's previous promise to restore the Egyptians' land after the famine.

Diemer's emendation and his criticism of the *Millstätter* poet are debatable. As noted, line 104, 15 is ambiguous; it does not necessarily contradict the preceding lines. Diemer was perhaps more influenced by his own conjectured emendation, namely to append the "missing" lines to the *Millstätter* text by drawing on the *Vienna/Vorauer* version, than by the *Millstätter* text as it stands; the *Vienna/Vorauer* version does indeed contradict the *Millstätter* account of Joseph's promise to the Egyptians.

As for Diemer's claim that there is a gap in the text, one cannot accept this without question. While the lines contained in the *Vienna/Vorauer* version, which are supposedly missing in the *Millstätter* text, closely follow the biblical text, treating, in addition to Joseph's relation with the Egyptian laymen, the sacerdotal immunity from the royal tax and Jacob's request to be buried in his native land, the Genesis poets frequently omit large sections of their biblical source and the omission in the *Millstätter* version causes no disturbance to the narrative flow. The

only essential information to be excluded, namely Jacob's impending death, is sup-
plied in any case by the heading at lines 105, 17-18.[34]

The *Millstätter* poet's extant account of Joseph's actions, as well as departing
from the *Vienna/Vorauer* version, obviously radically changes the biblical story.
One may assume, as Diemer did, that the poet inexplicably contradicts himself. Or
one might argue that as a result of his modification of the biblical text, the poet
felt compelled to omit or alter Joseph's buying all of the Egyptians' land for the
pharaoh, his imposing the royal tax, and his subjecting the Egyptians to permanent
servitude. If one assumes that the *Millstätter* poet was consistent, then this would
explain these omissions as well as why he neglected to treat the priestly freedom
from taxation. For in the *Millstätter* version as it now stands, everyone who offered
Joseph the nominal control of his land for the duration of the famine would be
exempt from exploitation, not only the priests (104, 12-13).

Even if one assumes that there is a gap in the text, the comparison of *Vienna
Genesis* lines 5,210-5,221 with lines 104, 7-15 of the *Millstätter Genesis* clearly
demonstrates that the differences between the *Millstätter* version and the
Vienna/Vorauer versions are too substantial to permit one merely to supply lines
from the latter to fill the hole in the former. There is little reason to assume that
the *Millstätter* poet would have suddenly reverted to a version identical to the
Vienna/Vorauer Genesis.

Finally, although Diemer's explanation of the gap is not implausible and even
has a certain elegance, the end rhymes to which he refers as the cause of the proposed gap, while similar, are by no means identical: "swerigen/nerigen (*Millstätter
Genesis*, 104, 15) versus "irwerigen/swerigen" (*Vorauer Bücher Moses*, ll. 1855-56).

In Diemer's favor, one must concede that the *Millstätter* poet's omission of
Jacob's sense of impending death, except in the title lines, is unmotivated. The
question of the existence of a gap in the text cannot, therefore, be answered with
any finality. One can only say that in its present version, the *Millstätter Genesis*
presents a far more unequivocal rejection of the imposition of servitude on free
men. Justice demands that they be left free under any and all circumstances.

The concern in the biblical Genesis epics with justice based on legal categories
is, as mentioned, an exception among the Early Middle High German poets, and
in the passages discussed above, the concept of *reht* is never explicitly evoked, but
only *sunte*, which I have construed as *unreht*. None of the other religious poets
connects just behavior with the absolute categories of law; rather, the more relative pairs of lords and servants and rich and poor are clearly the center of their
attention, and it is therefore to these social categories that we now turn to discover
their implications for the practice of justice.

2. *HÊRRE* AND *KNEHT* AND *RÎCH* AND *ARM*

A. *Der hêrre* and *der rîche* in "Vom Rechte"

In their admonitions to justice directed to the "lords" and the "rich," the Early Middle High German religious poets generally distinguish between these two categories. They may appear in the same work, but usually in different sections. Exceptions to this rule are few and are usually restricted to the purely adjectival use of the terms. Thus Heinrich von Melk combines *hêr* and *rîch*, along with *frî* in its — typically for Heinrich — moral sense:

> wer mac sich da vor entreden,
> swie riche oder swie her er si,
> daz er von solhen suhten belibe fri?[35]

And Der arme Hartmann says of Christ:

> So ist er dem vater al gelich   eben geweldich unde eben rich
> eben geweldich unde eben her,   weder minner noch mere.[36]

Usually, the poets contrast *der rîche* with *der arme* and *der hêrre* with *der kneht*, or occasionally with *der dienstman*, more rarely with *der scalc*. Heinrich von Melk again provides the exception to the rule when he sarcastically asks about a power-hungry priest:

> von wie getaner ordenunge
> sold er ze einem *herren* werden gehabt,
> fur daz er der welt hat widersagt,
> der vor des ein *armmensc* was? (my emphases)[37]

In order to demonstrate the use of the categories and their fairly strict division I would like to turn once again to a closer examination of "Vom Rechte." Unfortunately, an insightful analysis of the poem by Ingeborg Schröbler has canonized an interpretation that obscures the relations between *die hêrren* and *die rîchen* and the *knehte* and *die armen*. The identities of the "meister und sin chneht" mentioned in the poem have also been subject to misleading interpretations. Because Schröbler's interpretation and structural analysis of the poem have won such general acceptance, I will summarize her scheme as the starting point for the following discussion.[38]

Schröbler divided "Vom Rechte" into two parts: The first contains general teaching about duties ("eine allgemeine Pflichtenlehre") and the second, specific teachings for certain "estates" ("eine spezielle Pflichtenlehre für einzelne Stände").[39] After the prologue (ll. 1-12) on the nature of justice (see above, Chapter I), the first section of the poem, the general teaching about duties, begins with the division of the concept of *reht* into its three species or forms: *triuwe*, the Golden Rule, and *gewære sîn* (ll. 13-33) (see above, Chapter II).

Schröbler characterized lines 34–53 as a depiction of three perversions of the three forms of *reht*:

(1. *triuwe*)	(40)	mannechlich sinem vriunde *niht* gestat als er in geminnet hat.
(2. *gewære sîn*)		bi des iegelicher sinen moutwillen gechosot, so stat daz reht verbosot.
(3. the Golden Rule)		manneclich wil reht han,
	(45)	als sin gewalt ist getan,
		und wil daz im selben haben
		und wilz deheinem anderen geben.
		der site der sint dri,
		da ist rehtes niht bi.
	(50)	dar an wellent si gestan,
		von diu wirt des armen rede vil unrehte getan.
		die scheident ouch zware
		von dem rehten rihtære.[40]

The poet, according to Schröbler, then offers a more detailed discussion, including examples, of the three kinds of *reht*, beginning with the Golden Rule, then turning to *triuwe*, where Satan's fall is depicted, and finally to *gewære sîn*, where the poet describes the ordeal by fire. The author concludes this section with a small excursus on *avaritia* as the root of all evil (ll. 303–320).

The second part of the poem, interrupted by an excursus of some 50 lines on God's knowledge of our practice of *reht* (ll. 450–97), consists, in Schröbler's view, of a presentation of the "rights" and "duties" specific to three "estates:" lords (ll. 321–344), husbands and wives (ll. 345–416), and priests (ll. 417–449; 498–523).[41] The poem closes with a sort of summary, a final admonition, and a prayer (ll. 524–549).

For the sake of clarity, Schröbler's interpretation of the structure of the poem may be visualized as follows:

I. Prologue: The nature of *reht* (ll. 1–12)
II. General teaching on duties (ll. 13–320)
    A. The three forms of *reht* (ll. 13–33)
    B. Their opposites (ll. 34–53)
    C. Detailed discussion, with examples, of the three forms of *reht*:
        1. The Golden Rule (ll. 54–190)
        2. *Triuwe* (ll. 191–238)
        3. *Gewære sîn* (ll. 239–302)
    D. Excursus on *avaritia* (ll. 303–320)
III. Specific teaching to the estates (ll. 321–523)
    A. The lords (ll. 321–344)
    B. Husbands and wives (ll. 345–416)
    C¹. Priests (ll. 417–449)

D. Excursus on God's knowledge of man's practice of *reht*   (ll. 450-497)

C². Priests (ll. 498-523)

IV. Conclusion (ll. 524-549)

While few would dispute this general account of the structure of "Vom Rechte," its detailed execution is far from clear.[42] Indeed, Schröbler devoted the major part of an essay, "On the Limits of Understanding Medieval Literature," to the problems specifically encountered in a consistent structural analysis of the poem. She took a positive view and asserted that the difficulties with which readers feel confronted lie in our modern aesthetic categories and our resulting lack of understanding of medieval patterns of thought.[43]

Schröbler's positive comments are, in part, a response to earlier criticisms of "Vom Rechte." Carl von Kraus, for example, had been decidedly less generous to the author of the poem, accusing him of lacking "any schooling in logic" and of failing to bring to a satisfactory conclusion any thought that he had once begun.[44] Von Kraus especially objected to lines 68 to 190 of "Vom Rechte," in which he claimed the author contradicts himself.[45]

These lines in particular are the most illuminating for the meaning and relation of the concepts *der rîche* and *hêrre* and therefore merit very close attention. Schröbler, as shown, assigns them to the detailed discussion of the Golden Rule, which in her view begins at line 54 (section II. C. 1. in my reconstruction). The poet first castigates those who commit injustice (ll. 54 ff.) and then turns to the example of *der rîche man*, whose wealth God can at any time destroy (ll. 68-95). Lines 101-123 explain that God punishes the rich man for his *superbia* ("ubermuot"). The poet then describes how *der meister* and *der chneht* work together to clear the forest. Just as they must exert themselves to remove the largest roots in order to be able to plow the soil, so will God forcefully remove the hard, rich man who commits injustice (ll. 124-162). When *der meister* and *der chneht* come to harvest the land, they should equally divide its fruits for which they both have worked (ll. 163-176). Similarly, we should begrudge one another nothing and help each other in our need, for the *der hêrre* and the *chneht* both have one *reht* (ll. 177-190).

Von Kraus claimed that in lines 168 ff., on the equal division of the harvest, the poet has already forgotten his point of departure, namely that God had punished the rich man by seizing all his wealth and forcing him to clear the wilderness with his servant. The rich man is, therefore, entirely destitute and possesses as little as his *chneht*. By demanding that he share with his *chneht*, the poet assumes that the lord on the contrary must have something to share.[46]

Previous to Kraus, Wilhelm Scherer had also found this section of "Vom Rechte" unusual. He calls the poet "a demagogue" and "a revolutionary" because of what he saw as harsh criticism of the lords, and he sensed an experience of "class struggles" lurking behind the poem.[47]

Schröbler attempted to answer Kraus's objections to the poet's logic and perhaps refute Scherer's "revolutionary" characterization as well by a thematic division of lines 54-190 into three main, but intertwined parts: A) a discussion of *reht* and wealth, B) a symbolic narrative on land clearance and the division of its fruits, and C) an exegesis of this symbolic narrative.[48] Schröbler's structural analysis of lines 54-190 is so essential to her interpretation that a visual outline of her proposed divisions of this part of the text should be given as well:

A¹) *Der ríchtuom* (ll. 54–95):
    a.) The man who commits *unreht* is threatened with damnation (ll. 54–67).
    b.) The uncertainty of the rich man's wealth (ll. 68–95).
B¹) The symbolic narrative:
    Meister and *chneht* clear the land together (ll. 96–100).
A²) *Der ríchtuom*:
    Der ríche is punished for his sins (ll. 101–123).
B²) The symbolic narrative:
    Meister and *chneht* must work to remove roots (ll. 124–136).
C¹) The interpretation of the symbolic narrative:
    Only God can convert the *herter rícher man* (ll. 137–162).
B³) The symbolic narrative:
    When the *meister* and the *chneht* come to harvest the land they should equally divide its fruits (ll. 163–176).
C²) The interpretation of the symbolic narrative:
    So we should all live: *hêrre* and *chneht* should all love the same *reht* (ll. 177–190).

The contradictions of which Kraus complained and the revolutionary tenor that Scherer detected disappear, in Schröbler's view, if one sharply distinguishes these three strands of the poem.[49] Schröbler claimed that because Kraus had overlooked the symbolic character of the narrative on land clearance (B), he had misunderstood it as a literal continuation of the story of *der ríche man* (A). Kraus, in other words, had mistakenly followed Scherer in identifying *der ríche man* of section A and *der hêrre* of section C with *der meister* of section B.[50] In fact, *der meister* of the symbolic narrative is not the same as the *der ríche* or *der hêrre*, but only a symbol. The inconsistencies that Kraus imagined merely emphasize the necessity of maintaining the division in the poem into different narrative levels. To equate *der ríche man* with the symbolic *meister* would lead "to impossible consequences."[51]

Similarly, the demand that the harvest be equally divided appears only in the symbolic narrative (B) and not in its moral exegesis (C). While it is startling, Schröbler claimed, that such a demand should be made at any level of the narrative, it should by no means be literally understood, for such a demand "in the real world would be socially revolutionary in a way that appears inconsistent with the character of the poem."[52] The purpose of the symbolic narrative is rather to show that "lord and servant" should both participate in that *Recht*, namely the duty of reciprocity, that is revealed in the struggle against *Unrecht*.[53] Although it is true that the poet is not always clear in the execution of his plan, "it is obvious that the author . . . wants to make fundamental religious demands of people" and that he is not calling for the social order to be overthrown.[54]

Schröbler's explanation has achieved widespread approval.[55]   Speicher, in his commentary on the poem, accepts it without question,[56] as Maurer apparently had done in his edition when he divided lines 54-190 of "Vom Rechte" into six unequal strophes that almost exactly parallel Schröbler's structural analysis:

Schröbler	Maurer[57]
A¹ *ríchtuom* (ll. 54-95)	strophe 4 (ll. 54-67)
	strophe 5 (ll. **68**-95)
B¹ symbolic narrative (ll. **96**-100)	strophe 6 (ll. **96**-123)
A² (ll. 101-123)	
B² (ll. **124**-136)	strophe 7 (ll. **124**-136)
C¹ exegesis (ll. 137-162)	strophe 8 (ll. 137-162)
B³ (ll. **163**-176)	strophe 9 (ll. **163**-190,
	initial at l. **195**)
C² (ll. 177-190)	

Schröbler's recognition of the different strands in lines 54-190 of "Vom Rechte" has certainly advanced our understanding of the poem. Yet her insistence that despite the poet's use of gradual and therefore unclear transitions,[58] the symbolic (B) and exegetical levels (C) should be clearly separated from the general narrative on *der ríche* (A), distorts the poet's depiction of the connection between *der ríche, der meister,* and *der hêrre* and their relation to *der arme* and *der chneht* of the poem. No doubt, the author of "Vom Rechte" was concerned with making "fundamental religious demands" of his audience, but Schröbler's interpretation and Maurer's visual reconstruction of the poem conceal its equally important legal and rhetorical dimensions.

To justify this assertion, a line-by-line commentary on this section of "Vom Rechte" is necessary. I begin at line 68 because Schröbler's proposed division at line 54, in contrast to the manuscript initials, raises questions that are not pertinent to the argument.

Lines 68-95 (A¹, b. in my characterization of Schröbler's division), beginning with a sermonic call to attention, present a vivid picture of the transitory nature of all earthly wealth:

> **D**a vernement algeliche:
> nieman ist so riche,
> (70)   er muozze den richtuom verlan
> unde muoz sin ane gestan.
> swie der man daz geholot,
> daz got daz verdolot,
> daz im sin richtuom zergat,
> (75)   daz er sin niweht hat:
> swedir daz verbrinnit,
> daz der man gewinnit,
> oder er wird beroubet,
> sin richtuom so getruobet;

    (80)   swedir ez versinchet,
            in dem wazzir ertrinchet,
            oder sus chomet ein unheil,
            unde enleibet im sin deheinen teil,
            oder in begriffet der tot,
    (85)   so læt er ez danne durch got.
            swenne ez got niht mere wil bewaren,
            so læt erz noten varen.[59]

The poet utilizes traditional arguments, saturated with biblical imagery, as can be found in many other Early Middle High German poems.[60] Note, however, that wealth per se is not condemned by the poet. Rather, as Speicher has rightly commented, lines 68 ff. treat "the transitory and useless nature [of wealth] *sub specie aeternitatis,*"[61] in other words, the argument is eminently practical and morally neutral. The source of the man's wealth is irrelevant: "swie der man daz geholot" (l. 72). The poet merely states that there is no trust in worldly riches.

The lines immediately following are less clear:

            so geloubet er alerste sinem chnehte.
            so richtet got rehte,
    (90)   wan er uns nimet unde lat,
            als er des gewalt hat,
            bediu lutzzil unde vil.
            Daz tuot er also diche er wil,
            unz ez also ergat,
    (95)   daz der man niweht hat.[62]

Line 88, in particular, is problematic and raises three questions: To whom does the pronoun *er* refer, who is his *chneht*, and what does the verb *gelouben* mean? All previous commentators agree that *er* is most naturally identical to the previous *er* of line 87, which in turn unequivocally refers to the rich man. But the sudden appearance of the *chneht* is abrupt. Scherer thought that the *chneht* is identical to *der arme* of line 51 in the section on the opposites of the three *reht* (II. B.): "von diu wirt des armen rede vil unreht getan," etc. He understood *rede* in this line as "speech," and he then took *gelouben* in its usual Middle High German sense to mean "to believe." Line 88, therefore, could be translated as "Only then does he [the rich man] believe his servant [the poor man] and listen to what he says."[63]

Johannes Stosch, while accepting Scherer's interpretation of *er* and *chneht*, suggested a different meaning for *gelouben* and translated line 88 as: "Only then is the rich man *gentle and considerate* towards his servant; *he grants him a hearing,*"[64] an interpretation that was reaffirmed by Kraus and most recently — it would appear — by Vollmann-Profe.[65] Schröbler, however, had found the linking of *chneht* in line 88 to *der arme* of line 51 tenuous and confessed her inability to make sense of the line. She remarked that even if one grants Stosch's interpretation of *gelouben,* the line so understood seems to stand isolated and without context.[66]

Speicher, finally, agrees with Schröbler's rejection of the connection between *der arme* of line 51 and *der chneht* of line 88, but he otherwise dismisses Schröbler's hesitation and supplies the missing context by referring forward to lines 105-113, which discuss the cause of the rich man's downfall. Speicher suggests that through the loss of his riches, the rich man discards his pride and now (in line 88) meets the servant entrusted to him, but hitherto wronged, in Christian brotherly love.[67]

Speicher's explanation contradicts his own characterization of the passage, according to which lines 68-95 treat wealth "*sub specie aeternitatis*," whereas only in lines 101 ff., that is after the intervening commencement of the so-called symbolic narrative, does the poet discuss the moral consequences of amassing wealth and connect riches with injustice and sin.[68] The rich man of lines 68 ff., however, is not accused of any moral wrong to his servant or anyone else.

Speicher's view also strains the logic of the poem. If the *chneht* of line 88 cannot refer back to the previously mentioned *der arme* of line 51, how can it anticipate by 21 lines the, as yet unknown, injustice supposedly done to him by *der rîche*, but only vaguely described in line 109 ("im [the rich man] erbarmet niemans not")? The word *chneht* is never used in lines 101 ff.

Schröbler's hesitations are justified. There is no context that can motivate the sudden appearance of the rich man's *chneht*, for there is no mention in lines 68-95 of a possible injustice done to him that would explain why *der rîche man* only now ("alerste") is charitable towards him. Either line 88 is hopelessly obscure or the traditional explanations of *er*, *chneht*, and *gelouben* are simply wrong.

A solution to the puzzle may perhaps be reached if we look at the three problematic words in turn. Consider, first, the poet's previous use of the word *chneht*. It initially appears in line 5 where it is used in a religious and moral sense to mean the servant of God, the biblical "servus Dei": "von diu hiez er [God] den sinen chneht/ vil starke minnen daz reht" (ll. 5-6). In its second occurrence, line 66, the biblical phrase is even directly translated: "gotes chneht." From Scherer onward, commentators have ignored the poet's previous use of *chneht* as a biblical and moral concept and have simply assumed that in line 88, its third appearance, *chneht* suddenly has a social meaning: *chneht* as opposed to the *rîche*. As we have seen, this pairing, constructed by interpretation, is unusual in the Early Middle High German poems. Rather, *der rîche* is almost always combined with and contrasted to *der arme* and not the *kneht*.[69]

In view of the lack of convincing arguments to the contrary, one might perhaps better assume that the *chneht* of line 88 continues the poet's original usage and thus refers to the obedient servant of God. If this interpretation is right, however, the possessive adjective *sinem* modifying *chneht* as well as the pronoun *er* now indicate God and not the rich man: "Only then does God *geloubet* His servant."

This reading again raises the problem of the meaning of *gelouben*. Its usual Middle High German definition "to believe" is difficult, regardless of how one interprets *chneht*. As mentioned, Stosch had long ago suggested that the lines should be understood as "Only then is the rich man gentle and considerate towards his servant; he grants him a hearing." Stosch based his comments on the evidence of Karl Lucae whose conjectures about an alternative meaning of "gelouben" arose, in turn, in the context of his explaining some difficult lines in Wolfram's *Parzival*.[70] When Parzival's father Gahmuret declares that he must reject his mother's and brother's generous offer to stay with them, his mother pleads with him one last time:

> 'owê nu truoc dich doch mîn lîb:
> du bist och Gandînes kint.
> ist got an sîner helfe blint,
> oder ist er dran betoubet,
> daz er mir niht geloubet?'[71]

Lucae suggested that the obscure lines should be understood as "Is God, who could help me, blind or deaf that He does not grant my wish or listen to my plea?"[72] As in line 88 of "Vom Rechte," God is the subject of *gelouben*. Following Lucae's interpretation of *gelouben* in *Parzival*, one might, therefore, translate line 88 of "Vom Rechte" as: "Only then does God *grant the wishes or hear the plea* of His servant."

A grammatical objection to this interpretation might be raised by my understanding of the pronoun *er*, which now anticipates "got" in line 89, or, skipping back over the "er" in line 87 (i.e. the rich man), refers back to "got" in line 86. While a reference to the immediately previous noun or pronoun is, of course, the more frequent usage, the anticipatory usage was by no means unknown in Middle High German.[73] A slight change in the editor's punctuation makes this new interpretation fairly clear:

> swenne ez got niht mere wil bewaren,
> so læt erz noten varen͵ (instead of ';')
> so geloubet er alerste sinem chnehte͵ (instead of '.')
> so richtet got rehte, etc.

Who then is this devoted *chneht* or servant whose wishes God grants and whose pleas He hears and how does my interpretation of line 88 fit into the context of the passage? The servant is none other than the rich man himself, humbled and penitent, who, like Job, pleads with God to stop his destruction. God only answers His servant's call after his riches have been destroyed. In this, God judges justly, for He can take and bestow as He wishes, both little and much, and as often as He desires until His servant has nothing ("Vom Rechte," ll. 89-95), for unlike the many who unjustly identify *reht* with their power or *gewalt*, God's *gewalt* is by definition *reht*.[74]

In favor of this interpretation are these points: its uniting, in one syntactic unit, the rhyme words *chneht* and *reht* as is done in myriad other examples in Early Middle High German; its avoidance of an implied and otherwise unusual pairing of *der riche* and *der chneht* as social categories; its preservation of the poet's previous use of *chneht* as a religious concept, here applied specifically to the rich man; and its elimination of an unmotivated accusation against the rich man of dealing unjustly with his servant. In the context of the poem, finally, it preserves the character of the passage as a practical warning about the transitoriness of wealth; the moral condemnation comes only later.

We can now return to the discussion of the structure of the poem. Lines 96–100, set off by the scribe with a capital, introduce what Schröbler characterized as the "symbolic narrative" and are another source of difficulties in this section of "Vom Rechte":

> So hat der meister und sin chneht
> bede samt ein reht.
> ich weiz, si ensamet hin gant
> ein routin bestant:
> si routent mit den armen.[75]

The principle questions posed by these lines are: Who are the *meister* and the *chneht* and what is their relation to the previous description of the rich man's loss of wealth, or in grammatical terms, what is the force of the adverb "So" in line 96? Scherer and Kraus argued that "so" introduces the consequences of the rich man's divinely-imposed poverty and thus, as we have seen, identified him with the *meister* who now must clear his lands with his own labor, an interpretation that was also shared by Mackensen.[76] Ehrismann scarcely touched the question and simply stated: "The author has rural circumstances in mind; the lord (*meister*) and his servant are farmers who clear the forest together . . . ."[77] Gernentz vaguely spoke of a world depicted in the poem "that is extraordinarily complicated by the opposition between rich and poor, the difference between lord and servant, . . . and the coexistence of old property and new clearance."[78] He claims that the *meister* is the *hêrre*.[79] Erb spoke merely of "a farmer" and seemed not to identify him with either *der rîche* or the *hêrre*.[80]

Schröbler, of course, denied that the "so" in line 96 should be understood as showing the consequences of the impoverishment of the rich man (ll. 68 ff.) and instead claimed that the word, "untranslatable into modern German," introduces a new thought that draws the conclusion from "what was said in lines 54 ff. about the injustice of the powerful [des Gewaltigen]: 'Master [Meister] and servant therefore have one duty."[81] Schröbler's justification for this interpretation stems from her characterization of lines 96–100 as part of a symbolic narrative, which is continued in lines 124–136 and in lines 163–176, in which the demand for the equal division of the harvest (ll. 163 ff.) appears. Because this demand would be "socially revolutionary" in the sphere of real life and therefore incompatible with the character of the poem, the symbolic narrative should on no account be connected with the description of the rich man, which apparently does belong to the sphere of real life. The result of these assertions is clear: "the *meister* of line 96 is not the *rîche* of the previous section, and the *hêrre* of line 183 is not identical to the *meister* of line 164."[82] Schröbler's reading of lines 96–100 is thus determined by her ideological classification of the character of the poem and by her belief that the equal division of the harvest between *hêrre* and *chneht* would have been revolutionary at the time of its composition. In Schröbler's view, therefore, the *meister* and the *chneht* are merely symbols and need not be more closely identified. Nonetheless it is not by chance, claimed Schröbler, that the poet uses the words *meister* and *chneht*, for while they occasionally designate "the farmer and his servant, they more usually describe the relation between a superior, by virtue of an intellectual qualification, and the person entrusted to him."[83]

Vollmann-Profe has criticized some of the details of Schröbler's division of the text, and she questions whether section B, the symbolic narrative, is indeed symbolic. She nonetheless accepts Schröbler's view that the *meister* of line 96 is not to be confused with *der rîche* of Schröbler's section A.[84] Unfortunately, her translation obscures the matter by her inconsistent renderings of *meister* now as "der Herr" (lines 96 and 164; see also lines 323 and 327) and now as "der Meister" (line 125).

To summarize these conflicting views: the *meister* of line 96 has been seen as identical to the impoverished *rîche man* of lines 68 ff. (Scherer, Kraus, Mackensen) and/or the *hêrre* of lines 183 ff. (Ehrismann?, Gernentz), or he is simply a (symbolic) farmer who has no real connection with *der rîche* (Erb?, Schröbler, and, following, her both Speicher[85] and Vollmann-Profe, with some modifications).

Schröbler's characterization of the *meister* is problematic. It sways between identifying the *meister* and his *chneht* as merely a symbolic "farmer and his servant," both far removed from the social sphere of the *der hêrre*, and portraying the *meister* as the intellectual superior and moral guardian of his *chneht*. The latter characterization is certainly consonant with the poet's later use of *meister*[86] and is well founded in Early Middle High German literature where *meister*, as Schröbler had stated, most often refers to a person of spiritual, intellectual, or moral superiority.[87] But within the "symbolic narrative" of "Vom Rechte," *meister* nowhere has any connotation that indicates such a mental superiority over his *chneht*.

Schröbler's assertion, moreover, that *meister* and *chneht* occasionally designate "the farmer and his servant," which is crucial to her disassociating the *meister* of the symbolic narrative from the social sphere of the *rîche* or the *hêrre*, is also questionable. The classical dictionaries of Middle High German do not sustain this interpretation, but they are based primarily on sources that were written after the Early Middle High German period.[88] One must, therefore, attempt to glean some insights from the literature of the Early Middle High German period, but here too Schröbler's definition cannot be confirmed. In addition to meaning an intellectual superior, *meister* describes a hierarchical superior, usually in the spiritual realm.[89] But when *meister* explicitly appears within descriptions of the rural sphere, which is rare, it means the "master" of an animal and not a *chneht*.[90]

On three occasions, however, *meister* is used in a quite different sense. In the *Millstätter Genesis*, *meister* is associated with *hêrre* in a passage in which Jacob's sons tell their father about Joseph's success under the Pharaoh in Egypt:

> da ward er triut des chuniges   unde alles sinen gedigenes.
> Meister er wart   unde herre ubir allez lant.[91]

Meister here is some kind of hierarchical superior in the Pharaoh's household and he is also a *hêrre*.

In the *Vienna Genesis* version of these lines, the word *hêrre* is omitted, and Joseph has become the *meister* of Pharaoh's *gedigene*. Jacob's sons relate of Joseph:

> daz er trût ware des chuniges,
> meister alles sines gedigenes

> wî uber churz iouch lanch
> im unter tân was daz lant.[92]

The *gedigene* over which Joseph is *meister* usually means "retinue," the collected *degen* or warriors. In this passage, however, it seems to mean simply the king's followers or servants.

In the *Millstätter Exodus, meister* again appears, this time in connection with the description of the Egyptians' brutal treatment of the enslaved Israelites:

> Er wære gesunt oder siech   man entleib im niht;
> niemæn si nescherten   die den gewalt hebeten;
> die meister si blowen   unsanfte dwngen
> swa si senfte waren   den ir untertanen.[93]

Meister here refers to the overseers of the Israelites, who themselves are called *schalche*, as when they beg Pharaoh for mercy, saying:

> 'du entlibest uns weizgot   uns wære bezzer der tot
> wir sin dine schalche   du ruche uns ze behalten,
> entlibe uns herre etwaz   daz wir dienen desterbaz.[94]

The use of *meister* in these three instances seems to parallel some of the meanings of medieval Latin *magister*, from which *meister* was derived.[95]   Consider, for example, Chapter 18 of the "Capitula legibus addenda" from 818/819. Instructions are given for those *servi* who refuse to use "denarios bonos." The *servi*, regardless of whether they belong to the Church, a count or "nostri vassalli," will be punished with 60 lashes, a corporal version of the 60 *solidi*, the usual mulct imposed by the imperial ban. The capitulary then continues:

> Si magister eorum [servi] vel advocatus qui liber est eos vel comiti vel misso nostro iussus praesentare noluerit, praedictum bannum nostrum sexaginta solidorum conponat.[96]

Here *magister* designates the (free?) overseer of the *servi*.

In the well-known capitulary "De villis" (ca. 800), *magister* also means the "master" of the *servi*. In Chapter 29, he is made responsible for acting as an advocate to the *servus* whose legal case is conducted outside the jurisdiction of the estate: "servus habuerit noster forensicus iustitias ad querendum, magister eius cum omni intentione decertet pro eius iustitia."[97]   In Chapter 57 of the same capitulary, the limitations of the *magister*'s authority are made clear. The case is mentioned where a *servus* has something to report to the king:

> Si aliquis ex servis nostris super magistrum suum nobis de causa nostra vellet dicere, vias ad nos veniendi non contradicat.[98]

In the "Lex familiae" of Burchard of Worms, written over 200 years after the capitularies (1023–1025), *magister* appears to have a similar meaning.   Chapter 12 discusses the conduct of manorial justice:

> Ut in omnibus locis, ubicumque fieri possit, declinentur periuria, qualiscumque sit ex familia qui cum sotio suo sive in agro sive in vineis sive in illis levioribus

rebus iniuste fecerit, et se ad magistrum loci proclamaverit, volumus, ut illius loci
minister cum subiectis concivibus suis sine iuramento hoc determinet.[99]

The *magister* or *illius loci minister* (or, as an alternative reading calls him, *regens*)
seems here to be the local manager of a lord's estate with a limited jurisdiction
over the *subiecti concives*. He is, thus, perhaps close to what English ecclesiastical
sources of the eleventh century call a *firmarius* who

> was neither the delegate of the religious community nor a servant. He was the
> holder of a concession who for a certain period, most often for his lifetime,
> wielded the powers of the lord. . . . It does not appear that this process [of leas-
> ing land to a *firmarius*] . . . was employed in the English countryside alone. In
> Saxony and the Rhineland at the end of the twelfth century, manors owned by
> the Church were often granted for life or for a fixed period to a villicus in
> exchange for a pensio or fixed participation in provisioning the household.[100]

Whether Burchard's *magister* is indeed equivalent to a *firmarius* or *villicus*, he at
least has some jurisdictional rights (as well as duties) on a manor. He might, therefore, also be what Eike calls in the *Sachsenspiegel* a *bûmeister*, a manorial overseer
who was also entrusted with the execution of 'low justice' over *causae minores* or
less serious crimes.[101]

Whatever the passages quoted precisely mean by *magister* and regardless of
whether the conjectured parallels to the *firmarius*, *villicus*, or *bûmeister* are valid, the
outward similarity in their description of the function of the *magister* or *bûmeister*
to the description of the *meister* in the *Millstätter Exodus* is striking. In none of
these cases does *magister* mean "farmer" or *Bauer*; it seems, rather, to refer to a
(manorial) overseer, likely a man of free status, a lord not in the sense of a noble-
man, but of one who has authority over *servi*.[102] The *meister* in "Vom Rechte,"
which is, after all, preserved in the same collection as *Millstätter Exodus*, perhaps
designates such a *magister* or *bûmeister* and thus, at the same time, a lord and with
respect to his wealth, possibly a (formally) rich man. There is, therefore, no exter-
nal lexicographic reason to reject Scherer's original interpretation of *meister* in line
96 of "Vom Rechte" as the fallen rich man of lines 68 ff. Those scholars who
equated the *meister* with *der rîche* may well have been right in their intuition,
although the "Vom Rechte" poet's sometimes confusing style does not always
make the equation clear.

The fall from riches to poverty is a common theme in Early Middle High
German literature. One instance of this in the *Vienna Genesis* is remarkably similar to the situation described in "Vom Rechte." After their expulsion from
Paradise, Adam and Eve and their two sons were forced to work the land in order
to survive:

> in was bi den ziten
> sam nu ist sumelichen liuten
> die fon richtuomen
> zarmoten choment.
> die nechunden puwen,
> die sehent menege riuwe,

> die in danc muzen nemen
> swaz in got geruchet geben.
> sam tet Adam
> iouch sin wib lussam,
> muosen mit armuote
> liden ire not.[103]

Before continuing with the interpretation of the poem, let us first establish what conclusions may be drawn from what has been claimed so far. Lines 68-95 of "Vom Rechte" describe in very general terms the transitory nature of wealth and how a rich man can lose everything he has until God finally spares him. Lines 96 ff. then describe the consequence of the rich man's fall. I would like to suggest that at this point the general remarks on wealth become particularized. In other words, beginning with lines 96 ff., the poet offers an *exemplum*. Any rich man's wealth is in danger, regardless of his conduct, but now we hear the story of one particular rich man. As a result of his impoverishment (this would be the meaning of *so* in line 96), he must now himself help to clear the land. In this agricultural setting, *der rîche* is now individualized as a manorial overseer or master. He works together with his *chneht* (which word is used here for the first time, in connection with *meister*, in a mundane sense) and the other poor.

With the introduction of a sermonic *exemplum* in lines 96 ff., the author of "Vom Rechte" uses an approach to his theme that shifts constantly between the narrative of the rich man/*meister* and his servant clearing the land and the moral lessons to be drawn from his story. But first the poet interrupts his narrative to explain how his exemplary rich man has come to this pass. All wealth is ephemeral, but this rich man or *meister* lost his wealth for a specific reason:

> daz mohte uns wol erbarmen,
> daz der riche man zergat,
> daz er niht enhat.
> daz sage ich iu, wie daz stat,
> daz der riche man zergat:
> durch daz michil guot
> er cheret hohe sinen muot,
> er furhtet niht den tot,
> im erbarmet niemans not;
> die ubirmuot er hin treit,
> daz er si nidir nine leit,
> unz an den tach,
> daz danne chumet der gotes slach.[104]

The poet then draws a moral by comparing the rich man to a castellan:[105] no "burch" or stronghold is so mighty that it cannot be destroyed. Similarly, no walls are so high that someone could hide himself behind them from God's punishment (ll. 114-123).

After the moralizing explanation for the impoverishment of the rich man, the "Vom Rechte" poet returns to his narrative with a description of the work of the *meister* and *chneht* clearing the land of roots. When they come to a large stump, they exert themselves and carefully remove it with their tools (ll. 124-136). The poet pauses once again to draw a general moral about the hard man who commits injustice:

> als ez umbe den herten man stat,
> der daz unreht begat.
> swer den wil becheren,
> der muoz in rehte leren,
> er muoz in starche dwingen,
> an daz reht bringen,
> also der routære vil guot
> dem vil grozzen stoche tuot,
> der in des *dwing*et,
> daz er in von der erde bringet.[106]

The transitions here between the *exemplum* and its moral lesson are almost imperceptible, as is often the case in a good sermon. Explaining how *der herte man* must be forcibly taught, the poet slides back into his example to tell why the *routære* must remove the stump.[107] If he left it standing it would break his plow-share when he came to plow the land (ll. 143-152). Again a moral is drawn:

> also *ez* umbe den richen man stat,
> der daz unreht *be*gat;
> den mach nieman bedwingen,
> an de*hein* reht bringen,
> ez netuo got der guote
> mit etlicher note;
> oder ez avir etwie so chome,
> daz er in von der christenheit neme,
> daz diu christenheit geste,
> daz si nine zerge.[108]

God alone can bring the rich man who commits injustice back to the practice of *reht*, but sometimes God must remove him altogether. Note that *der ríche man* here no more refers to the *meister* clearing his land than did the comments about "the hard man who commits injustice." Instead, a general lesson is being taught about rich men who commit injustice.

It may be that *der herte man* "der daz unreht begat" is identical to the *der ríche man*, "der daz unreht begat;" this is immaterial to the interpretation of the passages. Speicher, however, assumes their identity and then claims that these lines represent a retreat from the poet's previous remarks:

> In the allegorical narrative it was necessary to remove the stump (ll. 128-136), but in its explanation it is said to be impossible to force *der ríche man* to justice— God alone can do that. Perhaps the conduct suggested in the symbolic narrative

seemed too revolutionary to the author so that he withdrew it in his explanation.[109]

In fact, these lines simply demonstrate the author's orthodoxy: The hard man must be forcibly taught, but — under the assumption that he is also the rich man — God alone is ultimately responsible for his reform or for removing him from Christendom altogether. God's power alone is just and God alone judges justly, as the poet had earlier affirmed:

> so rihtet got rehte
> wan er uns nimet unde lat,
> als er des gewalt hat,
> bediu lutzzil unde vil, etc.[110]

The poet again returns to the *meister* and his *chneht*. These are the lines that Schröbler claimed must be understood symbolically, for they would have been revolutionary if they had been intended for the real world:

> Sa cheren abir an daz reht,
> da der meister unde der chneht
> bede samt hin gant
> unde die routin bestant.
> so ez danne ze diu wirt,
> daz diu ruotin gebirt,
> si sulen ez fuoren samet heim,
> teilen ez alliz enzwei,
> wellent si rehte gevaren.
> si schulen sich vil wol bewaren,
> daz ir newederem werde mere,
> wand si arnent ez bede sere.
> si habent ez mit ir swaizze gewunnen,
> ez bedarf ir enwerdirz dem anderem enbunnen.[111]

In asserting that the equal division of the harvest was somehow revolutionary, Schröbler, and following her Speicher, was faithfully accepting Scherer's interpretation. But was the "Vom Rechte" poet's demand for the equal division of the harvest truly such an exception at the time of the composition of the poem? Two historians who commented on these lines of "Vom Rechte" did not seem to think so. Hans Fehr, a legal historian with a strong interest in literature, clearly took no exception to the poet's demand in his summary:

> If the lord ["der Herr"] clears the land with his servant and if they obtain any crops from the cleared land, then they must be divided equally between them. The crops must be shared. This is nothing more than the reaffirmation of the well-known principle: "Property is the reward for work. . . ."[112]

Günther Franz, one of the most respected German agricultural historians, once mentioned "Vom Rechte" in passing in a footnote. He, too, obviously did not think that the poet was unusual in his demands:

In the middle of the twelfth century, in the poem "Vom Rechte," . . . the master (that is to say the lord of the manor ["der Grundherr"]) still clears land together with his servant. They are supposed to share the yield, according to law [von rechtswegen]. Neither should try to take advantage of the other. Yet the poem also warns of a false equality and the pride of servants. Lucifer is given as deterrent example.[113]

Fehr and Franz, of course, give no more justification for their interpretations of lines 163-176 of "Vom Rechte" than do Scherer, Schröbler, or Speicher. To set their opinions, however knowledgeable, against those of the literary critics is merely to argue from authority that this section of the poem, if taken literally, is not "revolutionary." Fortunately, more historical evidence is available to prove this point.

It has long been recognized that in his example of the *meister* and *chneht* who clear the land, the "Vom Rechte" poet was describing an important contemporary phenomenon, namely the massive expansion of arable land that was taking place in Europe in the eleventh and twelfth centuries.[114] Gert Kaiser rightly saw the poet's demanding the equal division of the harvest from the reclaimed land does not contradict his carefully observing the distinctions between *hêrre* and *chneht*:

> The same thing is demanded in a market privilege from Radolfzell. There too the participation of serfs in the market was seen as necessary and desirable, as was here their participation in land clearance. Both required economic equality. At the same time, their legal bonds to the manor were strengthened.[115]

But one need not point to parallels in market privileges to explain the passage in "Vom Rechte." Hans K. Schulze gives an example of the privileges with which lords hoped to entice their serfs to the often difficult and isolated work of land reclamation, while at the same time preserving their social and legal status as unfree men. In a charter issued in 1152 by Bishop Wichmann of Naumburg, the enhanced rights and duties of those who would undertake the reclamation and colonization of some of the bishop's lands in the present-day Netherlands are described. The charter carefully adds that these rights do not entail a change of status:

> quicumque successores eorum fuerint et eadem bona optinuerint, sive liberi sive servi, sub quacumque lege vel moribus vivant, idem statutum et observent et faciant.[116]

There is, therefore, nothing revolutionary about the demand for the equal division of the harvest in "Vom Rechte," although it may have been a privilege restricted to those who reclaimed land. Schröbler's chief justification for distinguishing between *der meister, der rîche*, and *der hêrre* therefore appears untenable and her characterization of these passages in the poem as a symbolic narration, devoid of reality, equally so. The passages (C) that Schröbler understood to be the exegesis of the allegory (B) are better seen as the poet's moralizing conclusions drawn from his *exemplum*.

Aside from the historical information used to argue this point, it would in any case have been strange for the author of "Vom Rechte" to have invented as a "symbolic narrative" or a sermonic *exemplum* a story that did not reflect the reality of his audience's own lives. If the equal division of the harvest granted to those who reclaim land was only in the "realm of a parable," but otherwise unheard of, why should the audience have accepted the moral lessons that the poet draws from it? He might, of course, have been simply indulging in pure fantasy, as medieval allegorical writers often did. But land reclamation and the harvesting of crops hardly qualify as fantasy; they were in all probability well-known to the poet and his audience.   The poet's narrative is, therefore, firmly in the realm of reality.

The example of the *meister* and the *chneht* concludes in good sermonic fashion with some general lessons for all to learn ("wir allesamt):

> swer ze genaden wil chomen,
> der sol nieman niht nemen;
> er sol ouch nieman nihts erbunnen,
> des er mit rehte hat gewunnen.
> so sol der herre unde der chneht
> minnen daz selbe reht.[117]

That the final lesson of the poet's example should use the terms *hêrre* and *chneht* returns us to our starting point: What does "Vom Rechte" tell us about the Early Middle High German use of the categories *der hêrre* and *der rîche*? First, the terms are held distinct. Nowhere does the author simply substitute one for the other. They appear in different narrative strands in the poem, regardless of whether one follows Schröbler's scheme or accepts my proposed division into sermonic example and lesson. Second, despite their being distinguished in the poem, the categories are clearly related and can even refer to the same person. *Der rîche* can be a *meister* and thus a *hêrre* over a *chneht*, and the example of the impoverished *rîche* can be used to instruct listeners about *hêrren* and *chnehte* in general.

B. The *reht* of *die rîchen* and *die hêrren*

The conclusion reached in this long discussion of "Vom Rechte" must at first sight seem trivial. Of course *der rîche* can be a *hêrre* and of course the two may be conceptually related. Anyone who studies the Middle Ages already knows this. But Schröbler's division of lines 54-190 of "Vom Rechte" into the discussion of *der rîche*, the symbolic narrative of the *meister* and his *chneht*, and the exegesis of the narrative, which speaks of *der hêrre* and *der chneht*, was not an eccentric fancy. Schröbler rightly perceived that the author of the poem had carefully separated his comments on *der rîche*, *der meister*, and *der hêrre* and that he had nowhere explicitly called the lord *rîch* or the rich man *hêr*. But the poet's reason for distinguishing these different labels for what at times could be the same person lies in the different demands for *reht* that he and the other Early Middle High German poets make of *der rîche* and of *der hêrre*, and not in the ontological status of the different strands of narration.

What is the *reht* demanded of the rich man who commits *unreht*?   It is described *ex negativo* in the lines quoted above:

daz sage ich iu, wie daz stat,
daz der rich man zergat:
durch daz michel guot
er cheret hohe sinen muot,
er furhtet niht den tot,
im erbarmet niemans not.[118]

The rich man's wealth makes him proud, with the result that he no longer has
erbermede for other people, specifically *die armen*. To understand what the poet precisely means by this, however, we must turn to other Early Middle High German
poems. In Der arme Hartmann's version of the story of Lazarus and Dives,[119] for
example, the *unreht* of "ein riche man" is initially described in terms almost identical to those used in "Vom Rechte":

durh sin ubirmute   er netet neheine gute.
got er niht nevorhte, niht gutis er neworhte.
Do was ein vil arm man,   des newolder sich nicht irbarmen.[120]

Hartmann concludes the story of Dives' damnation with slightly more information about what is meant by "sich irbarmen:"

Diz bispelle   begonde wilen zelle(n)
Crist dem lute   zu einem dute;
daz wir unse almosen geben   al di wile daz wir leben;
unde der durftigen armen   lazen uns irbarmen
unde got vorhtin   unde gute werch wirchin.[121]

For a lengthy description of the "gute werch" that are here due from the rich
man, one must recall an earlier section of "Die Rede vom Glauben" where
Hartmann described the first counsel given by the Holy Ghost:

Diz ist des heiligen geistis rat: swer so den mit ime hat,
unsen herren got er vorhtet,   gute werch er wirket;
daz ubile er vermidet,   vil luzzil er genidet.
guter dinge er pliget,   sin alemose er gerne gibet
durh got den armen,   der beginnet er sich irbarmen.
daz er des nit nelæzet,   die hungerigen er æzet,
die durstigen er trenket,   siner sele da mite gedenket.
mit der siner hant   den nacketen git er sin gewant.
die ellenden geste   læzt er gerne reste(n)
in sinem hus,   die newiset er niwit dar uz.

Under sinem dache   da wirt er in ze gemache.
bei dem fure an siner flezze   da beginnet er si sezze(n)
unde git in sine spise,   der siechen beginnet er wisen;
vil wole er die beruchet,   die gevangen er suchet,
swa man si notet sere,   in dem karchere.
den tut er helfe unde trost   daz si werden irlost.

diz meistert alliz allir meist   der vil heilige geist.
der ist zerist unde lezist   allir meistere bezist,
der meisteret alle di dinc   di da gut unde reht sint.[122]

The author of "Die Hochzeit," which, as mentioned, is closely related to "Vom Rechte," makes various demands of the rich man, but central to these are works of mercy similar to those listed by der arme Hartmann. The "Hochzeit" poet says that the rich man is assured of heaven if he does these works and if he avoids *unreht*:

dar mohte der riche
chomen im selben sælichlichen,
wolde er die gewinne
teilen durch die minne,
den vrostigen solde er bewæten,
den hungerigen nerigen.
er solde den siechen
mit sinem guote suochen,
wisen den blinten
unde leren den tumben,
vaste die zite,
die man im gebiete,
die viere began,
die dar zuo schulen gestan,
sinen zehenten willichlichen geben,
er selbe christlichen leben,
der werlde guotes gunnen,
deheiner meineit sol er swerigen,
daz unreht sol er werigen.
diu gotes huos sol er zieren,
den ewarten eren,
der uns diu gotes wort sol leren,
da mit mugen die richen alle
chomen in die ewigen zelle.[123]

Both der arme Hartmann and the author of "Die Hochzeit" thus primarily define the *reht* of the rich man as the *opera misericordiae* as they are found in Matthew 25, 31-46. The biblical passage, which is a description of the Last Judgment, should be compared with these Early Middle High German renderings:

Cum autem venerit Filius hominis in maiestate sua et omnes angeli cum eo, tunc sedebit super sedem maiestatis suae. Et congregabuntur ante eum omnes gentes et separabit eos ab invicem sicut pastor oves quidem a dextris suis, hedos autem a sinistris. Tunc dicet rex his qui a dextris eius erunt: 'Venite benedicti Patris mei. Possidete paratum vobis regnum a constitutione mundi. Esurivi enim et dedistis mihi manducare, sitivi et dedistis mihi bibere, hospes eram et collexistis me, nudus et operuistis me, infirmus et visitastis me, in carcere eram et venistis ad me' (25, 31-36).

The *iusti,* repeating the list of good works, ask Christ when they did these things to him and he responds: "Amen dico vobis, quamdiu fecistis uni de his fratribus meis minimis, mihi fecistis" (25, 40). Those to his left, Christ condemns to Hell, repeating the works of mercy yet again, which they failed to do. The chapter concludes with the words: "Et ibunt hii in supplicium aeternum, iusti autem in vitam aeternam" (25, 46).

We have already seen how the works of mercy were considered one aspect of *iustitia* in early medieval Latin literature. The same is true for any Early Middle High German work that treats that *reht* which is due from the rich man. Thus in "Van der Girheit," der Wilde Mann continually castigates *der gire*, or the avaricious man, whom he also describes as "der riche,"[124] for his *unreht* in failing to show mercy to the poor. But "gereht" is that rich man who is described as follows:

> die wile dat der man duge
> so ge he zu godis diniste gerne,
> undi si dat he dat lerne
> dat he sin alimuse geve
> unde reine behalvi sunde leve,
> undi laze sich der armen
> durch den richen got irbarmen
> mit cledirn undi mit spisen.
> di sichen sal he wisen
> undi virsmen alli idilcheit.
> . . .
> so bezechint he den girehtin,
> di dat mit manheidi bisteit,
> alsi he sin unreht widerdeit.[125]

Similarly, the Old Testament paradigm of justice, Tobias ("her was gereht und ein gut man"),[126] is described by the Pfaffe Lamprecht as performing the works of mercy:

> Tobyas karte sinen sin   uppe daz himelisce gewin.
> die sichen unde auch die armen   die liez er sich irbarmen.
> . . .
> al unrehtes was ime leit: deme nachedeme gaf er daz cleit,
> dem hungerege gaf er daz er geaz,   zuo neiner gude was er laz.
> die gevangene troste er alle zit . . . .[127]

Compare also the "Uppsala Beichte." The penitent narrator, clearly a man of substance, lists his sins:

> der maze rethe,
> die mir min erwarthen dathen,
> di nebehilth ich mit gehorsame nie:
> des bekennen ich mich god hie.
> die mir hant gedinet,

> den han ich ungelonet.
> die miner herbergen gerden,
> vil selden ich di werthe.
> ich neliz mich nie irbarmen
> die sichen noch di armen.
> ich han minen zehenden ungegeben.
> unreht was ie min leben
> leider in allen enden.[128]

As one might expect from their biblical context, the *opera misericordiae* demanded of the rich also frequently appear in those Early Middle High German works that describe the Last Judgment in any detail. In the "Linzer Antichrist," for example, Christ first says to the "gotis druden," or those beloved of God:

> 'do ir iuch die armin
> liezint irbarmen,
> beide siechen unt gevangin suohtint
> unt die beruohtint:
> daz was alliz mir getan.'
> die dann zuo der winster sihit stan,
> ich weiz er sich an in richit,
> vil zornliche er <in> zuo sprichit
> 'wan iuch des unrehtes nan vil untiur,
> nu vart ir firfluochtin in daz ewigi viur
> daz dem divil gegerwit ist!'[129]

Of course, not all these passages describe the works of mercy as *reht* or their absence as *unreht*, although most do. Nor do they all explicitly state that it is the rich man who must have mercy on the poor. If, however, anyone is explicitly addressed or named, then it is the rich man, and because of the universal pairing of *der arme* and *der rîche*, for an Early Middle High German poet to say one is usually to imply the other. The passages quoted differ in detail, some mentioning, for example, alms-giving, or the tithe, or going to church, others follow the biblical list of the works of mercy more closely, while still others, like the "Vom Rechte" poet, speak merely of the need to have mercy. Yet the composite picture they present is clear. The similarity of terminology, even in widely distant dialects, is striking, and many of the poets presume knowledge on the listener's part to make their references understandable. The *reht* or *iustitia* which is due from the rich man is to have mercy on and to help the poor by sharing his wealth.

But what of the justice demanded of *der hêrre*? Again "Vom Rechte" can provide a useful, if enigmatic starting point. It will be recalled that after demanding that *der meister* and *der chneht* equally share the harvest, the poet once again drew a moral from his *exemplum*: "so sol der herre unde der chneht minnen daz selbe reht" (ll. 183-184) (Lord and servant should thus love the same justice). He continues:

> wellent si rehte gevaren,
> ieweder *sol* den anderen bewaren
> ubir alle sine not
> unz an sinen tot:
> so lebent si bede rehte,
> die herren unde die chnehte.[130]

Schröbler claimed that in these lines the poet is preaching the duty of reciprocity between the *herre* and the *chneht*:

> 'Herr und Knecht' must both engage in that 'Recht' revealed in the fight against 'Unrecht.' Reduced to a common denominator for both this is the reciprocity of duty . . . the content of each one's duty may differ.[131]

Changing "duty" to "justice," one can say that this is an accurate characterization of the poet's message, but it can be made more precise and the context of the reciprocal justice between the lord and the servant can be more closely defined.

We have seen that the division of the harvest that precedes the lines quoted above is not part of a symbolic narrative but a real demand made of *der meister* and *der chneht*. A similar demand for the division of one's goods was quoted above in the "Hochzeit" poet's description of the *reht* of the rich man (ll. 488-489). The "Hochzeit" poet also says that the "housherre" will be redeemed if he shares his wealth:

> Wande hie teilte ein housherre
> sinen richtuom vil verre
> undir sine chnehte,
> die dienent im mit rehte.[132]

Der Wilde Mann makes the same demand in "Von christlicher Lehre":

> Beati qui verbum dei audiunt
> et illud custodiunt.
> iz ist reht dat wirz u dudin,
> want iz kristinen ludin
> geschriven ist zu heile,
> dat ein iwelich mensce deile
> dem andiren dat he gudis kan.[133]

The "Vom Rechte" poet's demand that the *meister* and the *chneht* equally divide their harvest is merely another example of such sharing. But what is the moral the poet draws from this demand made of both *der hêrre* and *der rîche*, and what is "daz selbe reht" that *herre* and *chneht* should love? In part, it is simply a repetition of the demand to share and to help one's neighbor. More specifically, however, it refers to the reciprocity of judicial justice.

To glimpse this judicial aspect, one must first recall Schröbler's account of the general structure of "Vom Rechte." The story of the rich man's fall and the conclusions that the poet draws from it are part of the detailed explanation of the Golden Rule as defined in lines 20-23:

> Ein andir reht daz ist also getan,
> daz wir uns selben wellen *haben*,
> daz solten wir ein andir *geben*,
> wolden wir christlichen leben.[134] (my emphases)

The specific judicial implications of the Golden Rule are revealed only in the poet's description of its perversion:

> manneclich wil *reht han*,
> als sin gewalt ist getan,
> und wil daz im selbem *haben*
> und wilz deheinem anderen *geben*.[135] (my emphases)

What do the italicized phrases "reht haben" and "reht geben" mean here? The identical terms are used in strophe 11 of Noker's "Memento mori;"

> Ube ir alle eines rehtin lebitint,   so wurdint ir alle geladet in
> ze der ewigun mendin,   da ir iemer soltint sin.
> taz eina *hant* ir iu selben,   daz ander *gebent* ir dien armen.
> von diu so nemugen ir drin gen,   ir muozint iemer dervor sten.[136]
> (my emphases)

For Noker, to *have* the same *reht* for oneself as one *gives* to others is to live "eines rehtin," in one *iustitia*.[137]

It would seem that both Noker and the "Vom Rechte" poet are using *reht haben* and *reht geben* as a formula. Its background can perhaps be traced to the Latin formula *iustitiam facere et recipere*, whose meaning and development have been described by Hermann Krause.[138] The Latin formula was perhaps inspired, in part, by the frequent use in the Bible of the phrases *iustitiam facere* or *iustitiam et iudicium facere*.[139] The combination of the biblical phrase with the second part of the formula, *iustitiam recipere*, is an early medieval creation without precedent in either the Bible or in Roman law. The two parts of the formula are not synonymous, but antithetical: either one does justice or one receives justice. When the formula achieved a certain consistency of usage, its context also became clear, namely judicial justice.

Iustitiam facere most frequently refers to the justice that should be upheld by a judge or judicial official, but the broad sense of *iustitia* also allows the meaning that everyone should do justice. The subject of *iustitiam recipere* can also vary. It can refer to the judge, but more typically it has as its subject either the plaintiff or the accuser. Krause writes:

> There is no consistent assignment of each part of the formula to certain groups.
> . . . But there is one point in which all the lines converge: The judicial court.[140]

The uncertainty expressed by the varying subjects and objects of the formula, according to Krause, has its source in the early medieval concepts of the judge and his court:

> In this period, courts and judges are not a third power subordinate to other pow-
> ers as they are today. They are rather a general expression of lordship, the epito-
> me of public power. . . .[141]

The role of the judge, in other words, was not yet an institutionalized position:
almost every lord could be a judge over others and he could in turn be judged by
his peers. The formula *iustitiam facere et recipere*, thus, does not only mean that one
person must do justice and another receive it, but that in the context of the
medieval judicial court, one and the same person must be willing to do both, as
the occasion requires. Krause concedes the ambiguity: "Conceptual clarity is not
the purpose of the formula."[142] The general sense, however, is clear. The demand
that someone should *iustitiam facere et recipere* means that one should be prepared
to receive justice as well as render it: All are equally subject to the law.[143]

In the Merovingian era, the formula occurs most frequently in royal documents. But by the Carolingian period, it appears especially in connection with the
jurisdiction of the count or the ecclesiastical advocate. One capitulary gives the
formula in connection with the traditional objects of justice:

> De iustitiis ecclesiarum Dei, viduarum, orfanorum, minus potentium volumus
> atque omnimodis precipimus, ut omnes episcopi et abbates et comites secundum
> legem pleniter iustitiam faciant et recipiant.[144]

According to Krause, the formula is first used in the vernacular in the
Sachsenspiegel where it is most clearly rendered as "recht dun und recht nemen,"
although the formula also occurs as "rechtes plegen unde helpen" and in other
forms.[145]

Nowhere in the vernacular does the formula appear as *reht geben und reht haben*
as in the "Memento mori" and "Vom Rechte."[146] The use of the formula in the
vernacular in the eleventh and twelfth centuries would be an anomaly in any case;
its first unequivocal instance in German occurs, as mentioned, in the thirteenth
century. The principle *iustitiam facere et recipere* should, therefore, best be seen as
part of the conceptual background to the Early Middle High German poets' formula *reht geben und haben*, but not as identical to it. While *reht geben* probably has
a meaning similar to *iustitiam facere*, to render justice, used especially of a judge, *reht
haben* cannot be equated with *iustitiam recipere*, usually used of the plaintiff or
accuser. *Reht haben* more likely still refers to the judge, or any one in a position
of authority, when he himself is the subject or object of a suit. The judicial context of the formula in Noker's demand that we should all live "eines rehtin" suggests, as Gentry rightly perceived, that in one's capacity as judge, one should render the same justice to the poor ("dien armen reht geben") as one allows to be
rendered to oneself ("taz eina hant ir iu selben"). In other words, there should be
no *acceptio personarum* before the justice of the law.

This interpretation of the *reht haben* und *reht geben* seems confirmed in lines 54
ff. of "Vom Rechte," the introduction to the poet's detailed discussion of the
Golden Rule:

> wan swelhir den gewalt hat
> unde er daz unreht begat
> unde erz ubir einen anderen dolot
> da mit hat *er* verscholot
> den ewigen lib,
> ez si man oder wip,
> er newelle sich es buozzen
> under welle ez gare verlazzen,
> daz er nimmer mere getuo:
> daz reht horet dar zuo.
> hat er sich verwandelot,
> so verchiuset es got;
> also mag er werden gotes chneht.
> cheren abir an daz reht![147]

Gewalt here seems to refer to the lord's right of jurisdiction over his subjects, as well as to the lady's less formally defined power over her servants. The perversion of the Golden Rule, which the poet described in lines 44–47, therefore, involves a lord's thinking that his justice, that is his own accountability before the law (*reht haben*), is proportionate to his power or right to impose his justice on others (*reht geben*). The *reht* which he applies to himself is not the same which he gives to others. But as we have seen, it is only God's *reht* that is, by definition, synonymous with His *gewalt*:

> so rihtet got rehte,
> wan er uns nimet unde lat,
> als er des gewalt hat,
> beidiu lutzzil unde vil.[148]

God allows ("verdolen," l. 73) the rich man to lose his wealth because God judges justly. But the man who has *gewalt* and allows ("dolen," l. 56) injustice to occur to others will be damned. In the same way that the *meister* and the *chneht* divide the harvest of the reclaimed land, so should *hêrre* and *chneht* have one justice between them. The *hêrre*, especially, should see that the justice he "gives" in his capacity as judge is the same as that which he "has" for himself: "so sol der herre unde der chneht/ minnen daz selbe reht."

The *reht* that the "Vom Rechte" poet demands of *der hêrre* is thus a judicial justice, impartial and strictly applied to both lord and servant. This same ideal of the *reht* due from the lord is found throughout Early Middle High German literature. As in the poem "Vom Rechte," God also frequently provides the model of the just judge. The author of the "*Millstätter* Sündenklage," for example, contrasts God's impartial and incorruptible justice at the Last Judgment with the abuses of earthly judges:

> Obe ich daz reht vernime,   so ez die w<issagen ha>bent gescriben,
> so wirt da ein <her gerihte>,   ein urteil mit chreften,
> da<z ze jungest we>sen sol   uber dise werlt al.

> D<a nehilfet> diu liute   silber noch golt da<z rote
> noch> miete diu mære   noch phen<ninge swære>
> noch landreht noch phaht: da <rihtet got> mit siner chraft.
> Da nehilfet <spæhe> zunge   noch der herre sinem manne
> noch der man sinem herren,   swie breit im sin diu lehen.
> Der voget da nehilfet,   swie gare er bestrouffet
> den sinem armen vogetman,   er negetar da lut werden.
> Da rihtet got mit rehte   dem herren joch dem chnehte,
> der vrouwen joch der diwe. . . .[149]

If God is the exemplar of the lord's justice, the Antichrist is his negative model. In the "Linzer Antichrist," for example, a mirror image of the ideal of both lord and servant subject to one justice is presented.[150] The author writes of the Antichrist and his minions:

> Iedannoch sie sezint ein reht,
> daz muoz behaltin der herre joch der kneht,
> uber alliu diu lant.[151]

The Antichrist appeals especially to the venality of earthly rulers, both secular and ecclesiastical, plying them with "luxurious clothing" and "silver and gems:"

> kunige unt herzogin,
> bischofe unt phaffin,
> die da soldin biwachin
> di vil arme christenheit,
> di gewinnet er vil gereit
> mit sus getanin gebin:
> bose wirt der rehtin lebin.[152]

But the false order of the Antichrist's justice will be swept away at the Second Coming. Frau Ava, for example, writes:

> So chumet got in den luften   in siner magencrefte.
> so rihtet er rehte   dem herren unde dem chnehte.[153]

Bribery and other corruptions of justice will then be of no avail, says Frau Ava, in phrases almost identical to those of the "Millstätter Sündenklage:" "Da nehilfet golt noch scaz,   e bedahten wir iz baz!"[154] To those who loved God in thought, word, and deed, however, to those who conduct trials without bribery ("gerihtes ane miete phlegen"[155]), the heavenly reward is assured.

The poem "Vom Rechte" has provided a useful orientation for this sketch of the *reht* due from *der rîche*, namely works of mercy toward *die armen*, and the *reht* expected of *der hêrre* in his capacity as judge, namely strict and impartial justice towards his inferiors, the *knehte*. At the same time, we have seen in "Vom Rechte" that despite these different forms of justice demanded from *der rîche* and *der hêrre* and despite their usually being treated separately by the Early Middle High German poets, they can be one and the same person. Two questions now remain:

why do the poets distinguish the rich from the lords and what do the Early Middle High German ideals of *reht* tell us about the period in which the poems were written?

NOTES

1   Eggers, *Deutsche Sprachgeschichte*, 357. Eggers continues: "Im theologischen Sinne ist *reht* also ein Begriff, der 'Rechte' und 'Pflichten' gleichmäßig umfaßt, im Grunde genommen aber durch keinen dieser beiden Ausdrücke voll gedeckt wird" (ibid.). Eggers's comments are an accurate description of the conceptual connections between *reht* and "rights" and "duties," for *reht* is not equivalent to the latter two, but implies them. Eggers, however, nowhere states that *reht* means *iustitia*, which would seem to be the reasonable conclusion of his presentation.

2   See Chapter I on Gernentz and Kaiser.

3   Eike von Repgow, *Sachsenspiegel*, "Landrecht," III, 42, ed. Karl August Eckhardt, *MGH*, Fontes Legum, I, I.

4   "Do not be surprised that this book has so little to say about the law of *ministeriales*. Their law is so varied that no one can fully treat it."

5   Herbert Kolb, "Über den Ursprung der Freiheit. Eine Questio im Sachsenspiegel," *ZfdA* 103 (1974), 289-311.

6   "When man first made law, there were no *ministeriales*. For everyone was free when our forefathers came to this land [Saxony]. In my understanding, I cannot conceive it as consonant with truth that someone should belong to another, nor do we have any authority for such a view."

7   Sten Gagnér ("Sachsenspiegel und Speculum ecclesiae," *NM* 3 [1948], 82-103) makes a convincing argument that Eike, rather than directly relying on the Bible for his comments, utilized and directed his criticism toward the views found in Honorius's *Speculum ecclesiae* and in the Early Middle High German collection of sermons of the same name. The comparison between Eike's position and Early Middle High German poets may therefore not be as tenuous as one might have first suspected.

8   "Noah blessed two of his sons; to the third he said nothing about serfdom. Ham settled Africa with his family, Sem remained in Asia, and Japheth, our forefather, settled Europe. Thus Ham belonged to no one else."

9   Genesis 9, 25-27. Cf. also Kolb, 305-309.

10   In his commentary on the Book of Genesis, Rabanus provides a distillation of earlier solutions to the inconsistency: "De talibus [Ham's descendants] ergo dictum est: Ex fructibus eorum cognoscetis eos (Mat., 7, 20). Ideo et Cham in filio suo maledictus est, tanquam in fructo suo, id est, in opere suo. . . . Item quod Cham pecannte posteritas ejus damnatur, significat quod reprobi hic delinquunt, sed in posterum, id est, in futurum, sententiam damnationis excipiunt." *Commentarii in Genesim*, II, ix, *PL* 107, c. 526. Rabanus is quoting either Isidore (*Questiones in vetus testementum. In Genesim, PL* 83, c. 237) or perhaps the original argument from Augustine's *De civitate dei*, XVI, ii. As was noted in Chapter II, at

least prior to ca. 1100, biblical commentators proper never treated the purely historical consequence of Noah's curse of servitude.

11   "Our law also states that no one can make himself another's property without his heir's being able to renounce the act. How could Noah or Isaac have given another to servitude, when no one can do it to himself without preventing his heir's renouncing it?"

12   This last argument is justified by an interesting interpretation of Matthew 22, 15 ff. on rendering unto Caesar that which is Caesar's and unto God that which is God's. The Vulgate speaks of "Caesaris imago" on the coin (Math. 22, 20-21), to which Christ points to make his argument. Eike, alluding to Genesis 1, 25, comments "Latet den keiser sines bildes geweldich unde Goddes bilde gevet Godde" (III, 42, § 5) ("Let the emperor have control over his image and render the image of God, i. e. man, unto God"). See Hans von Voltelini's discussion: "Der Gedanke der allgemeinen Freiheit in den deutschen Rechtsbüchern," *ZRG* (*GA*) 57 (1937), 184-185.

13   "In truth, serfdom arose from force and captivity and from unjust domination, which in ancient times were transformed into an unjust custom that is now declared to be law."

14   Voltelini (185) calls Eike's remarks "revolutionary;" the characterization is certainly true for vernacular literature, although one should note that Eike's views on the injustice of servitude have clear precedence in the Latin tradition, particularly in those writers familiar with the arguments of natural law. See, e. g., the authors cited by Otto Gerhard Oexle in his discussion of the equality of humankind, such as Pelagius, Smaragdus of Saint Mihel, Jonas of Orleans, Atto of Vercelli, and Christian of Stabo ("Die funktionale Dreiteilung der 'Gesellschaft' bei Adalbero von Laon. Deutungsschemata der sozialen Wirklichkeit im frühen Mittelalter," *FMS* 12 [1978], footnotes 168 and 169). See, for example Atto's comment: "Servi enim non a Cham sed ab iniustitia et mundi iniquitate facti sunt" (*Epistula ad Ephesios*, 6,9, *PL* 134, col. 583, cited in Oexle, ibid.), a view completely different from the Early Middle High German biblical epics. Pelagius's views on freedom, however, had been long since declared heretical, and Voltelini remarks of Smaragdus that "er [verlangte nicht] . . . die Abschaffung der Sklaverei, nur die eigenmächtliche Gefangensetzung also die Sklavenjagd" (Voltelini, 207).

15   One might argue this from the fact that the form of the Joseph story in the *Vorauer Bücher Moses*, which otherwise diverge greatly from the *Vienna* and *Millstätter* versions, is not substantially different from that given in the *Vienna Genesis*. The relation between the three versions of the Joseph story is, however, fairly complex. See the stemmata and comments in Dollmayr (*Altdeutsche Genesis*, vi), Ursula Henning ("Altdeutsche Genesis, *VL* I, 279-284), or in Kathryn Smits (*Die frühmittelhochdeutsche Wiener Genesis* [Berlin: Erich Schmidt, 1972], 7-14). Usually a prototype *VMV is proposed from which all three epics are thought to have derived, with the *Vienna* and *Millstätter* versions together diverging in one direction and the *Vorauer* in another. In the passage to be discussed here, there is great similarity between the *Vienna* and *Vorauer* versions and

the two will therefore be treated as one. The *Millstätter* version, as we will see, is quite different.

The connections among the different versions are not made any clearer by the many editions that exist. Joseph Diemer's 1849 edition of the *Millstätter Genesis* remains unique. But there are two versions of the *Vienna Genesis*, Viktor Dollmayer's short-line edition, based primarily on the *Vienna* manuscript, and Kathryn Smits's (a pupil of Friedrich Maurer's) long-line edition, which incorporates many readings from the *Vorauer* version. The *Vorauer* version of the Joseph story also exists in two editions, one by Diemer (*Vorauer Joseph, SB der Wiener Akademie der Wissenschaften,* 47 [1864], 636-687) and P. Piper's composite edition of the *Vienna* and *Vorauer* versions ("Das Gedicht von Joseph nach der Wiener und der Vorauer Handschrift," *ZfdP* 20 (1888), 257-289; 430-474). There is no edition that includes all the variants among the three versions of the Joseph story. In the following discussion, I cite from Diemer's edition of the *Millstätter Genesis* and Dollmayer's edition of the *Vienna Genesis*. Only the more important variations will be noted between the *Vienna* text and the *Vorauer* version, for which I will rely on Diemer's edition.

16   Indeed, the *New Oxford Annotated Bible (RVS)*, ed. Herbert G. May and Bruce M. Metzger (New York: Oxford UP, 1977), refers to it as a "feudalistic system" (note to Genesis 47, 18-19).

17   They evidently still are. The *Oxford Annotated Bible*, for example, apologetically writes: "The narrator does not intend to sanction absolutism but only to praise Joseph for his wisdom in delivering the people" (note to Genesis 47, 25). The historical school of biblical criticism usually emphasizes the intended irony of the Jew, Joseph, having power over servile Egyptians. See, for example, Robert Davidson, *Genesis 12-50, The Cambridge Bible Commentary on the New English Bible* (Cambridge: Cambridge University Press, 1979): "It could be that to the writer this is but another illustration of Joseph's wisdom and political skill. It is also possible, however, that he is taking an ironic delight in tracing to Joseph a system which made slaves of the Egyptians, in the land in which the Hebrews themselves were to be slaves."

18   Bede, *In Pentateuchum comentarii. Genesis, PL* 91, xlvii, c. 272-73. Rabanus repeats Bede's explanation, *Commentarii in Genesim, PL* 107, II.

19   *Genesis,* ll. 5,190-5,205. "When the first year had passed, they [the Egyptians] pleaded with Joseph to have mercy on them and to help them, for they were very poor and had neither livestock nor money. Neither money nor clothing was left to them; they had nothing more than their own bodies and land. [They begged] that Joseph would take possession of them and use them for the benefit of the king. They would become the king's slaves and transfer their allodial lands to his power, if he would save them and give them seed to sow."

20   Cf. the *Vorauer* variant, ll. 896-98: "er li si fri besten, er ne wolte ir niht ze scalke tuon,/ **D**iz duhte in sunde, die er fri funde/ ob er si ze scalken tate durch dehein ir note" (Diemer, ed., "Vorauer Joseph").

21   In her edition of the *Vienna Genesis*, Kathryn Smits follows the *Vorauer* version and amends "fridelichen" to "frîlichen" (Smits, l. 2,612; see also Diemer, ed.,

"Vorauer Joseph," l. 900). Piper neglects to mention the variant in his composite edition and gives "fridelîchen" in line 1,776 ("Das Gedicht von Joseph nach der Wiener und der Vorauer Handschrift"). While admitting that the *Vienna* manuscript reading, "fridelichen," is not in itself objectionable, Smits claims that its implications, "a view to the future, to a more certain existence," would be out of context in the present passage, which she claims deals with the present crisis and Joseph's measures for its alleviation (Smits, 348). This distorts the tenor of the passage, for it is precisely Joseph's view to the future, that is the status of the Egyptians after the famine, which is under discussion. While the *Vorauer* variant "frilichen" also fits this context, I see no compelling reason to amend the *Vienna Genesis* version, which contrasts nicely with lines 5,220-21 on the opposite of peace (fride), namely forceful oppression.

22   *Wiener Genesis*, ll. 5,210-5,221. "He allowed them to remain free; he didn't want them as slaves. He considered it sinful that he should make those whom he had found free into slaves through any necessity on their part. He wanted them to remain free of domination when the famine had subsided so that they might peacefully go about their business and each could obtain enough to live if no one would oppress them."

23   Joseph Diemer, ed., *Millstäter Genesis und Exodus* (Vienna, 1849), II, 48. Diemer's remark actually refers to the *Millstätter* version, but is equally applicable to the *Vienna* text. Diemer was the first—and to my knowledge the last—to draw attention to this disagreement with the biblical text.

24   Sic. "Ere," as Diemer remarked (*Millstäter Genesis und Exodus*, II, 48) means "land" or "earth" (cf. Genesis 47, 20: "omnem terram Aegypti" and Ulrich Pretzel et al., "ere" in *Nachträge zum mittelhochdeutschen Wörterbuch* [Leipzig: Hirzel, 1979]) and should not be emended to "êre" (honor) as Piper does ("Das Gedicht Joseph," l. 1,784).

25   *Wiener Genesis*, ll. 5,222-5,227. "Joseph did not refuse whoever offered him his allod. He bought into the king's domination the many lands; up to the very territorial limits [of Egypt] he bought them for the king."

26   "nôt" seems to recall the biblical "prae magnitudine famis."

27   Cf. Hermann Krause, "Königtum und Rechtsordnung in der Zeit der sächsischen und salischer Herrscher," *ZRG* (*GA*) 82 (1965), 40: "Im negativen Spiegelbild ist ... das Unrecht nicht nur in der kirchlichen Bußdisziplin, sondern auch in der Rechtsordnung Sünde."

28   *Wiener Genesis*, ll. 5,252-5,255. "We know that all our salvation lies in your hands. Now deign to look upon us; we will gladly serve the king."

29   *Millstätter Genesis*, 104, 3. "They themselves would become his slaves and give their allodial lands in exchange for money."

30   Cf. *Wiener Genesis*, l. 5,221: "ub in nieman neduvnge."

31   *Millstätter Genesis*, 104, 7-15. "Joseph said that he would do only one thing; he did not want them to become slaves. He considered it sinful to enslave for the king's domination those whom he had found free. He said: 'Listen to me. I shall take control of your lands for the king until the famine subsides and thus you will be able to save yourselves. Truly you will have enough so that hunger will not

oppress you.' Whoever offered him his allod, he helped from the misery of hunger. The others had to swear service to him if they wanted to save their life [or body]."

32   Diemer, *Millstäter Genesis und Exodus*, II, 48.

33   Diemer in fact uses the slightly different *Vorauer* version because the *Vienna* version appears to have minor corruptions at this point.

34   *Millstätter Genesis*, "*Do jacob ze dem tode nahete sine zwene sun er zu im brahte:/ er bat in genote daz er si segenote.*"

35   "Von des Todes Gehugde," ll. 556–558 (*RD* III). "However *rich* or *lordly*, who can preserve himself that he remains free from such [sinful] desires?"

36   "Rede von dem Glauben," 17, 1–2 (*RD* II). "He is the same as the Father, equally powerful and equally *rich*, equally powerful and equally *lordly*, neither more nor less." *Rich* here obviously does not mean "wealthy." But nor can it simply be the divine epithet "potens," discussed in Chapter II in connection with Ris's study of the word *rich*, for the word "geweldich" clearly means *potens* here.

37   "Von dem gemeinen Leben," ll. 230–233 (*RD* III). "By what kind of *ordo* should he be considered a lord because he, who had been a pauper, had earlier renounced the world?"

38   At the same time a structural overview of "Vom Rechte" will permit the reader to see where those passages of the poem discussed above in Chapters I and II fit into its overall structure.

39   Ingeborg Schröbler, "Das mittelhochdeutsche Gedicht vom 'Recht'" *PBB* 80 (1958), 219. "Estate" (*Stand*) should not be confused with late medieval legal estates. Helmuth Stahleder has investigated the history of the word and concept and concludes that its use for medieval society prior to ca. 1350 is highly problematic: "Was heißt . . . 'Ständegesellschaft,' wenn nicht nur jeder Mensch vielen Ständen gleichzeitig angehört, sondern auch noch jeder Mensch, jede Familie ein eigener Stand ist? Der Begriff scheint untauglich zur Kennzeichnung einer Gesellschaft." Helmuth Stahleder, "Zum Ständebegriff im Mittelalter," *Zeitschrift für bayerische Landesgeschichte* 35 (1972), 565. The religious concept of "estate," on the other hand, is an entirely different matter and could be applied to quite different groups (see, for example, the literature on *ordo* cited in Chapter II).

40   "Vom Rechte," ll. 40–54. "Many a one does not help his friend as he was loved by him. Thereby everyone says whatever he pleases and justice is maligned. Many a one wants to have justice in proportion to his *gewalt* and wants to have it for himself and doesn't want to give it to anyone else. These are the three customs devoid of justice. They [who practice these customs] refuse to desist. Because of this, great injustice is done to the cause of the poor. These customs also truly divorce them from the just judge." The meaning of *gewalt* will be discussed below.

41   As mentioned in Chapter I, Schröbler considered *reht* to mean both "Recht" and "duty." She also maintained that the estates discussed in "Vom Rechte" were real social groups within the purview of its author; they are limited to only three because the author's society was comparatively uncomplicated (Schröbler, "Vom Rechte," 231). As Schröbler herself recognized, however, the author of "Vom

Rechte" uses categories that are theological and rhetorical in origin and not purely social.

42   See the alternative structural analyses by Gustav Ehrismann, *Geschichte der deutschen Literatur, II/i: Frühmittelhochdeutsche Literatur* (Munich: Beck, 1922), 196 and Peter Ganz, "Vom Rechte," *VL*.

43   Schröbler, "Von den Grenzen des Verstehens mittelalterlicher Dichtung," *GRM NF* 13 (1963), esp. 10-13.

44   Carl Kraus, "'Vom Rechte' und 'Die Hochzeit,'" *SB der Wiener Akademie der Wissenschaften* 123 (1891), 8. In his criticism of the author of "Vom Rechte," Kraus closely followed Wilhelm Scherer, *Geistliche Poeten der deutschen Kaiserzeit, QF* 7 (Strasbourg, 1875), 12.

45   Kraus, 9.

46   Kraus, 9.

47   Wilhelm Scherer, *Geschichte der deutschen Dichtung im elften und zwölften Jahrhundert, QF* 12 (Strasbourg, 1875), 52.

48   Schröbler, "Vom Rechte," 220-223.

49   Schröbler, "Vom Rechte," 222.

50   See Scherer, *Geistliche Poeten der deutschen Kaiserzeit*, 7-8.

51   Schröbler, "Vom Rechte," 223 and 223, ft. 1.

52   Schröbler, "Vom Rechte," 222.

53   Schröbler, "Vom Rechte," 222.

54   Schröbler, "Von den Grenzen," 10.

55   Gisela Vollmann-Profe (trs. and ed., *Frühmittelhochdeutsche Literatur* [Stuttgart: Reclam, 1996], 271-272), while accepting the basic tenor of Schröbler's division, quarrels with some of its details.

56   Stephan Speicher, *"Vom Rechte." Ein Kommentar im Rahmen der zeitgenössischen Literaturtradition*, (Göppingen: Kümmerle, 1986), 42, 48-49. Speicher, however, inexplicably diverges from Schröbler in stating that the entire section begins at line 50 and not line 54.

57   *RD* II, 156-157. Bold face numbers refer, as usual, to the manuscript initials. Maurer plainly had great difficulty in forcing "Vom Rechte" into a pattern of internally rhyming long-lines. To avoid obvious ruptures between his metric scheme and the syntax of the poem, he combined, for example, three instances of three short-line verses with triple rhyme into single long-line verses (ll. 13-15, 132-134, 439-441) with the result that his line numbering is different from all other editions. To avoid confusion, I have given the line numbers according to Schröder's edition.

Note that to follow Schröbler, Maurer had to abandon his stated editorial ideal of marking strophes according to the initials of the manuscript (*RD* II, 156), specifically at lines 54, 137, and 190.

58   Schröbler, "Vom Recht," 229 and "Von den Grenzen," 10-11.

59   "Vom Rechte," ll. 68-87. "Now listen everyone: No one is so rich but that he must let his wealth go and be without it, no matter how he acquired it. [No one is so rich] but that God allows his wealth to disappear so that he retains none of it. Either that which man has won burns or he is robbed, his wealth destroyed;

either it is sunk and made to drown in water or such a disaster comes that nothing remains to him; or death seizes him. He must give it up because of God. For if God will not preserve it, he must of necessity let it go."

60   Cf., e. g.: Matthew 6, 19: "Nolite thesaurizare vobis thesauros in terra ubi erugo et tinea demolitur, ubi fures effodiunt et ferantur. Thesaurizate autem vobis thesauros in caelo ubi neque erugo neque tinea demolitur et ubi fures non effodiunt nec furantur." See also the examples from other Early Middle High German poems given in Speicher, 44.

61   Speicher, 44.

62   "Vom Rechte," ll. 88-95. "*He* finally *geloubet* his servant. Thus God judges [or rules] justly. For God takes away and bestows as He has power, both much and little. He does this as often as He will until it happens that man possesses nothing."

63   "dann glaubt er erst seinem knechte (dem armen) und hört auf dessen rede." Scherer, *Geistliche Poeten*, II, 7.

64   (My emphasis): "Vielmehr meint der dichter: 'dann erst wird er milde, rücksichtsvoll gegen seinen knecht, schenkt ihm gehör.'" (Johannes) Stosch, "Noch einmal mhd. *gelouben*," *ZfdA* 34 (1890), 78.

65   Kraus, 98 and Vollmann-Profe, 159: "Dann erst begegnet er seinem Kneht freundlich." See also Vollmann-Profe's comments, 271.

66   Schröbler, "Vom Rechte," 220, ft. 3.

67   Speicher, 47.

68   Speicher, 44 and 50-51.

69   In addition to the passage from Heinrich von Melk, quoted above, there is another apparent exception that occurs in lines 861–866 of "Die Hochzeit:" "so chert *er abe sine*n muot,/ also noch der riche man *tuot*./ *der herre* des armen hat rat,/ er neruochit wie *ez umbe in* stat,/ und ouch der arme ubirgatt *des richen herren* rat." Both instances of "herre" in lines 863 and 866 are, however, editorial conjecture and in my opinion should be replaced by "der richen." (l. 863) and perhaps "gouten" (l. 866).

70   (Karl) Lucae, "Beiträge zur Erklärung des Parzival" *ZfdA* 30 (1886), 365-375.

71   Wolfram von Eschenbach, *Parzival. Studienausgabe*, ed. Karl Lachmann, 6th. ed. (Berlin: de Gruyter, 1964), 10, 18-23. "Woe is me! My body bore you and you are Gandine's child. Is God blind in His help or is He so deaf that He does not *gelouben* me?"

72   "ist got, der mir doch helfen könnte, blind oder taub, dass er mir nicht willfährt, meinen bitten nicht nachgibt?", Lucae, 366-67. Cf. Wolfgang Spiewok's translation: "Ist Gott erblindet oder ertaubt, daß er mich nicht erhört und mir seine Hilfe versagt?" (Wolfram von Eschenbach, *Parzival*, trs. Wolfgang Spiewok [Stuttgart: Reclam, 1981], I, 23).

73   See Paul, *Mittelhochdeutsche Grammatik*, 23rd ed. by Peter Wiehl und Siegfried Grosse (Tübingen: Niemeyer, 1989), § 403, 369: "Das Pronomen der 3. Person kann ein im selben Satz folgendes Nomen vorausnehmen. Es besteht Kongruenz zwischen Pronomen und Nomen. . . . [die] Konstruktion dient *in zahlreichen Fällen* der emphatischen Wirkung. . . ." (My emphasis).

74 See "Vom Recht," ll. 44-47: "manneclich wil reht han,/ als sin gewalt ist getan,/ unde wil daz im selben haben/ und wilz deheinem anderen geben." The purport of these crucial lines will be discussed in more detail below.

75 Vom Recht," ll. 96-100. "Thus the *meister* and his *chneht* together have one *reht*. I know that together they go to clear the land. They clear with the poor." Schröbler translated the line as "Sie gehen und roden mit der Kraft ihrer Arme" ("Von den Grenzen," 12). The instrumental use of *arme*, aside from in idioms meaning to embrace (e.g. "mit den armen umbevâhen"), is unknown to me in Early Middle High German (and not listed in the Middle High German lexica). Schröbler seems to be straining to avoid the occurrence of the word "poor" in what she considered to be a purely symbolic narrative (B), unconnected with the discussion of fate of the rich man (A).

76 Maria Mackensen, "Soziale Forderungen und Anschauungen der frühmittel-hochdeutschen Dichter," *Neue Heidelberger Jahrbücher, Neue Folge* (1925), 147.

77 Gustav Ehrismann, *Geschichte der deutschen Literatur*, 199.

78 Hans Joachim Gernentz, "Soziale Anschauungen und Forderungen einiger früh-mittelalterlicher geistllicher Dichter," *Weimarer Beiträge* 3 (1957), 415-16. The passage is, in part, an unacknowledged quotation of Hauck, *Kirchengeschichte* IV, 535 ff.

79 Gernentz, 417.

80 Ewald Erb, *Geschichte der deutschen Literatur von den Anfängen bis 1160*, I, part II of *Geschichte der deutschen Literatur von den Anfängen bis zur Geegenwart*, ed. Klaus Gysi, et al. (Berlin [East]: Volk und Wissen, 1964), 589-590.

81 Schröbler, "Vom Rechte," 223.

82 Schröbler, "Vom Rechte," 226.

83 Schröbler, "Vom Rechte," 226.

84 Vollmann-Profe, 271-272.

85 Speicher, 49.

86 See "Von Rechte," ll. 321-344 in which the *meister* is admonished to provide a model of behavior to his *chneht* and ll. 417-420 where the priest's role is described in similar terms: "**D**er ist der zweier ['wip und man'] meister —/ daz sol sin der briester:/ der sol sin zware ir vorleitære." The intellectual superiority of the *briester/meister* is also underlined in ll. 435-436 ff.: "**S**wa der [briester] abe cheret,/ der die schuolær leret," etc. Cf. also ll. 498-506 ff. in which moral and intellectual superiority are combined: "**D**er ist des rehtes meister/ daz sol sin der briester:/ der ist unsir liehtvaz;/ der bezeichent daz/ daz er uns sol sin/ mit aller slahte guotin./ er sol uns leren unde sagen,/ den rehten spiegel vor tragen, er sol uns leren," etc.

87 Cf. *meister* as a warrior's mentor: "Do sprach der herre erwin zu lupolde deme meister sin" (*König Rother*, l. 3666); Daniel as the *meister* of the elders: "Daniel was ein chint an den jaren,/ der in, also alt so sie waren, von got ze meister gesezzet wart" (Heinrich von Melk, "Das Priesterleben," ll. 458-460 [RD III]); *meister* as teacher: "iz si der meister odir der junger" ("Linzer Antichrist," l. 192 [RD III]); and *meister* as the master of a trade: "zwene rote bouge soltu tragen/

wol gesteinert unt ergraben./ die hat mir ze triwen gislagen/ ein biderber meister" (Heinrich von Melk, "Das Priesterleben," ll. 693-696).

Meister meaning a priest: "des aber die urchunde gebent die under den phaffen der meisterschaft pflegent" (Heinrich von Melk, "Das Priesterleben," ll. 424-25); "ube er [the sinner] die buozze geleistet/ die ime bevilhet sin meister" ("Die Deutung der Meßgebräuche," 37, 6 [*RD* II]); and Alber's *Tnugdalus* where Saint Patrick is referred to as "der meister hêre" (l. 116).

88   Pretzel's *Nachträge*, as was noted once before, provide many instances of Early Middle High German usage, but his examples are far from complete and in any case unidentified. His entry for *meister* lacks any definition of the word as "Bauer." Beate Hennig (*Kleines mittelhochdeutsches Wörterbuch*, 3rd. ed. [Tübingen: Niemeyer, 1998]) offers among other definitions "Aufseher" and "Vorsteher." As will be presently argued, these are perhaps the most relevant meanings for understanding this section of "Vom Rechte." Without context or citations, however, it is unclear what exactly Hennig intends by them.

89   God or Christ is frequently described as Satan's *meister*, as in the "Millstätter Sündenklage:" "Wol du heiligir Christ, du ein warer got bist,/ paradisi porta, meister des hellewarten"(1, 1-2 [*RD* II]); or in the *Vienna Genesis* where Satan says of God: "min meister ist gewaltich" (l. 42); or in the parallel passage in the *Millstätter Genesis*: "min meister ist gewalt(ich) in dem himmele, er wænet im muge niht sin widere:/ ich bin im ebenherre, undir im wil ich niht wesen mere/ . . . ./ ich wil mit minem chore im ebengewaltich wesen, an in sol ich immer genesen" (1, 22 ff.).

Satan, in turn, is called the *meister* of the infernal realm: "want er ist meister zi flize uber elliu hellewizze" ("Schopf von dem Lone," l. 54 (*RD* II); and Alber's *Tnugdalus*: "der dâ ze helle ist der meist,/ der tiuvel ist kein sîn genoz" (ll. 1292-93) and "ir [der tiuvel] meister ungehiuren" (l. 1327).

90   See, e.g., *Das Anegenge,* ll. 9 ff. where *meister* is used of Balaam (Numbers 22, 21 ff.): "nû beleite mîne sinne/ sam dû der eselinne/ ûf tæte ir munt,/ daz sî ir meister daz gotes wort lerte" and "Die Deutung der Meßgebräuche" (l. 177, *RD* II), in which Christ is called the *meister* of the lost sheep: "so ist er sîn meister guoter." "Hêrre," too, is sometimes used to name the master of an animal: "sî [diu kuo] hate ir hêrre nimmer gesehen" (Alber's *Tnugdalus*, l. 802).

91   *Millstätter Genesis*, 100, 28-29. "He became the friend of the king and all his followers. He became *meister* and lord over all the land." Cf. Genesis 45, 26: "Ioseph vivit et ipse dominatur in omni terra Aegypti."

92   *Wiener Genesis*, ll. 4,996-4,999. "That he was beloved of the king and *meister* over all his followers, and how far and wide, the land was subject to him."

93   *Millstätter Exodus*, ed. Diemer, 133, 10-13. "Be he healthy or sick, they spared him not. There was no one who had authority who did not torture them: they beat and roughly oppressed the *meister* wherever they were gentle to those subject to them." Cf. Exodus 5, 14: "Flagellatique sunt qui praeerant operibus filiorum Israhel ab exactoribus Pharaonis."

94   *Millstätter Exodus*, 133, 23-25. "'Unless you spare us, God knows, death were better for us. We are your slaves; deign to preserve us. Spare us something, lord, that

we might serve that much better." Cf. Exodus 5, 15: "Cur ita agis contra servos tuos?" The *Vienna Exodus* account is nearly identical to these two passages ("Exodus," ed. Hoffmann von Fallersleben, *Fundgruben für Geschichte deutscher Sprache und Literatur*, II Theil [Breslau, 1837], 97, 14-29).

95   Lexer, II, 2085. Lexer also suggests that German *meist* colored the sense of the word.

96   "Capitula legibus addenda," *MGH*, Cap. I, no. 136, c. 18.

97   "Capitulare de villis," *MGH*, Cap. I, no. 32, c. 29.

98   Ibid., c. 57.

99   "Lex familiae wormatiensis ecclesiae, *MGH*, Leges, IV, 1, no. 438, c. 12.

100   Duby, *Rural Economy*, 179-180.

101   *Sachsenspiegel*, "Landrecht," II, 13.

102   For the meaning of *meister* after 1200 cf. Siegfried Beyschlag's comments on Neidhart's use of *meister* and *meisterinne*: "Beide Wörter . . . bezeichnen bei Neidhard . . . Funktionen im landwirtschaftlichen Bereich, die noch nicht deutlich genug faßbar sind. . . . am ehesten [ist] auf "Bauer" und "Bauerin" als (zumindest) Verwalter eines Hofes, damit etwa "Dienstherr" und "Herrin" zu schließen" (Beyschlag, ed., *Die Lieder Neidharts* [Darmstadt: Wissenschaftliche Buchgesellschaft, 1975], 715). Beyschlag's cautious description of *meister* seems identical to the Early Middle High German usage of the *Millstätter Genesis* and *Exodus*. See Günther Schweikle, however, (*Neithart*, SM 253 [Stuttgart: Metzler, 1990], 58) who says that the identity of the *meisterinne* is "unsicher."

     In Wernher der Gartenære's *Helmbrecht*, a work from which one would expect more enlightening examples of agricultural social terminology, Helmbrecht the father is called "wirt" and not *meister* (e.g. l. 1775), which is used alone for Helmbrecht's errant son in conjunction with a servant (*knehte*), e.g. ll. 1,800-03 (*Helmbrecht*, Friedrich Panzer, 9th ed. by Kurt Ruh, [Tübingen: Niemeyer, 1974]).

103   *Wiener Genesis*, ll. 1,182-1,193. "At that time they were in the same situation as many people are today who come to poverty from riches. Those who cannot farm see much sorrow. They accept with thanks what God deigns to give them, as did Adam and his beautiful wife who in poverty had to suffer their misery." The *Millstätter Genesis* version is essentially identical to the *Vienna Genesis* at this point. Neither poem depends on the Bible which says only: "Emisit eum [Adam] Dominus Deus de paradiso voluptatis ut operaretur terram de qua sumptus est" (Genesis 3, 23).

104   "Vom Rechte," ll. 101-113. "We might well have pity that the rich man declines in prestige [falls] and that he now has nothing. But I will tell you why the rich man falls. Because of his many possessions he becomes proud; he fears not death, and he pities no one's distress. He carries his pride high and never lets it fall until the day comes when God punishes him."

105   Vollmann-Profe (272) claims that *der rîche* owned the castle described here and that its loss is another aspect of the rich man's downfall. This seems a very forced interpretation of the passage.

106   "Vom Rechte," ll. 137-146. "It is the same for the hard man who commits injustice. Whoever wants to convert him must teach him properly. He must force him and bring him back to justice in the same way that someone who clears land does to a large stump. He forces it so that he can remove it from the earth."

107   Schröbler considered these lines explaining the need for the stump's removal as part of the interpretation of the symbolic narrative (C). Surely they belong rather to the narrative itself.

108   "Vom Rechte," ll. 153-162. "It is the same for the rich man who commits injustice. No one can force him, return him to justice, unless God does it with many kinds of afflictions. Or it might happen that God removes him altogether from Christendom so that it will last and never decay."

109   Speicher, 58.

110   "Vom Rechte," ll. 89-92. See above for the entire passage.

111   "Vom Rechte," ll. 163-176. "But let us now return to justice. The master and the servant together go and sow the reclaimed land. When the land comes to bear fruit, they should together bring home the harvest and divide it all in two, if they would be just. They should be very careful that neither of them receives more, for they would suffer much by it. They won it with their sweat; neither of them need begrudge the other [his share]."

112   Hans Fehr, *Das Recht in der Dichtung* (Bern: Francke, 1931), 76. On the basis of the poet's emphasis of reciprocal "Treue" and "Recht," Fehr characterizes "Vom Rechte" as "die erste soziale Dichtung des Mittelalters" (Fehr, 76).

       Speicher at least recognizes the principle to which Fehr refers (without, however, citing him), but he still persists in thinking that "die hier erhobene Forderung [mußte] doch fast revolutionär klingen" (Speicher, 59). He gives no evidence or argument for this contention.

113   Günther Franz, *Geschichte des deutschen Bauernstandes vom frühen Mittelalter bis zum 19. Jahrhundert* (Stuttgart: Ulmer, 1970), 38, ft. 13a. As was noted in Chapter II, the fall of Lucifer is not so much a warning example as an etiological explanation and justification for the social divisions between *hêrre* and *chneht* and *frouwe* and *diu*.

114   See, for example, the description in Duby, *Rural Economy*, 61-87.

115   Kaiser, "Memento mori," 369-370.

116   Quoted in Hans K. Schulze, "Rodungsfreiheit," 546.

117   "Vom Rechte," ll. 179-185. "Whoever wants to come to grace should never take anything from anyone; nor should he begrudge anyone anything that has been justly acquired. Lord and servant should thus love the same justice."

118   "Vom Rechte," ll. 104-109.

119   See Doris Walch (*Caritas. Zur Rezeption des 'mandatum novum' in altdeutschen Texten*, [Göppingen: Kümmerle, 1973], 49-58) for the Latin biblical commentaries that inform Hartmann's construction of the story. Walch interprets this section of "Die Rede vom Glauben" as an instance of the virtue of charity and not justice, but as was shown in the review of justice in Chapter II, the two virtues are not necessarily distinct. One might note, moreover, that Hartmann does not mention "minne" or "liebe" in this section of the poem; he speaks only of *reht*.

120   "Rede vom Glauben," 159, 7-8, 160, 1 (*RD* II). "Because of his pride he did no
         good. He neither feared God, nor did he do any good work. There was a poor
         man, but he took no pity on him."

121   "Rede vom Glauben," 164, 1-5. "Christ once told this *exemplum* to give a moral
         to the people: We should give alms all the while we live. We should have mercy
         on the needy poor and fear God and do good works."

122   "Rede vom Glauben," 98, 1-10, 99, 1-9. "This is the Holy Ghost's counsel:
         Whoever follows it fears our Lord God and does good works. He avoids evil and
         envies little. He does good things and gladly gives alms to the poor for the sake
         of God, and he begins to have mercy on them. He never ceases to feed the hun-
         gry and give drink to the thirsty, and by so doing he remembers his own soul.
         With his own hand, he gives his cloak to the naked. He gladly lets foreign trav-
         elers rest in his home and he never turns them out. Under his roof he takes care
         of them. He has them sit down on the floor by his fire. He gives them to eat,
         and he visits the sick. He takes good care of them, and he visits prisoners wher-
         ever they are tortured in dungeons. He gives them help and comfort so that they
         will be redeemed. The Holy Ghost inspires this most. He is, first and last, the
         best of all masters. He inspires all things that are good and just."

123   "Die Hochzeit," ll. 486-490 (Schröder, ed., II). "There in heaven the rich man
         could appear blessed even to himself if he would divide his gain for the sake of
         love. He should clothe him who is cold and nourish the hungry. He should visit
         the sick with his wealth, guide the blind, and teach the uneducated. He should
         fast at those times, prescribed to him and keep those Holy Days on which one
         should fast. He should willingly give the tithe and live as a Christian. He should
         think well of all and never perjure himself. He should avoid injustice. He should
         give to churches and honor the priest who should teach us the word of God. By
         means of these things, all the rich will come to the heavenly chamber."

124   In particular in the allegory of the rich man's garden (strophes 7 ff. [*RD* III]).

125   "Van der Girheit," 8, 6-26 (*RD* III). "As long as the man has any strength, let him
         gladly go to church. See that he learns to give alms, live purely without sin, and
         have mercy on the poor, giving them food and clothing for the sake of God the
         rich. He should visit the sick and despise all vanity. . . . He will be called the just
         one, who manfully persists in proportion to his rejecting injustice."

126   Pfaffe Lamprecht, "Tobias," 6, 3 (*RD* II). "He was just and a good man."

127   "Tobias," 12, 1-6. "Tobias turned his thoughts to the reward of heaven. He
         showed mercy to the poor and the sick. . . . He hated all injustice: He gave his
         cloak to the poor, he gave food to the hungry; he was remiss in no good work.
         Prisoners he continually comforted. . . ."

128   "Uppsala Beichte," ll. 51-62 (Schröder, *Kleinere Dichtungen*, vol. II). "I never obe-
         diently held to the many pieces of advice which my priests gave to me: I con-
         fess that now to God. I did not reward those who served me. I never granted
         shelter to those who asked me. I never took mercy upon the sick or the poor. I
         neglected to pay the tithe. Unjust was my life through and through." Maurer,
         (6, 1, *RD* III) emends "rethe" to "rehte," which would give the first two lines
         quoted above the sense "The many kinds of justice which my priests advised me,"

etc. This, of course, would fit my thesis even better, but, unfortunately, there is no compelling reason for the emendation.

129 "Linzer Antichrist," ll. 1,121-1,131 (*RD* III). "'When you took mercy on the poor, visited the sick and the imprisoned, and cared for them, you did that all to me.' But those whom He sees to His left, I know that He will take vengeance on them. Angrily He will speak to them: 'Since injustice seemed unworthy of your attention, now go condemned to the eternal fire that is prepared for the devil!'"

130 "Vom Rechte," ll. 185-190. "If they would be just, each should protect the other in all his need up to his death: Thus they would live justly, both lords and servants."

131 Schröbler, "Vom Rechte," 222.

132 "Die Hochzeit," ll. 510-513. "For here a lord of the house divided his wealth among his servants who rightly serve him."

133 "Von christlicher Lehre," ll. 115-121 (*RD* III). "Blessed are they who hear the word of God and uphold it. It is right that we interpret this for you, for it is written for the salvation of Christian people that every man should share with another whatever he has."

134 "Vom Rechte," ll. 20-23.

135 "Vom Rechte," ll. 44-47. "Many a person wants to have justice in proportion to his *gewalt*, and wants to have it for himself and doesn't want to give it to anyone else."

136 "Memento mori," 11, 1-4 (*RD* I). "If you would all live in one justice then you would all be invited to eternal joy where you would ever remain. But you have one for yourselves and the other you give to the poor. Therefore they cannot go in but remain standing without." Schützeichel denies that "taz eina" and "daz ander" here refer to "daz recht" (*Das alemannische Memento mori*, 84-86). His eccentric interpretation of this passage will be discussed in next chapter.

137 Gentry also sees "taz eina" and "daz ander" as referring to *reht* and interprets the passage as meaning: "If they lead their lives according to two different sets of principles, if they practice one form of *justitia* towards those of their own class. . . because they stand to gain something and if they practice another form of *justitia* for the less powerful members of society. . . then they will be lost" ("Noker's Memento mori and the Desire for Peace," 48).

138 Hermann Krause, "Mittelalterliche Anschauungen vom Gericht im Lichte der Formel: iustitiam facere et recipere, Recht geben und nehmen," *BAW SB, Heft* 11 (1974).

139 Krause, 6-7.

140 Krause, 19.

141 Krause, 23.

142 Krause, 53.

143 Krause, 23-24.

144 *MGH,* Cap. I, no. 90, chap. 1, quoted in Krause, 29, ft. 101.

145 Krause, 38-40.

146 Krause (5) does mention, however, a tripartite formula using "haben," which sometimes also occurs: "Recht haben, geben und nehmen." Unfortunately, he offers no comments on its meaning.

147 "Vom Rechte," ll. 54-64. "For whoever has power and commits injustice and allows it to happen to someone else, he will lose eternal life, be he man or woman, unless he desires to do penance for it and to renounce it so that he never does it again. Justice demands this [literally: justice belongs to this]. If he has changed, then God will ignore his injustice. Thus he can become the servant of God. Let us, therefore, turn to justice!"

148 "Vom Rechte," ll. 89-92

149 "Millstätter Sündenklage," 17, 1- 22, 2 (*RD* II). "If I have heard rightly what the prophets have written, then there will be a great court, a plenary judgment, which in the end shall encompass all of this world. There, neither silver nor red gold will help people, neither great bribes nor heavy coins, neither territorial law nor imperial law: God will judge in His power. There, neither a quick tongue will help, nor the lord his vassal, nor the vassal his lord, however great his fief. The [ecclesiastical] advocate will be of no help. However much he forces his miserable assistant, he will not dare to speak. There God will judge with justice the lord and the servant, the lady and the servant girl."

150 Erich Klibansky wrote that the "Linzer Antichrist" (as well as the Hamburger "Das jüngste Gericht") shows both a detailed acquaintance with theological accounts of the Last Judgment and with aspects of contemporary legal procedure ("Gerichtsszene und Prozeßform in den erzählenden deutschen Dichtungen des 12.-14. Jahrhunderts," *Germanische Studien*, 40 [1925], 28-30.

151 "Linzer Antichrist," 45, 1–3 (*RD* III). "And then they set one form of justice over all the lands that the lord and the servant must uphold."

152 "Linzer Antichrist," 22, 10-16. "Kings and dukes, bishops and priests who should watch over the poor Christians — the Antichrist wins them easily to his side with such gifts. The life of the just becomes wretched."

153 "Das jüngste Gericht," 20, 1-2 (*RD* II). "God will come in His majesty through the clouds. Then He will justly judge lord and servant."

154 "Das jüngste Gericht," 28, 1. "Neither gold nor treasure will help then. If only we had earlier thought better of it!"

155 "Das jüngste Gericht," 22, 6.

CHAPTER IV

Conclusion

1. *ORDO* AND RHETORIC

In discussing the Early Middle High German authors' views of *reht* or *iustitia*, I have scarcely mentioned any Early Middle High German prose works. However, one of them, the *Speculum ecclesiae* (ca. 1130-1150), the first complete collection of sermons in the German vernacular, offers important insights into how and why the Early Middle High German authors used certain social categories in their descriptions of *reht*, and it therefore deserves particular attention. The sermons contained in the *Speculum ecclesiae* are typical of those written in the German vernacular before ca. 1170, in that they are mostly translations and adaptations of Latin originals. The Latin sources are also, for the most part, drawn from the traditional early medieval authorities: Augustine and the Pseudo-Augustinian sermons, Gregory the Great, and Bede. Notable exceptions in the German collection are the use of some contemporary French preachers' Latin sermons and Honorius Augustodunensis's sermon collection, the *Speculum ecclesiae*, from which Kelle, the first modern editor of the Early Middle High German *Speculum*, borrowed the title.

The German *Speculum ecclesiae* consists of about 70 sermons and exhortations, preceded by seven liturgical pieces and closing with a vernacular *Pater noster*. The sermons are arranged according to the liturgical calendar, beginning with Advent and ending on Saint Martin's. They are mostly intended for major feasts and saints' days, with only a few to be preached at Sunday services.

The purpose of the collection is clear. From scattered remarks by the anonymous author, one can deduce that the *Speculum* was conceived as an ancillary work for preachers. The author writes, for example: "Hec predicis in quocumque festo beate Marie velis,"[1] or "Nomina quemcumque martirem uelis, in uniuscuiusque matiris festo hoc predicare poteris,"[2] or sometimes more specifically, "Hec dicas in inventione sancte crucis."[3]

The sermons can be divided by length into long, approximately three to five printed pages, medium, one and one half pages, and short exhortations, which are less than one printed page.[4]   On the basis of length, one can also distinguish between the translator/compiler's uses of sources.[5] In general, the longer sermons are straightforward translations of near-contemporary French preachers, especially Hildebert of Le Mans and Ivo of Chartres. The sermons of medium length are usually freer translations of Gregory the Great, Bede, Rabanus Maurus, and especially, Honorius. The short exhortations, finally, are perhaps original compositions.

Stephan Speicher has denied that the Early Middle High German sermons showed any interest in moral or social questions, and he claims that as a rule, the sermons were more concerned with the propagation of fundamental dogmas of the faith.[6] Since the *Speculum* collection is for the most part unoriginal, one should not expect extensive commentary on current issues, and in this respect, Speicher is no doubt right. Furthermore, the liturgically-based, model character of the collection would make any treatment of specific contemporary questions out of place. But the sermons contained in the *Speculum ecclesiae* by no means treat only Church dogma, and the author's concern with moral and, by implication, social questions is evident throughout, beginning with the first long piece, the "Pura confessio," which is an admission of countless moral failings:

> Ich begihe dem almahtigim got, daz ich mich uersundet han mit nîde, mit hazze, mit vientsefte, mit vrbunne, mit bisprâche, mit luge, mit lugen urkvnde, mit maineidin, mit hinterkosunge, mit divue, mit roube, mit ubeln ratin, mit zorne, mit lanchrâche, mit uberâzze . . . .[7]

Most pertinent to my subject, however, is a sermon found near the end of the collection, following those for feast and saints' days, with a theme from the Psalms: "**U**enite fillii, audite me, timorem domini docebo uos."[8] The source for this sermon has long been recognized to be the "Sermo generalis" from Honorius's collection, the *Speculum ecclesiae*.[9] In Honorius's liturgical cycle, the "Sermo generalis" falls before the Lenten season. Honorius addresses different groups, beginning with "sacerdotes," then turning to "judices," "divites," "pauperes," "milites," "mercatores," "agricolae," and finally to the "conjugati." The different categories that Honorius uses are similar to those found in many Early Middle High German poems, especially in the works of Heinrich von Melk. Each of the groups is admonished to avoid those sins particularly associated with its "order." The "Sermo generalis" closes with a long exhortation to all to practice virtue and charity and to do penance and fasting for Lent.

The categories of the "Sermo generalis" that most closely resemble those with which the Early Middle High German poets were concerned in their admonitions to *reht* are, of course, the judges, the rich, and the poor. While Honorius does not specifically devote a section to lords and servants, he begins the sermon by stating that his audience includes "divites vel pauperes, domini vel servi,"[10] the typical Early Middle High German categories. The *servi* are never admonished, but the *domini* are in their function as judges, and in much the same fashion as the Early Middle High German poets address *hêrren*.

In the Early Middle High German version of Honorius's sermon, the translator/adapter generally follows his Latin model, but he diverges from or modifies

Honorius's text at certain telling points. In the address to the judges, the German author has selectively translated the Latin original:

> Nv spreccen wir ziv, rihtare, die got, der rehte rihtare, gesezzet hat ze uursten simme liute. Div wort des ewigen rihtares scult ir niht ungerne uernemen, so gewinnet ir hie rihtuom un*de* êre un*de* enphâhet dort daz ewige lôn. Irne scult nimmer durch miete gerihten unrehte. Dem armen scult ir wole rihten, daz ir iht entrihtet werdet der ewigen genaden, wan div heili*ge* scrift sprichet: Iudiciu*m* sine mi*sericordi*a ei, q*ui* n*on* fac*it* mi*sericordi*am. 'Er wirt uerteilet an urteile, der hie ane barmunge rihtet.' Allez ubil scult ir uermiden, so verre so ir muget, dem guoten scult ir nach uolgen. Ist daz ir danach arbeitet, so werdet ir gechronet uon dem oberosten rihtare. Welt auer ir die armen uerdrucchen, so werdet ir an der uorhtlichen urteile des almahtigen gotes gestozzen in die grimmigen helle.[11]

The German author has simplified and shortened Honorius's text, omitting the latter's injunctions to protect the clergy, widows, children, and the poor, as well as the property of the Church. The German version also excludes Honorius's command to the judges to eliminate thieves, bandits, and plunderers and his call for the severe punishment of the guilty ("Expedit enim ut unus pereat quam ipse multos perdat"[12]). The quotation in Latin from the Epistle of James has been slightly changed in order more clearly to emphasize the role of the judge: "Qui non facit misericordiam" becomes "who *judges* here without mercy." Where Honorius warns of oppressing the "populus Dei," the German substitutes "die armen." In sum, the German translator has narrowed the focus of the Latin text to concentrate on the typical ideal of the *reht* demanded from *hêrren* as found in the Early Middle High German poems, namely, with God as model, impartial justice for all and the avoidance of bribes. In two respects, however, the vernacular author, by closely following his Latin source, diverges slightly from the Early Middle High German poets. First, the German author repeats Honorius's clear command to show mercy, which, although an important aspect of the early medieval conception of justice, is rarely mentioned in the poets' treatment of the secular practice of judicial justice. Second, the vernacular text follows Honorius in speaking of *die armen* ("pauperes") as the object of justice and not the more typical *knehte*. Again, in view of the early medieval emphasis on justice for the poor, one should hardly find this surprising. Indeed, as we have seen in Noker's "Memento mori," it is especially "ter armo man" who has need of *reht*. Perhaps because the German author never explicitly mentions *die hêrren*, he felt no need to name their usual opposite, *die knehte*.

In the Early Middle High German version of Honorius's address to the rich, a more substantial alteration of the source occurs:

> Nu manen wir ivch, riche, den got den werltlichen richtuom hat uerlihen den armen ze troste. Gedenchet darane, daz ir nachent in dise werlt bechômet un*de* nachent deruon sceiden muozzet. Den ríchtuom muozzet ir hie lazzen; uon div sendet in hin uure bi den armen, daz ir in dort uindet. Ir scult den hungerigen muosen, den dvrstenten trenchen, den ellenden herbergen, den nachenten uazzen, den siechen beruochen, den trurigen trosten. Tuot ir daz, so wirt iwer richtuom gemeret i*n* dirre werlt un*de* uindet in dort, da ivn niemen genemen mac.[13]

The German version begins with a literal translation of Honorius, reminding the rich that they came naked into this world and that naked they will leave it. It also repeats Honorius's appeal to self-interest: by distributing some of his wealth to the poor, the rich man will find treasure in heaven and honor and wealth on earth. But the German author entirely ignores Honorius's other enticements to the rich, as well as his warnings, in order to concentrate on the typical Early Middle High German conception of the *reht* due from the *die rîchen*, the *opera misericordiae*. Honorius had demanded a quite different list of good works from the rich, in which the Church and the lord's civic duties played a central role and the works of mercy were only partly implied:

> Ecclesias debetis libris, paliis et allis ornamentis decorare, lapsas vel destructas restaurare, praebendas Deo servientium ampliare, per hoc orationes eorum comparare, pontes et plateas aedificare, per hoc vobis viam ad coelum parare; pauperibus et egenis et peregrinis hospitia, victus et vestitus necessaria praebere, per hoc vobis aeternas divicias emere.[14]

In his comments to the poor, Honorius exhorted them patiently to bear their misery and to pray for those who give them alms. He concluded with a story of a pious hermit who witnesses the wretched death of a pauper who is immediately received in heaven. Coming to a rich man's house, the hermit sees a crowd of *nobiles* around the rich man's death bed. Demons come and seize the rich man who pleads to God for mercy, but to no avail.

In the Early Middle High German version, the *exemplum* is omitted and Honorius's text reduced to two sentences: "Die armen sculen ir armuot gedulteclichen tragen: darumbe enphahet si daz ewige lon. Daz almuosen, daz in die lute gebent, daz sculen si lôsen mit ire gebete."[15] As in the Early Middle High German poems, the poor are less the subject of the writer's admonitions to *reht* than the object.

The similarities between the German author's adaptation and modification of Honorius's "Sermo generalis" and the Early Middle High German poets' treatment of *reht* are both striking and revealing. Consider first the *Speculum* author's use of social categories. He repeats all of Honorius's social classifications, but only in the case of the *rihtare* and *die rîchen* do the typical Early Middle High German ideals of *reht* appear: the impartial judicial justice due from judges and the works of mercy expected of the rich.

Georges Duby wrote of Honorius's social concepts that:

> To carry the message home, to ensure that the seed being sown will fall on fertile ground, the mirror—that tool of reformation—had to be tilted at the proper angle towards each of the many faces in the crowd of listeners. Accordingly a fine social analysis was needed . . . .[16]

Honorius offers only a modest selection of social categories compared with those used in the first half of the tenth century by Rather of Verona in his *Praeloquia*.[17] The *Praeloquia*, like Honorius's "Sermo generalis" and its Early Middle High German adaptation, is an example of a "Ständelehre" or teaching for the different estates. Rather discusses the duties of the "milites," "negotiatores," "causidici," "iudices," "ministri publici," "mercenarii," "domini," "servi," "divites," "mendici," "coniuges," "reges," "episcopi," and many others. As Ingeborg Schröbler has remarked, Rather's categories are a sometimes confusing mixture of social function, legal status, family and marital status, secular and ecclesiastical rank, as well as age and sex, as is also true of Honorius's "Sermo generalis" and its Early Middle High German adaptation.[18]

As "Ständelehren," Rather's *Praeloquia*, Honorius's "Sermo generalis," and the Early Middle High German *Speculum ecclesiae* are only partly based on their authors' perception of their social surroundings, contrary to what Duby seems to have implied.[19] A more formative influence on these works was the early medieval *ars praedicandi*. It is, therefore, mistaken to speak of "a fine social analysis" determining any of these authors' social classifications. On the contrary, they are all selectively repeating and modifying the traditional social classifications of sermonic practice, which readily mixed legal and social status, function, and sex, as can be clearly seen in the first extensive and most influential early medieval guide to preaching, Gregory the Great's *Regula pastoralis*.

James Murphy describes Gregory's work as "essentially a treatise on ecclesiastical administration, broadly conceived."[20] One of the most important duties of the bishop was, of course, to preach regularly, and Gregory was careful to include in his work numerous suggestions and practical advice on delivering sermons. Murphy writes that Gregory had

> no intention of providing a new rhetorical theory for preachers. Part Three [of the *Regula pastoralis*] . . . deals with subject matter, not rhetorical form. . . . Gregory lists thirty-six pairs of opposed "characters" and then proceeds to write a brief sermonette that would be suitable to deliver to each pairing. There is no further discussion of the problem that any number of these diverse characters might be present at one time in an audience.[21]

Gregory's list of character pairs is as diverse as Rather's, including men and women, the young and the old, subjects and prelates, the married and the single, the learned and the ignorant, and such moral descriptions as "the kindly disposed and the envious," and "the humble and the haughty."[22] These disparate pairings are primarily the product of considerations from moral theology; their chief sources were biblical and patristic categories, not an astute social analysis.

Honorius and his German interpreter are thus heirs to an old tradition of sermonic composition, the chief function of which was, by definition, moral instruction. Its social categories were based on the traditional objects of such instruction. To be sure, in the course of the Middle Ages, Gregory's characters were continually varied and modified. The "negotiatores," for example, whom Rather mentions, were absent from Gregory's list of character pairs, and in general, Gregory's moral pairs gradually became subsumed under different social categories.

The fact that the sermonic social classifications were rhetorical and moral in origin does not preclude their being considered reasonably adequate descriptions of real social orders. The writers of sermons had a practical goal in view: to persuade their audiences to lead a Christian life. Their categories, therefore, had to reflect, at least in part, the reality of their audiences' conception of their own society. But one would be mistaken in imagining that the preachers' social classifications arose from an attempt to give the medieval equivalent of an objective sociological analysis of their society. In the first place, such an abstract analysis would have seemed irrelevant to one concerned with improving and converting his listeners. And, as is still the case with modern secular social classifications, ideology and personal inclinations and interest cannot help but determine the categories chosen.[23] There is no division and classification of society into different groups independent of a person's goals in undertaking such an analysis and removed from the tradition in which the observer stands.

In his version of Honorius's "Sermo generalis," the author of the Early Middle High German *Speculum ecclesiae*, while repeating Honorius's categories, was, in turn, selectively modifying and adapting them for his own purposes, which seem to have been nearly identical to those of the Early Middle High German poets. By this process of adaptation, the content of Honorius's admonitions to the judges and the rich more closely reflected that of the poets' exhortations to the practice of *reht* directed to *die hêrren* and *die rîchen*.

But what of the poets' social classifications? They, too, seem to have been selected from a broad range of sermonic character pairings, as first given by Gregory the Great. In fact, in Gregory's *Regula pastoralis*, two chapters are devoted to how one should preach to the needy and the rich and to servants and lords.[24] Neither chapter mentions the practice of justice, as specified by Early Middle High German authors, whether judicial impartiality or the works of mercy. But both contain themes that are reflected in many of the Early Middle High German poems. Thus, in Gregory's suggestions as to how the needy and the rich are to be admonished, he especially concentrates on the danger of the rich man's "elatatio" and "superbia," much as the "Vom Rechte" poet and Der arme Hartmann had condemned the *übermuot* of *der rîche*. And in his chapter on lords and servants, Gregory writes of the lords: "illi admonendi sunt ut cognoscant se conservos esse servorum,"[25] just as in "Vom Rechte," the poet writes:

> der meister ist guot,
> der selbe guotiu werch tuot
> unde den chneht so mit heizzet varen.
> der wil den tumben bewaren. . .
> der bedenche sich enzit,
> daz er reht vor vare
> unde die menege beware.[26]

The traditional and sermonic character of the Early Middle High German poets' categories, *die hêrren* and *die knehte* and *die rîchen* and *die armen*, however, is most readily seen not in the content of the poets' admonitions, but simply in the paired form of their categories. The poets used these paired forms despite the fact that they showed no more interest in addressing *die armen* and *die knehte* than did the author of the *Speculum ecclesiae*, as is evident from his summary and highly abridged treatment of Honorius's address to the *pauperes*. The servants and the poor are merely the objects of the practice of the *reht* that the poets demand from the rich and the lords. The paired forms are thus, in origin, a rhetorical device and not the product of a disinterested social analysis, a conclusion that is strengthened not only by the occasional suggestions, as in "Vom Rechte," that the rich man and the lord are the same person, but also by the historical fact that the medieval lord was indeed usually rich. Murphy's comment about Gregory's characters thus applies equally well to the Early Middle High German authors' admonishments to justice: the poets were obviously unconcerned that their different categories might describe one and the same person in their audience. The question posed above at the end of Chapter III, as to why the poets separate the two categories of the rich and the lords, finds its answer in the traditional rhetorical practice of sermonic composition.

2. HISTORY AND *REHT*

If the Early Middle High German poets' divisions of society that serve as the basis for their demanding one form of justice from one group and another from a second are rhetorical in origin, then one might well ask whether these demands themselves are not purely traditional and thus, perhaps, irrelevant to the historical situation in which they arose. Was Heinz Rupp, in fact, correct in saying that, in general, the Early Middle High German poems contain ideas which had been the common property of Christianity since the Patristic era and that there is no clearly discernible evidence of contemporary events or concerns in the poems?[27] An answer to the question that served as the starting point for this discussion of the concept of *reht* in Early Middle High German literature, namely what is the relation between this literature and its historical context, must now be sought.

A. *Die frîen* and *die scalce*

The answer in the case of the least prevalent of the Early Middle High German social pairs, the *frîe* and the *scalce*, is fairly simple. These concepts are not typical sermonic categories, but, as has been shown, descriptions of legal status that have been infused with theological ideas on sin and the origin of servitude. In spite of the claims of some social historians, the continued relevance, to at least 1150, of the divisions between the free and the unfree has been affirmed. The seriousness with which especially the authors of the biblical epics treated these categories has been demonstrated by the sometimes substantial changes imposed in their rendering of the biblical story of Joseph and the Egyptians. The transformation and expansion of the pairing of *frî* and *scalc* from a simple binary combination in the accounts of Noah's curse in the *Vienna* and *Millstätter Genesis* epics to the more differentiated description contained in the *Vorauer Bücher Moses* suggest, furthermore, that the concern with this legal/religious pair was, in part, a response to the contemporary problems incurred by the rise in status in the twelfth century of the *ministeriales* or knights.

B. *Die rîchen* and *die armen*

The relation between historical trends and concerns and the dominant Early Middle High German social categories, *die rîchen* and *die armen* and the *hêrren* and the *knehte*, must be approached more tentatively and speculatively. The pairing of the rich and the poor is most clearly traced to Gregory's sermonic characters, the "inopes et divites," although it is unlikely that Gregory's *Regula pastoralis* was the immediate source. Regardless of how they were transmitted, certain of the themes that Gregory had suggested for preaching to the rich and the poor were clearly followed by at least some of the Early Middle High German poets. But the content of the *reht* due from *der rîche*, the works of mercy, was absent from Gregory's sermon to the "inopes et divites" in the *Regula pastoralis* and present only in a limited and subordinate manner in such contemporary Latin sermons as Honorius's "Sermo generalis." It would seem, therefore, that in consistently describing the *reht* due from *der rîche* in these terms, both the author of the German *Speculum ecclesiae* and the Early Middle High German poets were following a common tradition that slightly diverged from the usual sermonic treatment of the rich and the poor.

While there is no one particular source for the equation of the rich man's justice and the *opera misericordiae*, we have seen that one aspect of the early medieval concept of *iustitia* related the practice of justice to the favorable treatment of the poor. The Bible provides the dominant influence here, in particular the canonical version of the works of mercy as described in Matthew 25, 31-36, where those who perform such works are called the "iusti" and promised redemption.[28]

Biblically-inspired injunctions and categories were also seen to have played an important role in the concern for the *pauperes* expressed in the Carolingian capitularies. The capitularies, however, were usually addressed not to the *divites*, but to such magnates or *potentes* as the counts, bishops, or *missi dominici*, and they tended to concentrate on the fair administration of judicial justice, not the works of mercy.

In Early Middle High German literature, the early medieval concern with the justice due from the *powerful* to the poor, defined by the works of mercy, thus came to be applied to the biblical and sermonic categories of the *rich* and the poor. Perhaps this combination was simply the result of rhetorical considerations: "the rich" provide a clearer contrast with "the poor" than do "the powerful." Or perhaps the fact that the works of mercy generally require wealth was the motivating factor.

The exact source of the conceptual change from the Carolingian "potentes" to the Early Middle High German *die rîchen* and of the modified content of the *iustitia* due from Gregory's "divites" can perhaps not be found. Michel Mollat has written that "Twelfth-century thinking on the subject of poverty derived from traditional patristic writings about justice as well as on charity."[29] The Early Middle High German poets could have imbibed this thinking through at least two currents, monastic spirituality and episcopal practice. Monks, the dominant spiritual influence of the early Middle Ages, had continually emphasized the importance of the works of mercy, which had been prominently enshrined in the Rule of Saint

Benedict.[30] And throughout the early Middle Ages, bishops were exhorted to be "fathers of the poor." At the bishop's gate, Mollat writes, "the poor received food and clothing, sometimes from his own hand."[31]

Yet despite the importance of tradition in the formation of the Early Middle High German poets' concept of the *reht* due from the rich to the poor and regardless of the fact that their concept of this *reht* seems to have been common throughout Europe in the twelfth century, one can draw certain historical conclusions from their poems. First, the poets and sermon writers clearly admonish laymen and not monks or ecclesiastic leaders to practice *reht* toward the poor. They speak directly to *die rîchen* (who are also *hêrren*) not in learned Latin, but in their own vernacular language and in their own terms. Thus, in the Holy Roman Empire, it was probably the Early Middle High German authors who first widely publicized the European-wide transformation of traditional episcopal and monastic duties and ideals into a new code of ethics for the lay aristocracy. Because of the complicated legal and social status of most of the German knights, this was not yet a chivalric code: knights receive relatively little attention in the purely religious Early Middle High German works.[32] But it was clearly becoming such in the second half of the twelfth century. Alber's *Tnugdalus*, it may be recalled, described the *reht* due from the Irish lord and knight Tungdalus as the practice of the works of mercy towards *die armen*, as well as judicial impartiality.[33]

Second, to the Early Middle High German poets, poverty was not merely a traditionally conceived object of moral concern, but a social reality with which they clearly felt themselves confronted. As I have tried to show, the "Vom Rechte" poet's portrait of the fall of the manorial *meister* from riches to poverty, although used as a sermonic *exemplum*, is described in realistic and contemporary terms. The same poet's concern with contemporary poverty can also be seen in those lines that Schröbler had characterized as an "excursus" on avarice, but that in fact reflect the obverse side of his ideal of justice:

> Nieman ist gotes chint,
> wan die daz reht wurchundi sint.
> die anderen sint von den gesunderot.
> vil ist, des mich wunderot,
> daz sich der hunt archman,
> niht verdenchen chan:
> 'diu erge daz ist schante,
> diu ist laster und sunte.'
> swenne der arge man zergat,
> daz er des libes nine hat,
> so riwet in sin richtuom;
> er nehat den lon noch den ruom.
> so stat er *in d*er helle,
> es *ist* wunder, waz der gotes sun sin zuo d*er* christenheit welle,
> liez *er* in einen heiden wesen,
> er mohte alsam wol genesen.

> wan unmæzzige erge
> ist gruntveste aller ubele.[34]

The development of a code of aristocratic ethics and the recognition of the problem of poverty, while not confined to the Early Middle High German poets, can be seen as their response to contemporary spiritual and intellectual trends as well as to such social phenomena as the widespread famines in the empire in the early twelfth century.[35] The traditional and sermonic nature of the categories that the poets use in their description of their ideal of *reht*, prevent, of course, any historical localization of these concerns. *Dives* and *pauper, der rîche* and *der arme* are too static in their development and too vague in content to permit specific conclusions about when and where they were used, and the works of mercy are, of course, far too general to be described as a response to any one particular crisis.[36] In general, therefore, the historical context of the poets' addresses to the rich can only be seen in very broad terms. But what Mollat has written of the early medieval conciliar decisions for the relief of the poor can also be said of the Early Middle High German poems: the frequency and the ubiquity of the poets' demands for justice toward the poor show "the persistence of the problems with which they deal."[37] That the poets' categories should have been in use from biblical times is not so much an example of the longevity and persistence of a *topos*, but a human tragedy.

C. *Die hêrren* and *die knehte*

To a certain degree, the Early Middle High German pairing of *die hêrren* and *die knehte* also permits only general conclusions to be drawn about their historical context, for these categories, too, are largely biblical and sermonic in origin. Unlike *der rîche* and *der arme*, however, *hêrre* and *kneht* are not relatively neutral translations (in this case, of *dominus* and *servus*), but are, in part, influenced by feudal concepts and changes in the status of the unfree (*kneht* meaning sometimes slave, knight, or an unspecified servant).[38] Although their scope of reference is wide, it is not nearly as vague as that of *die rîchen* and *die armen*.

Similarly, while the content of the *reht* due from *der hêrre*, impartial judicial justice, is biblically inspired and the most typical early medieval definition of *iustitia*, the poets seem to tailor their description of judicial justice to contemporary concerns. First, as we have seen, the peculiarities of medieval procedure led to the poets' emphasis on honesty and good faith in the practice of justice. Second, and more important, the poets' central concern with the avoidance of bribes and the abuse of judicial *gewalt* are perhaps a reflection of the corruption caused by the devolution of jurisdiction and changes in the concepts of judicial punishment and fines.

Georges Duby gave a very clear picture of the collapse in parts of France of the Carolingian public administration of justice and the usurpation of judicial rights and profits by local lords.[39] While the German-speaking lands had been spared the full extent of the catastrophes suffered by the western portions of the Carolingian empire, significant changes in the nature of imperial judicial institutions, sometimes similar to those that occurred in France, did take place. Already during the reign of Charlemagne, a class of magnates had arisen whose power, according to Heinrich Fichtenau, was measured less by aristocratic lineage than "by the possession of 'much wealth' or by an office which permitted its holder to acquire it."[40] Fichtenau continues:

> Once the older order of rank and status had been destroyed, . . . the race for money and property became the guiding motive of many public officials. They no longer shared an impersonal ideal of justice, but were intent upon grasping for their families whatever there was to be grasped.[41]

The venality of these Carolingian lords and judges had already been indirectly castigated in the Old High German poem "Muspilli."[42] As in the Early Middle High German poems, the Antichrist provides a negative model for judges when the anonymous author speaks of the corruption by means of "rewards" or "miata" of judicial justice:

> ni uneiz der uuenigo man, uuielihan uuartil er habet,
> denner mit den miaton marrit daz rehta,
> daz der tiuual dar pi kitarnit stentit.[43]

In the Early Middle High German period, *miete* had become a *terminus technicus* for such judicial bribes.[44]

The devolution of jurisdiction in the eleventh and twelfth centuries further contributed to the corruption of justice. While the famous *dicta* of the great thirteenth-century French jurist Phillipe de Beaumanoir that "Every baron is sovereign in his barony" and that "Every lord has all justices—high and low—in his fief . . . . Fief and justice—it is all one"[45] did not apply with equal force in the twelfth-century Empire (if they were valid even in France), the judicial rights of the German manorial lords were indeed increasing. As we have seen, the lords' *servi* were slowly beginning to enjoy more rights as legal persons and not things, but the less powerful *liberi*, who in the Carolingian era had, at least theoretically, been subject to the authority of the "public" institutions of the hundred court or the comital or ducal courts, increasingly came under the "private" jurisdiction of those manorial lords from whom they rented their lands or among whose estates their own property or allods were located.[46] Local manorial lords, unrestrained by public officials, thus came to wield increasingly greater judicial power over both the free and the unfree living on or among their lands.[47]

In theory, the judicial function of these lords, like that of most medieval *iudices*, was restricted to their role as presiders over a trial. Judgment, it will be recalled, was rendered by the peers of the accused, and consensus between the judgment-finders and the presiding judge was theoretically the means as well as the ideal of medieval law. According to Hanna Vollrath, this judgment by peers became in a sense equivalent to an act of modern legislation, for precedent or custom was all important in medieval law.[48]

The system was obviously an easy prey to the abuses of a powerful lord, especially with respect to the imposition of fines or punishments. In the early medieval period, a complicated and exact schedule of monetary tariffs, the aim of which was the avoidance of the blood feud, had determined the punishment for various delicts, but this system of composition had begun to break down by the eleventh century. For example, the lord/judge, even when he accepted the judgment of the accused person's peers, could sometimes usurp their right to pronounce sentence,[49] and many judges began to exercise "a new principle of discretionary mulcts."[50] At the same time, the fines themselves were changing in nature. Starting under Henry IV, the imperial rulers had hoped to impose a more lasting semblance of peace and order by instituting a new and vigorous public prosecution of crime. Judges were encouraged to replace the original fines, measured in monetary terms, with the corporal punishments imposed by "blood justice."[51]

A situation had thus developed in which a local lord had won jurisdiction over a wide class of dependents, and in proportion to the extent of his *gewalt*, he might possess broad discretion in pronouncing sentence.[52] In view of these various changes in the administration and pursuit of justice, one can see how a wealthy and powerful person could, with a well-timed "gift" or "reward" (the original meanings of *miete*), avoid the punishment required by law, while a corrupt judge could easily threaten the poor and the powerless under his jurisdiction, who were more than ever subject to the caprices of a partial judge.

The arbitrary nature of the judge's power was later nicely illustrated by the thirteenth-century author, der Stricker. In his admonitory tale "Der Richter und der Teufel," the greed of a *rihtære* surpasses that of the devil himself. A judge meets the devil on the way to the marketplace and boasts to him, saying:

> ich hân gewaltes hie sô vil,
> swaz ich iu leides tuon wil,
> daz mac mir nieman erwern.[53]

The judge threatens the devil with the loss of life and property ("lîb unde guot"), if he does not do his will and show him his trade.[54] Together they go to the marketplace, but the devil refuses the livestock and even children that various people carelessly wish upon him or in Hell, even though the judge encourages him to seize whatever he can. The two then come upon the quintessential example of the object of early medieval justice, a poor widow, both sick and old ("beidiu siech und alt"), who complains to the judge of his ill-treatment in terms that should by now be readily familiar:

> 'wie was dir sô rihtære,
> daz du sô rîche wære
> und ich sô arm bin gewesen,
> und du niht trûwetest genesen,
> dune habest mir, âne schulde
> und âne gotes hulde,
> mîn einigez küelîn genomen,
> dâ ez allez von solde komen,
> des ich armiu solde leben?'[55]

The widow concludes by calling on God to send the judge to the devil who this time readily accedes to the request and seizes the judge.

In the Early Middle High German period, the emphasis on the rights of the powerless and the poor and the ideal of the just judge found a memorable expression in the story of the Emperor Trajan found in the *Kaiserchronik*, the source of which can perhaps be traced to Honorius's "Sermo generalis." Honorius had concluded his address to the "iudices" with the *exemplum* of a "quidam rex," who, while hurrying off to war, is interrupted by a widow who asks that the king vindicate her son. The king promises to deliver judgment upon his return, but accedes to the widow's request for an immediate inquest when she reminds him that he might be killed in battle and then receive no credit for the judgment. When he eventually dies, the king, as a pagan, must suffer the torments of Hell. One day, many years later, Saint Gregory the Great, while passing the king's former house, sees his effigy and remembers the justice he had rendered to the widow. He laments the king's fate in prayer for three days. On the third day, an angel appears to him to announce that his request has been heard by God and the king redeemed to dwell in Paradise.[56]

The *exemplum* was repeated verbatim in Latin in the Early Middle High German *Speculum ecclesiae*, but in the *Kaiserchronik* it was much expanded — perhaps beyond the limits of its already questionable orthodoxy[57] — and turned into the greatest Early Middle High German paean of the just judge, the Emperor Trajan who although a pagan received the reward of Heaven. The author's initial description of Trajan as an impartial judge uses the typical Early Middle High German categories and phrases:

> er rihte vil rehte
> dem hêrren unde dem cnehte,
> von der armen diete
> nam er nehain miete.[58]

The military expedition to which Trajan is rushing is brought within historical memory by being portrayed as a defensive action against "die laidigen Nortmann." Trajan is thus seen fulfilling one of the primary duties of the medieval king, the defense of his people. A widow comes to him to appeal for the rights of her slain son. Vacillating between his duties as defender and judge, Trajan is convinced by the widow's long speech to turn first to justice. He discovers the murderer of her son and has him brought to his court. The accused defends himself by saying that the widow's son had slain his brother:

> Er sprach: 'hêrre, er hête mir vil ze laide getan,
> des ich guoten geziuch hân.
> ich ermane dich, hêrre, wol:
> er was mîn rehter scol,
> er sluoc mir den bruoder mîn.
> mit dînen hulden sol iz von rehte âne gerihte sîn.'[59]

The accused man thus appeals to his right of self-help or feud: his brother has been slain. He, therefore, could by right kill the slayer. But Trajan spurns the primitive justice of the feud and says that the accused should have appealed to him first:

> 'wande mih Rômære
> lobeten ze rihtære;
> mînes gerihtes hâstû dich underwunden.'[60]

Trajan then closely follows the procedural ideals of medieval law, first by consulting the judgment of his retinue and then by imposing the usual sentence demanded by blood justice for manslaughter:[61]

> an den selben stunden
> mit rehter urtaile
> der fursten algemaine
> hiez er im daz houbet ab slahen,
> der frowen hiez erz tragen.[62]

As in Honorius's version, Gregory the Great later prays for the pagan emperor's redemption. He is admonished by an angel that his request is "unreht," but then the angel says to him:

> 'ich sage dir, Gregôrî, waz dû tuo.
> dû bist ain wârer gotes scalch;
> nû habe von gote den gewalt,
> daz dû den haiden lâzest lîden
> daz er gearnet habe mit dem lîbe,
> oder daz dû der sêle iemer phlegest
> unt siben suhte dar zuo nemest,
> daz dir der niemer buoz nemege werden,
> unz dû doh sulst ersterben.'[63]

Gregory willingly suffers the plagues for the sake of Trajan and the emperor's soul is snatched from the devil's clasp.

The poet concludes the story of Trajan by addressing all kings:

> Nû suln alle werltkunige
> dâ bî nemen pilide,
> wi der edel kaiser Trajân
> dise genâde umbe got gewan,
> want er rehtes gerihtes phlegete
> di wil er an dirre werlte lebete.
> der selben genâden suln si gewis sîn,
> behaltent si an ir gerihte mînen trähtîn.[64]

Like the Early Middle High German poets' ideal of the justice due from the rich man, their insistence on the impartial justice due from the lord, while not original, is significant for its consistency and for its being clearly presented in the

vernacular and thus contributing to the development and diffusion of an aristocratic code of ethics that was applied to the greatest as well as to the lowest of
lords, such as the manorial master in "Vom Rechte."[65] Even more than the works
of mercy expected from the rich, the judicial *reht* due from lords also perhaps
reflected specific historical changes, in particular, those in the administration and
nature of justice which arose in the Empire in the course of the eleventh and
twelfth centuries.

3. CONCLUSION: *MINNE UND REHT*

Occasionally, one can glimpse traces of the changed nature of judicial justice, as
when the "Vom Rechte" poet and Noker use the formula *reht nemen und haben* as
a response to those lords who had one justice for themselves and rendered another to their powerless dependents. A second example of a formula reflecting contemporary concerns can again be found in the "Memento mori," and this poem,
once considered be the quintessential expression of the unpolitical and "Cluniac"
spirit of Early Middle High German literature, can provide a fitting last example
of the Early Middle High German use of *reht*.

Hugo Kuhn, it will be recalled, was one of the first scholars to reject the validity of the "Cluniac" label for Early Middle High German literature and to suggest that these poems were, in some instances, eminently concerned with this
world. Kuhn had provocatively chosen the representative poem the "Memento
mori" to illustrate his thesis.[66] He by no means denied the penitential character
of the "Memento mori," but he no longer saw the crux of the poem in its negative threat of damnation, contained in the first six strophes, but in the positive
appeal to *reht* in its middle strophes. This section, from which portions have
already been quoted, had always presented difficulties, not least because of a presumed corruption of certain lines:[67]

7.   Got gescuof iuh alle, ir chomint von einim manne.   50
     to gebot er iu ze demo lebinne mit minnon hie ze wesinne,
     taz ir warint als ein man, taz hant ir ubergangan.
     habetint ir anders niewit getan, ir muosint is iemer
          scaden han.

8.   Toh ir chomint alle von einim man, ir bint iedoch geskeidan
     mit manicvalten listen, mit michelen unchusten.   60
     ter eino ist wise unde vruot . . . .

9.   . . . .   tes wirt er verdamnot.
     tes rehten bedarf ter armo man, tes mag er leidor niewit
     han,er nechouf iz also tiuro, tes varn se al ze hello.

10.   Gedahtin siu denne, wie iz vert an dem ende!
     so vert er hina dur not, so ist er iemer furder tot.   70
     wanda er daz reht verchoufta, so vert er in die hella.

da muoz <er> iemer inne wesen,   got selben hat er hin
   gegeben.

11.   Ube ir alle einis rehtin lebitint,   so wurdint ir alle geladet in
        ze der ewigun mendin,   da ir iemer soltint sin.
        taz eina hant ir iu selben,   daz ander gebent ir dien armen.   80
        von diu so nemugen ir drin gen,   ir muozint iemer dervor sten.[68]

According to Kuhn, Noker in these strophes first reminds his audience of the
original paradisical form of community, namely a life "mit minnon." Because we
have transgressed God's command to love one another, we should at least live
according to *reht*, by which the poet, as we have seen, especially means the preservation of judicial justice for the poor man and not merely for the rich lords. If we
could at least live "einis rehtin," then we still might obtain the eternal delights of
Heaven.

The source of Noker's existential alternative *minne* or *reht*, Kuhn argued, is the
juridical formula appearing in the vernacular as "mit minne oder mit reht."
Following Dietrich Schäfer's discussion of the formula, Kuhn interpreted it as the
vernacular equivalent of the Latin formula "consilio vel judicio."[69] According to
Schäfer and, before him, Homeyer, the formula describes the two different means
of avoiding strife, in particular the blood feud: litigants should resolve their disagreements either by *consilium* (*minne*), namely amicable agreement, or by *iudicium* (*reht*), formal judicial justice. If, and only if, these peaceful methods should fail,
could one then proceed to the self-help of the feud.

Kuhn also appropriated some remarks by Hans Hirsch and claimed that as a
means of avoiding the blood feud and favoring the cause of the poor, who had
most to fear from both legal abuses and the violence of the feud, the ideals of the
formula *consilio vel iudicio* might also be connected with Henry IV's espousal of the
Peace of God movement in the late eleventh-century Empire.[70] Far from being
an exemplary instance of putatively Cluniac asceticism, the "Memento mori," in
Kuhn's view, has a definitely mundane concern with the avoidance of violence and
for furthering the cause of the weak, and this concern can be historically local-
ized.

Kuhn admitted that the first use of the vernacular equivalent of *consilio vel iudicio*, "mit minne oder mit reht," was universally attributed to Gottfried von
Strasbourg (early 13th century) and that the first appearance of the German formula in an unequivocally legal text occurs even later, namely in the *Sachsenspiegel*.
Its use in the "Memento mori," wrote Kuhn, is exceptionally early and was obviously without immediate resonance.[71]

Kuhn's interpretation of the "Memento mori" first appeared in 1950, and as
we have seen, literary historians have gradually accepted his rejection of the
Cluniac label. But, in general, they have ignored Kuhn's discussion of the concepts of *minne* and *reht*. In 1962, Kuhn's ideas came under a full attack by Rudolph
Schützeichel in his monograph devoted to the "Memento mori."[72] Although
agreeing with Kuhn that the key to understanding the poem lay in its central stro-

phes on *reht* and that Noker was clearly concerned with contemporary abuses and their rectification, Schützeichel claimed that Noker's *reht* had little to do with judicial justice and the legal oppression of the poor. Instead, the *reht* that the poor man had such need of and whose sale led to eternal damnation referred, according to Schützeichel, to the sacraments and church offices.[73] Schützeichel justified this claim by interpreting lines 72-73 of the poem, "wanda er daz reht verchoufta, so vert er in die helle," as the vernacular equivalent of the Latin phrase "iustitiam vendere," which the radical anti-simoniac, Cardinal Humbert of Silva Candida, had used to describe the selling of church offices.

This new interpretation of *reht* as "sacrament" is fraught with difficulties and has not found general acceptance. I could discover no other instance of "reht verkoufen" referring to simony or even of *reht* alone clearly meaning sacrament in any text prior to at least the thirteenth century.[74] Simony is generally left unmentioned by the Early Middle High German poets, with the usual exception, of course, of Heinrich von Melk, who attacked it in no uncertain terms, but never by using the phrase "reht verkoufen." "Reht verchoufen" seems, rather, simply to mean "to sell (judicial) justice," an interpretation that is confirmed by a passage in Isidore's *Sententiae*, which I think more closely parallels Noker's concerns than the anti-simoniac tracts to which Schützeichel refers:

> Qui recte judicat, et praemium inde remunerationis expectat, fraudem in Deum perpetrat, quia *justitiam*, quam gratis impertire debuit, acceptione pecuniae *vendit*.[75] (my emphasis)

Humbert's radical views on simony, which Schützeichel sees mirrored in the "Memento mori," were not generally accepted even by the papal party. Indeed, they were later condemned by the Church, for they presumed that not merely the buyer of church offices, but also the recipients of those simoniacs' sacraments would be damned, a presumption that Schützeichel claimed was expressed in the poem by the line "tes varn se alle ze hello."

Schützeichel's interpretation demands quite different and, to a certain degree, distinct understandings of the word *reht* within the "Memento mori" itself.[76] Thus, in line 64, *reht* refers to the poor man's subjective rights,[77] but, as I have also tried to show, *reht*, especially in the oldest Early Middle High German poems, such as the "Memento mori," seldom means "subjective right," for which the poets generally use *gewalt*. In line 72, Schützeichel claims that *reht* means "the sacraments in the most general sense,"[78] which, as noted, is particularly problematic. Finally, in line 76, *reht* is used "in the sense of *ordo*, the order of the early Church as a loving community of all Christians."[79] But we have seen that while conceptually related to *ordo*, *reht* is not equivalent to it; rather, the one concept implies the other. It is hard to accept these vacillations in meaning, which are in themselves uncertain, between a fairly concrete definition, "sacrament," and the more abstract definitions, "subjective right" and "just order."[80]

Schützeichel's interpretation of *reht* has found little sympathy, but his refutation of Kuhn's claims has been generally accepted and the debate on "minne oder reht" in the "Memento mori," or for that matter in any of the Early Middle High

German poems, has been presumed closed. Schützeichel's arguments, however, need to be looked at in a more critical light, especially his understanding of *reht* and *minne*.

Schützeichel argued that the juridical meaning of the concepts *minne* and *reht* would have been obscure to an eleventh-century lay audience. Like Kuhn, he accepted Schäfer's contention that the terms in their legal sense were the vernacular equivalent of the Latin phrase *consilio vel iudicio* and that they were restricted to ecclesiastical jurisdiction.[81] Schützeichel claimed further that the Latin formula was used only in a limited fashion at the height of the Investiture Conflict and then, only by the pope or his legates. His specific examples are Henry IV's oath at Canossa, where the formula appears in the variant "aut iustitiam secundum iudicium eius aut concordiam secundum consilium eius," a letter from Gregory VII, also from 1077, "aut cum iustitia aut cum misericordia," and the Concordat of Worms (1122), "consilio aut iudicio."[82] Belonging to the remote sphere of papal jurisdiction, argued Schützeichel, the formula would not have been readily understood in its German form in the eleventh century in any case, for *minne* does not suggest *consilium*; but "amor" or "charitas." There is nothing in the history or etymology of "minne" to suggest any legal meaning.[83]

Schützeichel further contended that neither the Latin formula, *consilio vel iudicio*, nor the vernacular, *minne oder reht*, had anything to do with the Peace of God movement in the Empire.[84] He concluded his dismissal of Kuhn's thesis with a fact that Kuhn himself had had to concede, namely that the vernacular formula was unknown to Early Middle High German and was first used only in Gottfried's *Tristan*, that is at least 125 years after the "Memento mori." The unequivocally legal use of the vernacular formula, again as Kuhn had been forced to admit, first became widespread even later, after its initial appearance in the *Sachsenspiegel*, in the *Schiedsgerichte* or courts of arbitration of the thirteenth and fourteenth centuries.[85]

To summarize these arguments against Kuhn: the formula *consilio vel iudicio* had a narrow juridical meaning, was initially restricted to high ecclesiastical jurisdiction, and was, therefore, by implication obscure to laymen; it was unrelated to the imperial Peace of God movement, and, most importantly, only later made its appearance in the vernacular. To interpret Noker's use of *minne* and *reht* as an early instance of the formula, therefore, cannot be justified.

These claims about the formula cannot be sustained. As Hermann Krause made clear in an article published after the appearance of Schützeichel's monograph, the Latin formula *consilio vel iudicio* is in fact unrelated to the vernacular *mit minne oder mit reht*.[86] *Consilio vel iudicio* refers not to the two preferred means of solving disputes and avoiding feuds, but is rather a description of procedural law. It describes the usual course of a trial in which the presiding judge should first consult with his councilors. After this *consilium*, the formal judgment or *iudicium* is then pronounced.[87] The *consilium* is thus not opposed to the *iudicium*, but merely precedes it in time, as can be seen in the order of the terms in the formula and in the fact that the phrase is usually given as *consilio et iudicio*. The disjunctives "vel" or "aut ... aut" were rarely used in the formula, and except in one or two uncertain cases, they had lost, in typical medieval Latin fashion, any disjunctive meaning and should be understood as equivalent to "et."[88]

There is no one Latin predecessor to the vernacular formula *mit minne oder mit reht*. Rather, the Latin writers used different, but semantically clearly related concepts, which, unlike the formula *consilio vel iudicio*, always implied a distinct contrast in solving disputes. The one element implies some sort of amicable agreement, the other a strictly just, if not forced, settlement. Thus one finds "secundum iustitiam vel secundum gratiam," or "aut cum iustitia aut cum misericordia," or "iudicium vel concordia," or "per amicabilem compositionem vel per iustitiam," or "jure vel amore," ("amor," of course, being precisely the Latin equivalent of *minne*, which Schützeichel had claimed was devoid of legal connotations).[89]

These concepts, amicable agreement or justice according to the strict interpretation of the law, were by no means as obscure as Schützeichel had suggested. They were already widely used in the Carolingian period, a fact which Schützeichel had conceded, while at the same time dismissing them as mere "Vorformen" of the formula *consilio vel iudicio*.[90] The concepts also appear to have been in widespread use in western France in the eleventh century, where amicable arbitration, or "concordia," was more prevalent than formal judicial trials.[91] In the Anglo-Norman *Leges Henrici Primi* from the early twelfth century, a variant of the formula occurs numerous times, for example, "vel amore . . . vel iudicio," "ex amore [or] . . . per iudicium," "vel iudicio . . . vel amore," or, most succinctly, "Pactum enim legem vincit et amor iudicium:" "For an agreement supersedes the law and amicable settlement (or love) a court judgment."[92] The concepts, finally, also were known in the vernacular, or at least in the English vernacular, as early as the tenth century. They appear, for example, in 997 in the laws of King Aethelred where it is stated that "when a thegn has two choices, love or law (*lufe odde lage*), and he chooses love, it shall be binding as judgement."[93]

There are, it is true, fewer examples of the concepts from the Empire in this earlier period. In addition to Gregory VII's letter of 1077, quoted above, which uses the phrase "aut cum iustitia aut cum misericordia," one might point to Henry IV, who counseled the archbishop of Augsburg and his cathedral chapter to settle their dispute "non coactus, sed quasi fraterna charitate."[94] In itself, however, the relative paucity of the concepts in the legal documents of the Empire does not mean much, for it is a commonplace of legal historians that there is an overwhelming dearth of secular legal sources for the Empire from the end of the Carolingian period to the demise of the Salian dynasty. When the sources again become more numerous, our concepts are there to be found, starting in the late twelfth century in southwestern Germany where the relevant terms were usually "amicabilis compositio vel iudicium."[95]

While these examples are not all from ecclesiastical sources, they nonetheless clearly show the influence of Church doctrine, a fact which helps to explain the intent of the concepts. As well as naturally opposing the blood feud, the Church, in certain circumstances, also tried to avoid the strict judicial application of the law. On the one hand, a formal trial could be expensive and time-consuming, and on the other, the Church recognized that many courts were unable to enforce their judgments. In western France, for example, for which there is good documentation, there were countless instances of ecclesiastical or monastic institutions negotiating with their lay adversaries on questions of property ownership. The religious litigants, prior to any formal legal proceedings, frequently proposed a compromise or they awarded their opponents with gifts or promises of spiritual benefits.[96] The advantages of such friendly, non-judicial settlements were clear: in addition to avoiding the expenses and uncertainties of a formal trial, both sides felt vindicated and there was, thus, less likelihood that the dispute might arise again.[97]

The variety of concepts used in Latin to express what was later called *mit minne oder mit reht* implies something about their juridical status prior to their assuming more consistent and regular forms in the thirteenth century. In discussing the concepts as they appear before that time, one should perhaps avoid referring to a rigid "formula" at all. Instead, one might better infer from the concepts a general tendency, theologically, ethically, and practically motivated, to prefer some kind of friendly settlement to the vagaries or dangers of law. In discussing such phrases as *iure vel amore*, one should thus distinguish between their later development in formal courts of arbitration into strictly legally-binding juridical formulas and the intellectual background that gave rise to them.[98] In other words, prior to and laying the foundation for the legal formula, *mit minne oder mit reht*, the concepts *iure vel amore*, or their equivalents, were general, practical, and ethical injunctions and not legally-binding formulas.

What of Schützeichel's dismissal of the connection between the Peace of God movement and such concepts as *iure vel amore*? Hans Hirsch, as noted, had implied such a connection as early as 1922. Karl Bader, in a study that Schützeichel mentioned but did not discuss, was even more explicit. Speaking of the medieval courts of arbitration, the richest sources of the vernacular formula *mit minne oder mit reht*, Bader characterized them as "a byproduct of both the Peace of God and the *Landfrieden* movements."[99] Another legal historian, Hans Hattenhauer, even criticized Kuhn's cautionary statement that the formula was missing from the earlier Peace of God proclamations. Hattenhauer wrote that the absence of the formula in imperial proclamations is "no genuine *argumentum e silentio*," for the formula clearly appears in later *Landfrieden* documents, and the Peace of God and the *Landfrieden* were no different in their purposes, namely "the securing of peace and the struggle against feuds."[100]

We are left then with Schützeichel's argument against Kuhn based on the late appearance of the vernacular formula, namely in Gottfried's *Tristan*. Was the pairing of the concepts *minne* and *reht* or their conceptual equivalents unknown in the German vernacular prior to the thirteenth century? In their later, strictly legally-binding sense, yes; in their former, more ethical sense, one must answer no. In the *Vienna Genesis*, for example, the poet writes that Joseph, after having been unjustly imprisoned for desiring his master Potiphar's wife, wants to speak to the Pharaoh to convince him of his innocence. Joseph "gebot ioch bat in [Pharaoh] mit minnen."[101] The contrast is between a formal command ("gebieten") and an amicable settlement ("minne"). In the Millstätter version of the same story, from the early twelfth century, the terms used are more familiar: Joseph "wolde *mit reht und mit minnen* siner unschulde . . . innen bringen."[102] In the *Millstätter Exodus*, as well, similar concepts indicating strict justice and amicable persuasion appear. Moses and Aaron tell Pharaoh that he must free the Israelites, for God has told them:

> . . . .   daz solt er durch reht tun,
> unde tæte erz niht mit minnen   er wrde sin bedwngen
> uon dem oberisten gote . . . .[103]

More general examples include *König Rother*, in which the poet tells of the unruly giant Widold, whom his master King Asprian must pacify "mit drowe unde mit minnen,"[104] and in the widest sense of the formula, which, as we saw, could sometimes be expressed as "secundum iustitiam vel secundum gratiam," one might cite Heinrich von Melk, who says of Rome: "man vindet da dehein zuversiht/ rehtes noch genaden."[105]

As a point of logic, refuting Schützeichel's arguments against Kuhn does not, of course, prove the validity of Kuhn's thesis. Was he justified in describing the words *minne* and *reht* in the "Memento mori" as parts of a legal formula? Since in both Latin and in the vernacular the concepts do not appear to have had a strictly juridical meaning prior to the late twelfth century, one must concede that Kuhn's interpretation, in its narrow sense, was mistaken. Gentry, furthermore, has also shown that there is no exclusive contrast in the poem between *minne* on the one hand, and *reht* on the other. Noker, on the contrary, admonishes his audience to practice *reht* on the basis of *minne*.[106]

Gentry's conclusion is perhaps an even more profound indication of the connection between Noker's ideals and those of the imperial Peace of God movement, which, contrary to disparaging strict justice, actively demanded it by enforcing summary punishment of both nobles and serfs.[107] Neither the "Memento mori" nor those examples gathered above from other Early Middle High German poems favor one concept, whether *minne* or *genade*, over another, whether *reht*, or *gebot*, or *drowe*. Rather, these passages indicate that both strict justice and love should be exercised. This ideal is not at all dissimilar to the poets' preaching that rich lords should render both the works of mercy and strict and impartial justice to their dependents. The powerless dependents of the lords, *die knehte*, had less to fear from strictly applied justice than from a justice corrupted by bribes from the rich, and these poor dependents had ample need of the love (*caritas*) or the works of mercy from their rich masters. One should therefore speak of "minne *und* reht" in the Early Middle High German poems and see these concepts as embodying a demand that was anything but otherworldly. In this respect, Kuhn's insights were indeed valid.

The late R. W. Southern wrote of twelfth-century Europe that: "One common need at this time dominates the whole scene of human government, whether secular or spiritual: the need for justice."[108] The Early Middle High German religious poems amply reflect this need, and their preaching on the concept of *reht* or *iustitia* to the rich lords was an attempt to satisfy it.

NOTES

1   *Speculum ecclesiae. Eine frühmittelhochdeutsche Predigtsammlung*, ed. Gert Mellbourn (Lund: Gleerup, 1944), 97, 21-22. See Mellbourn's informative introduction, XXI-XXXIII.

2   *Speculum*, 90, 21-22.

3   *Speculum*, 104, 22.

4   Mellbourn, ed., *Speculum*, XXIV.

5   Mellbourn, ed., *Speculum*, XXVII.

6   Speicher, *Kommentar*, 119.

7   *Speculum*, 4, 4-8. "I confess to almighty God that I have sinned with envy, with hatred, with enmity, with jealousy, with calumny, with lying, with false witness, with perjury, with gossip, with theft, with robbery, with evil advice, with anger, with revenge, with gluttony," etc.

8   *Speculum*, 138, 29.

9   *PL* 172, cols. 862-870. See Anton Schönbach, "Studien zur Geschichte der alt-deutschen Predigt. Erstes Stück: Über Kelle's 'Speculum ecclesiae," *SB der kaiser-licher Akademie der Wissenschaften* (Vienna) 135 (1896), 124.

10   Honorius, col. 861. The Latin text, in fact, reads: "Hodiernum sermonem, fratres karissimi, debetis omnes intentissima aure percipere, quia hodie dicturus sum vobis quomodo divites vel pauperes *Domini*, vel servi, viri vel mulieres, ad gaudia aeterna possitis pertingere" (my emphasis). I have emended both punctuation and orthography so that "Domini" ("of the Lord") becomes "domini" ("lords") and is contrasted with "servi," which seems better to fit the syntax and sense of the sentence.

11   *Speculum*, 140, 7-19. "Now we are speaking to you, judges, whom God has appointed to be leaders of His people. Do not disdain to hear the words of the eternal judge. [Listen and] you will obtain here and now wealth and honor, and there [in Heaven], you will receive the eternal reward. You should never judge unjustly for the sake of a bribe. Judge the poor man well so that you will not lose eternal grace. For Holy Scripture says: Judgment without mercy for him who does not show mercy. [In German] 'He shall be condemned without judg-ment who here judges without mercy.' You should avoid all evil as much as you can and you should pursue goodness. If you toil for that, then you will be crowned by the highest judge. But if you oppress the poor, then you will be cast by the fearful judgment of almighty God into terrible Hell."

12   Honorius, col. 383.

13   *Speculum*, 140, 32-141, 7. "Now we are admonishing you, rich men, to whom God has granted worldly wealth as a comfort for the poor. Remember that you came naked into this world and that you shall leave naked. You must leave your wealth here. Therefore distribute it widely to the poor so that you may find it there [in Heaven]. You should feed the hungry, give drink to the thirsty, give shelter to the stranger, clothe the naked, take care of the sick, and comfort the sorrowful. If you do these things, then your wealth will increase in this world and you shall also find it there where no one can take it from you."

14   Honorius, col. 864.

15   *Speculum*, 141, 7-8. "The poor should patiently bear their poverty: for that they shall receive the eternal reward. They should pay back with prayers the alms that people gave to them.

16   Duby, *The Three Orders*, 251.

17   *PL* 136.

18   Schröbler, "Vom Rechte," 233.

19   Schröbler, however, claims, as Duby does of Honorius, that Rather's social distinctions are primarily traceable to his socially highly-differentiated environment in upper Italy in the tenth century.

20   James J. Murphy, *Rhetoric in the Middle Ages: A History of Rhetorical Theory from St. Augustine to the Renaissance* (Berkeley: University of California Press, 1974), 292.

21   Murphy, 294.

22   See Murphy, 294-95.

23   This point is the main thrust of the discussion of the rise of the concept of the three orders in Duby's book by the same name as well as of Bumke's treatment of the concept of knighthood in his *Studien zum Ritterbegriff*.

24   *Regula pastoralis*, Part Three, chap. II ("Quomodo admonendi sint inopes et divites") and chap. V ("Quomodo admonendi servi et domini"), *PL* 77, cols. 52-53 and 56.

25   Ibid., col. 56.

26   "Vom Rechte," ll. 323-326, 332-334. "That master is good who himself does good works and commands his servant to follow him: he desires to protect the ignorant . . . . Let [the master] remember in time that he should by right lead and protect everyone."

27   Rupp, *Deutsche religiöse Dichtungen*, 276 and 278.

28   See also Isaiah 58, 7-8, in which a partial list of the works of mercy is associated with the practice of justice.

29   Michel Mollat, *The Poor in the Middle Ages*, trs. Arthur Goldhammer (New Haven: Yale, 1986), 110.

30   *Regula benedictina*, 4, 14-19. See also Mollat, 45-49.

31   Mollat, 39.

32   See Bumke, *Studien zum Ritterbegriff*, 130-148.

33   See above, Chapter I, and *Tnugdalus*, ll. 1,750 ff. Alber's *Tnugdalus* is particularly significant because of its transitional character. It repeats many of the themes of the Early Middle High German poems as well as anticipating those of the high courtly period. Except for Nigel Palmer's fine study which, however, mostly concentrates on the later transmission of the story of Tnugdalus, Alber's poem has been generally neglected by literary historians.

34   "Vom Rechte," ll. 303-320. "No one is God's child except those who do justice. The others are divided from them. It surprises me greatly that that dog, the miserly man, cannot remember that avarice is scandalous, contemptuous, and sinful. When the avaricious man dies and has nothing left, then he regrets that he possessed riches. He now has neither reward nor fame. Seeing him standing there in Hell, it surprises me why the Son of God should ever have wanted him

for Christianity. Had He made him a heathen, he would have as likely been saved; for extreme avarice is the source of all evil."

Lester K. Little has argued that the replacement of pride by avarice in the hierarchy of vices is an indication of the changes effected by the transformation of a pre-commercial society into one based on exchange ("Pride Goes before Avarice: Social Change and the Vices in Latin Christianity," *American Historical Review* 76 [1971], 16-49). "Vom Rechte," however, provides a counter-example of Little's thesis, for while its author castigates avarice, he never mentions merchants, money, or commercial transactions and he describes the rural sphere alone.

35   See, for example, F. Curschmann, "Hungersnöte im Mittelalter," *Leipziger Studien* 6 (1900), 1-218.

36   See, however, Mollat, 26-30, where the particular difficulties experienced by the early medieval poor, sick, widows, and orphans are described. The traditional nature of these categories should not blind us to the real problems experienced by these people.

37   Mollat, 26.

38   Rupp, despite his claim that the Early Middle High German poems are basically devoid of historical content, remarked on this fact on numerous occasions. See, e.g., *Deutsche religiöse Dichtungen*, 190-91.

39   Duby, "The Evolution of Judicial Institutions."

40   Heinrich Fichtenau, *The Carolingian Empire: The Age of Charlemagne*, trs. Peter Munz (New York: Harper and Row, 1964), 112.

41   Fichtenau, 112.

42   Cf. also the injunctions contained in the capitularies, such as "Duces, comites et iudices iustitiam faciant in populos, misericordiam in pauperes, pro pecunia non mutet aequitates, per odia non damnent innocentes." (*MGH*, Cap. I, no. 121).

43   "Muspilli," 66-68 (Braune and Ebbinghaus, *Althochdeutsches Lesebuch*). "The man without means does not know what judgment he will receive, for standing nearby in hiding is the devil who hinders [*marrit*] with rewards [the practice] of justice."

The Old High German verb *marren* is perhaps one source of the Latin verb "marrire," meaning "to impede" or "to disturb," that is frequently used in the Carolingian capitularies to describe the perversion of judicial justice. Cf., for example, Chapter 1 of the "Capitulare missorum generale:" "Et nemo per ingenium vel austutiam prescriptam legem, ut multi solent, vel sibi suam iustitiam marrire audeat vel prevaleat, neque ecclesiis Dei neque pauperibus nec viduis nec pupillis nullique homini christiano" (*MGH*, Cap. I, no. 33). This passage also offers an interesting glimpse of how judges attempted to have one justice for themselves and render another to the poor, precisely the abuse that Noker and the "Vom Rechte" poet attacked by using the formula *reht han und geben*.

44   See, for instance, the examples cited above in Chapter III from "Die Millstätter Sündenklage" and Frau Ava's "Das jüngste Gericht." *Miete* was also used in the description of simony. Cf., for example, Heinrich von Melk's "Das Priesterleben"

where the poet writes of the priests "die hiut chouffent unt verchoufent/ unt durch miete toufent/ unt den scaz nement von der erde" (ll. 359-361, *RD* III).

45   Phillipe de Beaumanoir, *Coutumes de Beauvaisis*, secs. 1043 and 295, quoted in Berman, *Law and Revolution* (Cambridge: Harvard, 1983), 325.

46   See the classic account by Georg Meyer, "Die Gerichtsbarkeit über Freie und Hintersassen nach ältestem deutschen Recht." Cf. also the more recent critical discussion of the phenomenon by Jürgen Weitzel, *Dinggenossenschaft und Recht*, vol. I, 716-723.

47   Cf. also K. S. Bader's remarks on the development of the lord's jurisdiction over the *villae*: "Das Herrschaftsrecht im Dorf erscheint als Zwing und Bann in den Quellen; die Herrschaft über das Dorf findet ihre maßgebliche Begründung in gerichtlichen Befugnissen. Zwing und Bann, das Recht, im Dorfe zu gebieten oder zu verbieten, sind regelmäßig mit niedergerichtlichen Gerechtsamen verbunden. Alles, was auf dem Gebiete eines Dorfes lebt, unterliegt diesem niederen Gerichtsbann ohne Rücksicht auf die grundherrliche und hofrechtliche Lage des Einzelnen" (Bader, "Staat und Bauerntum im deutschen Mittelalter," in Theodor Meyer, ed. *Adel und Bauern im deutschen Staat des Mittelalters* [Leipzig: Koehler und Amelang, 1943], 115).

48   Vollrath, "Herrschaft und Genossenschaft im Kontext frühmittelalterlicher Rechtsbeziehungen."   See also Hermann Krause, "Königtum und Rechtsordnung in der Zeit der sächsischen und salischen Herrscher."

49   Julius Goebel, *Felony and Misdemeanor*, 95.

50   Goebel, 198-99.

51   Hans Hirsch's book *Die hohe Gerichtsbarkeit im deutschen Mittelalter* is still the best discussion of this profound change in the nature of criminal justice and punishment.

52   Already in the capitularies there were clear warnings against this practice, for example: "Ut iudices secundum scriptam legem iuste iudicent, non secundum arbitrium suum" ("Capitulare missorum generale," chap. 26).

53   Der Stricker, "Der Richter und der Teufel," ll. 33-35 (*Verserzählungen*, II, ed. Hans Fischer, rev. ed. Johannes Janota, [Tübingen: Niemeyer, 1977]. "My power [or rights] is [are] so great here that whatever pain I choose to inflict upon you, no one can prevent me."

54   Ibid., l. 39.

55   "Der Richter und der Teufel," ll. 181-189. "'What were you thinking, judge, when you were so rich and I was so poor, that you did not trust yourself to survive, but that you had to take from me my only calf, without my being guilty and without God's approval. Why did I have to lose everything from which I, poor one, should have lived?'"

56   Honorius, cols. 863-864.

57   See the informative discussion in Friedrich Ohly's *Sage und Legende in der Kaiserchronik* (1940; rpt. Darmstadt: Wissenschaftliche Buchgesellschaft, 1968), 119-128.

58   *Die Kaiserchronik*, ed. Edward Schröder, *MGH*, DChr I, i, ll. 5,845–5,848. "He judged very justly both lord and servant. From the poor people he demanded no bribes."

59   *Die Kaiserchronik*, ll. 5,963–5,968. "He spoke: 'Lord, he injured me; I have good witness of that. I remind you, lord, he was my legal debtor, for he slew my brother. With your permission, there should justly [or by right] be no trial.'"

60   *Die Kaiserchronik*, ll. 5,973–5,975. "'For the Romans have recognized me a judge; you have circumvented my court.'"

61   In medieval law "manslaughter" was defined not by intention, but by being committed in public. It was considered a lesser crime than "murder," which referred to a secret and unfaithful killing. Manslaughter was punished by the respectable punishment of decapitation, while murders were ignominiously killed by the wheel or hanged.

62   *Kaiserchronik*, ll. 5,976–5,979. "Following the just judgement of all the princes, Trajan immediately commanded the accused man's head to be cut off and brought to the lady."

63   *Kaiserchronik*, ll. 6,058–6,060. "'I shall tell you, Gregory, what you can do; for you are a true servant [slave] of God. Receive now from God the right either to let the pagan deservedly suffer for his life, or you can forever take his soul into your care. But you will then receive seven plagues from which you will never obtain relief until you die.'"

64   *Kaiserchronik*, ll. 6083–6090. "Now all the kings of this world should heed this example of how the noble Emperor Trajan won God's mercy because he conducted his court justly while he lived in this world. They, too, can be certain of mercy if they remember my Lord God at their courts."

65   Joachim Bumke, in his analysis of the late twelfth-century author Wernher von Elmendorf, suggests that Wernher's poem, in its divergence from its Latin source and in the similarity of its treatment of certain ethical categories (including *reht*) to that of the thirteenth-century *Der wälsche Gast* by Thomasin von Zirclaere, is an indication of the continuity of an orally-propagated code of ethics for lords. Bumke writes: "Wir kennen die Vulgärtradition der Fürstenlehre nicht: daß es sie aber gab, läßt die übereinstimmende Konzentration bei Thomasin und Wernher, die mit den gelehrten Tugendkatalogen nicht viel gemein hat, deutlich erkennen" (Bumke, "Die Auflösung des Tugendsystems bei Wernher von Elmendorf," *ZfdA* 88 [1957], 50). Might not the Early Middle High German poems have been an important constituent factor in the development of this "Vulgärtradition"?

66   Hugo Kuhn, "Minne oder reht."

67   See Gentry, "*Vruot . . . verdamnot?* Memento mori, vv. 61-62," *ZfdA* 108 (1979), 299–306. Kuhn suggested a radical solution to the problem by entirely eliminating the questionable lines 61-62 as an interpolation. Gentry convincingly argues that Kuhn's emendation is unnecessary, and he suggests an emendation that draws on some supposedly spurious lines at the end of the poem. The problems posed by lines 61-62, however, do not materially affect the following discussion.

68 "Memento mori," strophes 7-9 (*RD* I). "God created you all, you all come from one man. He commanded you all to live this life in love, that you might be as one man, but you have transgressed that command. Even had you done no other wrong, you would suffer for this transgression. Although you come from one man, yet you are different through many ruses and through much evil. The one man is wise and good . . . for that he is damned. The poor man has need of *reht*, but unfortunately he cannot have it unless he pays dearly for it. For that they must all go to Hell. If only they thought how it will all end! Thus he must leave and is dead forever, for he sold *reht* and therefore must go to Hell where he shall always remain: he has betrayed God himself. If you would all live *einis rehtin* then you would all be invited to eternal joy where you would stay forever. But the one you have for yourself and the other you give to the poor. Therefore you can never go to Heaven but must always remain outside of it."

69 Dietrich Schäfer, "Consilio vel judicio = mit minne oder mit rechte," *SB der königlich-preußischen Akademie der Wissenschaften* (1913), 719-733. See also Homeyer, "Über die Formel 'der Minne und des Rechts eines Andern mächtig sein,'" *Abhandlungen der königlichen Akademie der Wissenschaften zu Berlin, Philosophische und Historische Abhandlungen* (1866), 29-55.

70 Hirsch, *Die hohe Gerichtsbarkeit im deutschen Mittelalter*, 77 ff. and 150-157.

71 Kuhn, 111.

72 Rudolph Schützeichel, *Das alemannische Memento mori. Das Gedicht und der geistig-historische Hintergrund* (Tübingen: Niemeyer, 1962).

73 Schützeichel, 76-86.

74 Schützeichel also indirectly concedes this by the tentative form of his claim: "*iustitiam vendere* (was im Mittelhochdeutschen *reht koufen*, bzw. *verkoufen* heißen würde)" (Schützeichel, 81).

75 Isidore, *Sententiae*, II, chap. lvi (*PL* 83).

76 See Gentry, "Noker's *Memento mori* and the Desire for Peace," 33.

77 Schützeichel, 84.

78 See Schützeichel's summary of his book in "Justitiam vendere," *Literaturwissenschaftliches Jahrbuch NF* (1964), 5.

79 Schützeichel, 84.

80 As mentioned above in Chapter III, Schützeichel denies that the two instances of "daz" in lines 79-80 of the "Memento mori" refer to *reht*. Instead, he seems to argue that "daz" indicates material possessions: "So umständlich oder schwerfällig die Stelle [Strophe 11] auch . . . konstruiert sein mag, so erinnert sie ganz deutlich an Ananias und Saphira aus der Apostelgeschichte [Acts 5, 1 ff.], die zwar Besitz verkaufen, den Erlös auch zu einem Teil 'zu Füßen der Apostel legten,' den anderen Teil aber zurückbehielten und von Gott auf das Härteste — nämlich mit dem Tode — bestraft wurden. Die Handlungsweise des Ananias und der Saphira steht nahe bei der Simonie, wie man sie auffaßte, nämlich als eine zu starke Einwirkung irdischer Dinge auf die geistlich-religiöse Sphäre. So wird aber auch diese schwierige und bisher nicht befriedigend gedeutete Stelle der 11. Strophe mit einem Schlage durchsichtig und verständlich . . ." (Schützeichel, 86).

The comparison of lines 78-80 of the "Memento mori" with the similar lines 46-47 of "Vom Rechte," however, has shown that the two poems are in fact using a formula, *reht han und geben*, which is perhaps related to the Latin formula *iustitiam facere et recipere*, and which refers to the practice of impartial justice. Schützeichel's belief that Noker is alluding to the story of Ananias and Saphira, who are never mentioned by the Early Middle High German poets, is unlikely. If there is a biblical allusion in strophe 11 of the "Memento mori," then it is more probably to the popular parable of Dives and Lazarus. After criticizing the rich lords for having one justice for themselves and giving another to the poor, Noker writes: "von diu so nemugen ir drin gen, ir mouzint iemer dervor sten" (ll. 81-82). He seems here to be reminding his audience of the fate of Dives who because he failed to do justice to Lazarus must stand in pain outside the gates of Heaven.

81   Schützeichel, 68-72.

82   Schützeichel, 71.

83   Schützeichel, 70-71.

84   Schützeichel, 72-73.

85   Schützeichel, 73.

86   Hermann Krause, "*Consilium vel iudicio*; Bedeutungsbreite und Sinngehalt einer mittelalterlichen Formel" in *Speculum historiale*, ed. by Clemens Bauer et al. (Freiburg/Munich: Karl Alber, 1965), 416-438.

87   Krause, 422 ff. Compare the description of Trajan's trial of the widow's son's murderer in the *Kaiserchronik*.

88   Krause, 428-430.

89   All examples from Schäfer, 723, 725, 727, 729, 732. It is interesting to note that the judicial content of *iustitia* was so strong that it could be freely exchanged with *iudicium*.

90   Schützeichel, 72.

91   See Stephan D. White, "'*Pactum . . . Legem Vincit et Amor Iudicium*:' The Settlement of Disputes by Compromise in Eleventh-Century France," *American Journal of Legal History* 22 (1978), 281-308.

92   All examples from *Leges Henrici Primi*, ed. and trans. by L. J. Downer (Clarendon: Oxford), 73a; 54, 2; 45, 1a; 49a; the translation of 49a appears on page 165.

93   Quoted in Doris M. Stenton, *English Justice between the Norman Conquest and the Great Charter 1066-1215* (Philadelphia: American Philosophical Society, 1964), 7. See also Harold J. Berman, *Law and Revolution*, 74 ff.

94   *MGH*, DHIV, 483.

95   See Karl S. Bader, "Arbiter arbitrator vel amicabilis compositor. Zur Verbreitung einer kanonistischen Formel in Gebieten nördlich der Alpen," *ZRG (KA)* 46 (1960), 239-276.

96   See White, "The Settlement of Disputes by Compromise in Eleventh-Century France."

97   Such non-judicial settlements did not necessarily lead to an informal court of arbitration under the aegis of a third party. Rather, as White's examples from western France show, no arbitrator need have been invoked if the parties could

come to a mutually satisfactory agreement. For this reason, the legally established judicial authorities on occasion discouraged and even outlawed such agreements: they stood to lose financially from them.

98 See Hermann Krause, "Minne oder recht," *HRG*.

99 Bader, 271 and 271, ft. 105.

100 Hans Hattenhauer, "'Minne und recht' als Ordnungsprizipien des mittelalter-lichen Rechts," *ZRG* (*GA*) 80 (1963), 333, ft. 34.

101 *Wiener Genesis*, l. 2,462. "Joseph commanded and begged him in love."

102 *Millstätter Genesis*, 84, 2 (my emphases). Joseph "wanted by justice or by love to make his innocence known."

103 *Millstätter Exodus*, 135, 29-31. "He should do that by justice, and if he would not do it in love, he would be forced by God on high."

104 *König Rother*, l. 763. "With threats and by love."

105 Heinrich von Melk, "Von dem gemeinen Leben," ll. 400-401 (*RD* III). "There is no certainty there, neither of justice nor of mercy."

106 Gentry, "Noker's *Memento mori* and the Desire for Peace," 44-53.

107 See Hirsch, 150-157.

108 R. W. Southern, *The Making of the Middle Ages* (Tiptree, Essex: Arrow Books, 1959), 152.

Bibliography

1. Primary Vernacular Sources

Das Anegenge. Ed. Dietrich Neuschäfer. Munich: Fink, 1966.

Das Annolied. Ed. and trs. Eberhard Nellmann. 2nd ed. Stuttgart: Reclam, 1979.

Braune, Wilhelm. Ed. *Althochdeutsches Lesebuch.* 16th ed. Ernst A. Ebbinghaus. Ed. Tübingen: Niemeyer, 1979.

Eike von Repgow. *Sachsenspiegel.* Ed. Karl August Eckhardt. MGH, Fontes Legum, I, I.

"Exodus." Ed. Hoffmann von Fallersleben. *Fundgruben für Geschichte deutscher Sprache und Literatur.* II Theil. Breslau, 1837.

Die altdeutsche Exodus. Ed. Edgar Papp. Munich: Fink, 1968.

Altdeutsche Genesis. Ed. Viktor Dollmayr. Halle: Niemeyer, 1932.

Hartmann von Aue. *Iwein.* Ed. Ludwig Wolf. Berlin: De Gruyter, 1968.

Heinrich von Melk. Ed. Richard Heinzel. Berlin, 1867.

Der sogenannte Heinrich von Melk. Ed. Richard Kienast. Heidelberg: Winter, 1946.

"Das Gedicht von Joseph nach der Wiener und der Vorauer Handschrift." Ed. P. Piper. *ZfdP* 20 (1888). 257-289; 430-474.

Die Kaiserchronik. Ed. Edward Schröder. *MGH. DChr* I, i.

König Rother. Eds. Theodor Frings and Joachim Kuhnt. Bonn/Leipzig: Kurt Schroeder, 1922.

Lucidarius. Ed. Felix Heidlauf. DTM 28. Berlin, 1915.

Maurer, Friedrich. Ed. *Die religiösen Dichtungen des 11. und 12. Jahrhunderts.* 3 Vols. Tübingen: Niemeyer, 1964-1970.

Millstäter Genesis und Exodus. Ed. Diemer, Joseph. 2 Vols. Vienna, 1849.

Siegfried Beyschlag. Ed. *Die Lieder Neidharts.* Darmstadt: Wissenschaftliche Buchgesellschaft, 1975.

Otfrids Evangelienbuch. Ed. Oskar Erdmann. 6th ed. Ludwig Wolff. Tübingen: Niemeyer, 1973.

"Rígsthula." Ed. Hans Kuhn. *Edda.* Vol. I Heidelberg: Winter, 1962. 280-287.

Schröder, Werner. Ed. *Kleinere deutsche Gedichte des 11. und 12. Jahrhunderts.* 2 Vols.
Tübingen: Niemeyer, 1972.

Speculum ecclesiae. Eine frühmittelhochdeutsche Predigtsammlung. Ed. Gert Mellbourn. Lund:
Gleerup, 1944.

Der Stricker. "Der Richter und der Teufel." *Verserzählungen.* Vol. II. Ed. Hans Fischer.
Rev. Ed. Johannes Janota. Tübingen: Niemeyer, 1977.

Suchier, Hermann. Ed. *Reimpredigt.* Halle, 1879.

Visio Tnugdali. Lateinisch und altdeutsch. Ed. Albrecht Wagner. Erlangen, 1882.

Vorauer Bücher Mosis. Ed. Joseph Diemer. *Deutsche Gedichte des 11. und 12. Jahrhunderts.*
Vienna, 1849.

"Vorauer Joseph." Joseph Diemer. Ed. *SB der Wiener Akademie der Wissenschaften.* 47
(1864). 636-687.

Wernher der Gartenaere. *Helmbrecht.* Ed. Friedrich Panzer. 9th Ed. Kurt Ruh.
Tübingen: Niemeyer, 1974.

Die frühmittelhochdeutsche Wiener Genesis. Ed. Kathryn Smits. Berlin: Erich Schmidt,
1972.

2. Primary Latin Sources

Alcuin. "De virtutibus et vitiis liber." *PL* 101. 613-638

Anonymous. "De duodecim abusionibus saeculi." *PL* 4. 947-960.

Aristotle. *"Art" of Rhetoric.* Trs. John Henry Freese. *LCL.* Cambridge, MA: Harvard,
1926.

——————. *Athenian Constitution. Eudemian Ethics. On Virtues and Vices.* Trs. H.
Rackham. *LCL.* Cambridge, MA: Harvard, 1952.

——————. *Nichomachean Ethics.* Trs. H. Rackham. *LCL.* Cambridge, MA: Harvard,
1934.

Augustine. *De civitate Dei.* Eds. B. Dombart and A. Kalb. CC XLVIII. Turnhout:
Brepols, 1955.

——————. *Confessionum libri XIII.* Ed. Lucas Verheijen. CC XXVII. Turnhout:
Brepols, 1981.

——————. *De diversis questionibus LXXXIII.* Ed. Almut Mutzenbecher. CC XLIVA.
Turnhout: Brepols, 1975.

——————. *De doctrina christiana.* Ed. Joseph Martin CC XXXII. Turnhout: Brepols,
1962.

——————. *De ordine.* Ed. W. M. Green. CC XXIX. Turnhout: Brepols, 1970.

Avitus. *De spiritalis historiae gestis.* Ed. R. Peiper MGH AA 6.2.

Bede. *Comentarii. in Pentateuchum. PL* 91. 189-394.

Cicero. *De inventione.* Trs. H. M. Hubell. *LCL.* Cambridge, Ma.: Harvard, 1949.

——————. *De re publica.* Trs. Clinton Walker Keyes. *LCL.* Cambridge, Ma.: Harvard,
1928.

Eichmann, Eduard. Ed. *Kirche und Staat.* Vol. I 1925; rpt.: Munich: Schöningh, 1968.

The Institutes of Gaius. Trs. by W. M. Gordon and O. F. Robinson with the Latin text of Seckel and Kuebler. Ithaca: Cornell, 1988.

Gregory the Great. *Moralia in Job*. Ed. M. Adriaen. CC CXLIII. Turnhout: Brepols, 1979.

——————. *Regula pastoralis. PL* 77. 9-128.

Leges Henrici Primi. Ed. and trans. by L. J. Downer. Clarendon: Oxford.

Hincmar. "De regis persona et regio ministerio." *PL* 125. 833-856.

Honorius Augustodunensis. *Imago mundi. PL* 172. 115-188.

——————. *Summa gloria*. MGH. Libelli de lite. III.

——————. *Speculum ecclesia. PL* 172. 807-1108.

Isidore of Seville. *Questiones in vetus testamentum. PL* 83. 207-424.

Isidore. *Sententiae. PL* 83. 537-738.

Justinian's Institutes. Trs. Peter Birks and Grant McLeod with the Latin text of Paul Krueger. New York: Cornell, 1987.

Plato. *The Republic*. Vol. I. Trs. Paul Shorey. *LCL*. Cambridge, MA: Harvard, 1930.

Rabanus Maurus. *Commentarii in Genesim. PL* 107. 439-670.

Wilhelm A Eckhardt. Ed. "Die Capitularia missorum specialia von 802," DA 12 (1956). 498-516.

3. **Secondary Literature**

Amos, Thomas L. "Monks and Pastoral Care in the Early Middle Ages." Thomas F. X. Noble and John J. Contrenti. Eds. *Religion, Culture, and Society in the Early Middle Ages*. Kalamazoo, MI: Medieval Institute Pubs., 1985. 165-180.

Arnold, Benjamin. *German Knighthood. 1050-1300*. Oxford: Clarendon, 1985.

Bader, Karl S. "Staat und Bauerntum im deutschen Mittelalter." Theodor Meyer. Ed. *Adel und Bauern im deutschen Staat des Mittelalters*. Leipzig: Koehler und Amelang, 1943. 109-129.

——————. "Arbiter arbitrator vel amicabilis compositor. Zur Verbreitung einer kanonistischen Formel in Gebieten nördlich der Alpen." *ZRG (KA)* 46 (1960). 239-276.

Barraclough, Geoffrey. *The Origins of Modern Germany*. New York: Norton, 1984.

Batany, J. "Le vocabulaire des catégories sociales chez quelques moralistes français ver 1200." Ed. D. Roche and C. E. Labrousse. *Ordres et classes*. Paris: Mouton. 1968. 59-92.

Berman, Harold J. *Law and Revolution: The Formation of the Western Legal Tradition*. Cambridge: Harvard, 1983.

Bosl, Karl. "Freiheit und Unfreiheit." *Vierteljahrszeitschrift für Sozial- und Wirtschaftsgeschichte* 44 (1957). 193-219.

——————. "Herrscher und Beherrschte im deutschen Reich des 10. - 12. Jahrhunderts." *SB BAW*, Phil-Hist., Heft 2 (1963). 3-29.

—————. "Potens und pauper. Begriffsgeschichtliche Studien zur gesellschaftlichen Differenzierungen im frühen Mittelalter und zum 'Pauperismus' des Hochmittelalters." (1963) Rpt. in: Bosl. *Frühformen der Gesellschaft im mittelalterlichen Europa*. Munich: Oldenburg, 1964. 106-134.

—————. "Gesellschaftsprozeß und Gesellschaftsstrukturen im Mittelalter." Bosl and Eberhard Weis. *Die Gesellschaft in Deutschland von der fränkischen Zeit bis 1848*. Munich: Martin Lurz, 1976. 11-130.

Brown, Peter. "St. Augustine." Ed. Beryl Smalley. *Trends in Medieval Political Thought*. Oxford: Blackwell, 1965. 1-21.

—————. *Augustine of Hippo*. Berkeley: University of California, 1969.

—————. "Society and the Supernatural: A Medieval Change." *Daedalus* 104 (1975). 133-151.

Brunner, Heinrich. *Deutsche Rechtsgeschichte*. (1906) Rpt.: Berlin: Duncker und Humbolt, 1961.

Brunner, Otto. *Land and Lordship: Structures of Governance in Mediaeval Austria*. Trs. Howard Kaminsky and James van Horn Melton. Philadelphia: University of Pennsylvania, 1992.

Bumke, Joachim. "Die Auflösung des Tugendsystems bei Wernher von Elmendorf." *ZfdA* 88 (1957). 39-54.

—————. *Studien zum Ritterbegriff im 12. und 13. Jahrhundert*. Heidelberg: Winter, 1964.

Carlyle, R. W. and A. J. Carlyle. *A History of Mediaeval Political Theory in the West*. New York: Barnes and Noble, 1953.

Chenu, M.-D. "The Platonisms of the Twelfth Century." *Nature, Man, and Society in the Twelfth Century*. Trs. Jerome Taylor and Lester K. Little. Chicago: University of Chicago, 1968. 49-98.

Christes, Johannes. "Christliche und heidnisch-römische Gerechtigkeit in Augustins Werk 'De civitate Dei.'" *Rheinisches Museum für Philologie* 123 (1980). 163-177.

Clark, Mary T. "Augustine on Justice." *Revue des Études Augustiniennes* 9 (1963). 87-94.

Congar, Yves. "Les laïcs et l'ecclésiologie des 'ordines' chez les théologiens du XIᵉ et XIIᵉ siècles." Ed. Giuseppe Lazzati and Cosimo D. Fonseca. *I laici nella "societas christiana" dei secoli XI et XII*. Milan: Sociatà editrice vita e pesiero, 1968. 83-117.

Cotta, Sergio. "Droit et justice dans le De libero arbitrio de St. Augustin." *Archiv für Rechts- und Sozialphilosophie* 47 (1961). 159-172.

Cowdrey, H. E. J. *The Cluniacs and Gregorian Reform*. Oxford: Oxford University Press, 1970.

Curschmann, F. "Hungersnöte im Mittelalter." *Leipziger Studien* 6 (1900). 1-218.

Davidson, Robert. *Genesis 12-50. The Cambridge Bible Commentary on the New English Bible*. Cambridge: Cambridge University Press, 1979.

Dilcher, Gerhard. Review of Gerhard Köbler. *Das Recht im frühen Mittelalter*. *ZRG* (*GA*) 90 (1973). 267-273.

Duby, Georges. *Rural Economy and Country Life in the Medieval West*. Trs. Cynthia Postan. Columbia, SC: University of South Carolina, 1968.

—————. "The Evolution of Judicial Institutions." *The Chivalrous Society*. Trs. Cynthia Postan. Berkeley: University of California, 1977. 15-58.

——————. "The Origin of a System of Social Classification." *The Chivalrous Society*. 53-57.

——————. *The Three Orders*. Tr. Arthur Goldhammer. Chicago: University of Chicago, 1980.

Dumézil, Georges. "La Rígsthula et la structure sociale indo-européenne." *Revue de l'histoire des religions* 154 (1958). 1-9.

Eckhardt, Wilhelm A. "Die Capitularia missorum specialia von 802." *DA* 12 (1956). 498-516.

Eggers, Hans. *Deutsche Sprachgeschichte*. Vol. I. *Das Althochdeutsche und das Mittelhochdeutsche*. Reinbeck: Rowohlt, 1986.

Ehrismann, Gustav. "Die Wörter für 'Herr' im Althochdeutschen." *Zeitschrift für deutsche Wortforschung* 7 (1905-06). 173-202.

——————. *Geschichte der deutschen Literatur*. II/i: *Frühmittelhochdeutsche Literatur*. Munich: Beck, 1922.

Erb, Ewald. *Geschichte der deutschen Literatur von den Anfängen bis 1160*. I. Part II of *Geschichte der deutschen Literatur von den Anfängen bis zur Geegenwart*. Ed. Klaus Gysi, et al. Berlin (East): Volk und Wissen, 1964.

Ewig, Eugen. "Zum christlichen Königsgedanken im Frühmittelalter." *Spätantikes und fränkisches Gallien*. Ed. Hartmut Atsma. Munich: Artemis, 1976. 3-71.

Fehr, Hans. *Das Recht in der Dichtung*. Bern: Francke, 1931.

Fichtenau, Heinrich. *The Carolingian Empire: The Age of Charlemagne*. Trs. Peter Munz. New York: Harper and Row, 1964.

Fleckenstein, Josef. "Zur Frage der Abgrenzung von Bauer und Ritter." Ed. Reinhard Wenskus et al. *Wort und Begriff "Bauer"*. Göttingen: Vandenhoeck und Ruprecht, 1975. 246-253.

Franz, Günther. *Geschichte des deutschen Bauernstandes vom frühen Mittelalter bis zum 19. Jahrhundert*. Stuttgart: Ulmer, 1970.

Freytag, Hartmut. *Kommentar zur frühmittelhochdeutschen Summa Theologiae*. Munich: Fink, 1970.

——————. Review of Gisela Vollmann-Profe. *Von den Anfängen bis zum hohen Mittelalter. Wiederbeginn volkssprachlicher Schriftlichkeit im hohen Mittelalter (1050/60-1160/70)*. *ZfdA* 117 (1989). 132-140.

Gagnér, Sten. "Sachsenspiegel und Speculum ecclesiae." *NM* 3 (1948). 82-103.

Ganshof, F. L. *Feudalism*. Trs. Philip Grierson. New York: Harper and Row, 1961.

Gentry, Francis G. *Triuwe and vriunt in the Nibelungenlied*. Amsterdamer Publikationen zur Sprache und Literatur 19. Amsterdam: Rodopi, 1975.

——————. "*Vruot . . . verdamnot*? Memento mori, vv. 61-62." *ZfdA* 108 (1979). 299-306.

——————. "Noker's *Memento mori* and the Desire for Peace." *ABäG* 16 (1981). 25-62.

——————. *Bibliographie zur frühmittelhochdeutschen geistlichen Dichtung*. Berlin: Erich Schmidt, 1992.

Gernentz, Hans Joachim. "Soziale Anschauungen und Forderungen einiger frühmittelhochdeutscher geistlicher Dichter." *Weimarer Beiträge* 3 (1957). 402-428.

Gilsenan, Michael. *Recognizing Islam: Religion and Society in the Modern Arab World*. New York: Pantheon, 1982.

Goebel, Julius. *Felony and Misdemeanor.* 1937; rpt: Philadelphia: University of
Pennsylvania, 1976.

Graus, Frantisek. "Über die sogenannte germanische Treue." *Historica* I (1959). 71-121.

——————. "Die Gewalt bei den Anfängen des Feudalismus und die
'Gefangenbefreiung' der merowingischen Hagiographie." *Jahrbuch für
Wirtschaftsgeschichte* I (1961).

——————. "Herrschaft und Treue. Betrachtungen zur Lehre von der germanischen
Kontinuität." *Historica* 12 (1966). 5-44.

——————. "Verfassungsgeschichte des Mittelalters." *HZ* 243 (1986). 529-589.

Grubmüller, Klaus. "Nôes Fluch. Zur Begründung von Herrschaft und Unfreiheit in
mittelalterlicher Literatur." Ed. Dietrich Huschenbett et al. *Medium Aevum deutsch.
Kurt Ruh Festschrift.* Tübingen: Niemeyer, 1979. 99-119.

Grundmann, Herbert. "Freiheit als religiöses, politisches und persönliches Postulat im
Mittelalter." *HZ* 183 (1957). 23-53.

Hallinger, Kassius. *Gorze-Kluny.* 2 vols. Rome: Herder, 1950/51.

Hattenhauer, Hans. "'Minne und recht' als Ordnungsprizipien des mittelalterlichen
Rechts." *ZRG GA* 80 (1963). 325-344.

Hennig, Beate. *Kleines Mittelhochdeutsches Wörterbuch.* 3rd. ed. Tübingen: Niemeyer,
1998.

Hill, Thomas. "Rígsthula: Some Medieval Christian Analogues." *Speculum* 61/1 (1986).
79-89.

Hirsch, Hans. *Die hohe Gerichtsbarkeit im deutschen Mittelalter.* 1922; rpt.: Darmstadt:
Wissenschaftliche Buchgesellschaft, 1958.

Hoffmann, Werner. *Altdeutsche Metrik.* Stuttgart: Metzler, 1967.

Homeyer. "Über die Formel 'der Minne und des Rechts eines Andern mächtig sein.'"
*Abhandlungen der königlichen Akademie der Wissenschaften zu Berlin, Philosophische und
Historische Abhandlungen* (1866). 29-55.

Jacobs, Herman. *Die Hirsauer.* Cologne: Böhlau, 1961.

Kaiser, Gert. "Das Memento mori. Ein Beitrag zum sozialgeschichtlichen Verständnis der
Gleichheitsforderung im frühen Mittelalter." *Euphorion* 68 (1974). 337-370.

Kartschoke, Dieter. *Geschichte der deutschen Literatur im frühen Mittelalter.* Munich: DTV,
1990.

Kauffmann, Friedrich. "Aus dem Wortschatz der Rechtssprache." *ZfdP* 46 (1918). 153-
209.

Kelsen, Hans. "Aristotle's Doctrine of Justice." Ed. James J. Walsh and Henry Shapiro.
Aristotle's 'Ethics:' Issues and Interpretations. Belmont, Ca.: Wadsworth, 1967.

Kern, Fritz. *Kingship and Law in the Middle Ages.* Trs. S. B. Chimes. New York: Harper
and Row, 1970.

Klibansky, Erich. "Gerichtsszene und Prozeßform in den erzählenden deutschen
Dichtungen des 12. -14. Jahrhunderts." *Germanische Studien* 40 (1925).

Köbler, Gerhard. "Richten — Richter — Gericht." *ZRG (GA)* 87 (1970). 56-113.

——————. *Das Recht im frühen Mittelalter.* Cologne: Böhlau, 1971.

Kolb, Herbert. "Himmlisches und irdisches Gericht in karolingischer Theologie und
althochdeutscher Dichtung." *FMS* 5 (1971). 284-303.

————. "Über den Ursprung der Freiheit. Eine Questio im Sachsenspiegel." *ZfDA* 103 (1974). 289-311.

Kraus, Carl. "'Vom Rechte' und 'Die Hochzeit.'" *SB der Wiener Akademie der Wissenschaften* 123 (1891).

Krause, Hermann. "*Consilium vel iudicio*. Bedeutungsbreite und Sinngehalt einer mittelalterlichen Formel." Ed. Clemens Bauer et al. *Speculum historiale*. Freiburg/Munich: Karl Alber, 1965. 416-438.

————. "Königtum und Rechtsordnung in der Zeit der sächsischen und salischen Herrscher." *ZRG (GA)* 82 (1965).

————. "Mittelalterliche Anschauungen vom Gericht im Lichte der Formel: iustitiam facere et recipere, Recht geben und nehmen." *SB Bayrische Akademie der Wissenschaften. Heft* 11 (1974).

Kroeschell, Karl. *Haus und Herrschaft im frühen deutschen Recht*. Göttingen: Otto Schwartz, 1968.

————. "Recht und Rechtsbegriff im 12. Jahrhundert." *Probleme des 12. Jahrhunderts*. Vol XII of *Reichenauer Vorträge und Forschungen*. Konstanz: Thorbecke, 1968. 309-335.

————. "Verfassungsgeschichte und Rechtsgeschichte." *Der Staat. Beiheft* 6 (1983). 47-77.

Kuhn, Hugo. *Dichtung und Welt im Mittelalter*. Stuttgart: Metzler, 1969.

————. "Gestalten und Lebenskräfte der frühmittelhochdeutschen Dichtung." *Dichtung und Welt im Mittelaler*. 112-132.

————. "Minne oder reht." *Dichtung und Welt im Mittelalter*. 105-111.

LeGoff, Jacques. "Les trois functions indo-européennes, l'historien et l'Europe féodale." *Annales ESC* 34 (1979). 1187-1215.

————. "A Note on the Tripartite Society, Monarchical Ideology, and Economic Renewal in Ninth- to Twelfth-Century Christendom." *Time, Work, and Culture in the Middle Ages*. Trs. by Arthur Goldhammer. Chicago: University of Chicago, 1980. 53-57.

Little, Lester K. "Pride Goes before Avarice: Social Change and the Vices in Latin Christianity." *American Historical Review* 76 (1971). 16-49.

Lottin, D. O. "La concept de justice chez les théologiens du moyen âge avant l'introduction d'Aristote." *Revue Thomiste* 44 (1938). 511-521.

Lovejoy, Arthur. *The Great Chain of Being*. Cambridge, Mass.: Harvard, 1936.

Lucae, (Karl). "Beiträge zur Erklärung des Parzival." *ZfdA* 30 (1886). 365-375.

Luscombe, D. E. "Conceptions of Hierarchy before the 13th Century." Ed. Albert Zimmermann. *Soziale Ordnungen im Selbstverständnis des Mittelalters*. *Miscellanea Mediaevalia*. Vol. 12/1. Berlin: De Gruyter, 1979. 1-19.

Lütge, Friedrich. *Geschichte der deutschen Agrarverfassung vom frühen Mittelalter bis zum 19. Jahrhundert*. Stuttgart: Eugen Ulmer, 1963.

Mackensen, Maria. "Soziale Forderungen und Anschauungen der frühmittelhochdeutschen Dichter." *Neue Heidelberger Jahrbücher*. *Neue Folge* (1925). 133-171.

Mäder, Eduard Johann. *Der Streit der Töchter Gottes*. Bern/Frankfurt: Lang, 1971.

Mähl, Sybille. *Quadriga virtutum*. *Die Kardinaltugenden in der Geistesgeschichte der Karolingerzeit*. Cologne: Böhlau, 1969.

Manz, Louis. *Der Ordo-Gedanke.* Stuttgart: Kohlhammer, 1937.

Maurer, Friedrich. "Über Langzeilen und Langzeilenstrophen in der ältesten deutschen Dichtung." (1950) *Dichtung und Sprache.* 174-194

————————. "Salische Geistlichendichtung." (1953) *Dichtung und Sprache.* 168-173.

————————. "Langzeilenstrophen und fortlaufende Reimpaare." (1959) *Dichtung und Sprache.* 195-213.

————————. *Dichtung und Sprache des Mittelalters.* 2nd. ed. Bern: Francke, 1971.

Meißburger, Gerhard. *Grundlagen zum Verständnis der deutschen Mönchsdichtung im 11. und 12. Jahrhundert.* Munich: Fink, 1970.

Meyer, Georg. "Die Gerichtsbarkeit über Unfreie und Hintersassen nach ältestem Recht." *ZRG (GA)* 2 (1881), 83-114 and *ZRG (GA)* 3 (1882), 102-126.

Mitteis, Heinrich. *Deutsche Rechtsgeschichte.* Rev. by Heinz Lieberich. Munich: Beck, 1966.

Mollat, Michel. *The Poor in the Middle Ages.* Trs. Arthur Goldhammer. New Haven: Yale, 1986.

Murphy, James J. *Rhetoric in the Middle Ages: A History of Rhetorical Theory from St. Augustine to the Renaissance.* Berkeley: California, 1974.

Nehlsen-von Stryk, Karin. "Die Freien im Frankreich als ungelöstes Problem der Rechts-, Sozial- und Verfassungsgeschichte." Ed. Dieter Simon. *Ius commune.* Frankfurt a. M.: Klostermann, 1987. 427-441.

Oexle, Otto Gerhard. "Die funktionale Dreiteilung der 'Gesellschaft' bei Adalbero von Laon. Deutungsschemata der sozialen Wirklichkeit im frühen Mittelalter." *FMS* 12 (1978). 1-54.

————————. "Die 'Wirklichkeit' und das 'Wissen.' Ein Blick auf das sozialgeschichtliche Œuvre von Georges Duby." *HZ* 232 (1981). 61-91.

————————. "Tria genera hominum. Zur Geschichte eines Deutungsschemas der sozialen Wirklichkeit in der Antike und im Mittelalter." Ed. Lutz Fenske et al. *Institutionen, Kultur und Gesellschaft im Mittelalter. Josef Fleckenstein Festschrift.* Sigmaringen: Thorbecke, 1984. 483-550.

————————. "Deutungsschemata der sozialen Wirklichkeit im frühen und hohen Mittelalter." Ed. Frantisek Graus. *Mentalitäten, Vorträge und Forschungen XXXV.* Sigmaringen: Thorbecke, 1987. 65-117.

Ohly, Friedrich. *Sage und Legende in der Kaiserchronik.* 1940; rpt. Darmstadt: Wissenschaftliche Buchgesellschaft, 1968.

————————. "Vom geistigen Sinn des Wortes im Mittelalter." *ZfdA* 89 (1958). 1-23.

Olberg, Gabriele von. "Zum Freiheitsbegriff im Spiegel volksspachlicher Bezeichnungen in den frühmittelalterlichen Leges." Ed. Dieter Simon. *Ius commune.* Frankfurt a. M.: Klostermann, 1987. 411-426.

Palmer, Nigel F. *"Visio Tnugdali." The German and Dutch Translations and their Circulation in the Later Middle Ages.* Munich: Artemis, 1982.

Paul, Hermann. *Mittelhochdeutsche Grammatik.* 23rd ed. by Peter Wiehl and Siegfried Grosse. Tübingen: Niemeyer, 1989.

Pelikan, Jaroslav. *The Growth of Medieval Theology (600-1300).* Vol. 3 of *The Christian Tradition.* Chicago: University of Chicago, 1978.

Peterson, Thomas Virgil. *Ham and Japeth: The Mythic World of Whites in the Antebellum South.* Methuen, N.J., 1978.

Pretzel, Ulrich. *Mittelhochdeutsche Bedeutungskunde.* Heidelberg: Winter, 1982.

——————, et al. *Nachträge zum mittelhochdeutschen Wörterbuch.* Leipzig: Hirzel, 1979.

Ris, Roland. *Das Adjektiv reich im mittelalterlichen Deutsch. QF NF* 40. Berlin: de Gruyter, 1971.

Rösener, Werner. "Bauer und Ritter im Hochmittelalter." Ed. Lutz Fenske et al. *Institutionen, Kultur und Gesellschaft im Mittelalter.* Sigmaringen: Thorbecke, 1984. 677-692.

Rupp, Heinz. *Deutsche religiöse Dichtungen des 11. und 12. Jahrhunderts.* 2nd. ed. Bern/Munich: Francke, 1971.

Sackur, Ernst. *Die Cluniacenser in iher kirchlichen und allgemeinen schriftlichen Wirksamkeit bis zur Mitte des 11. Jahrhunderts,* 2 vols. (1892/94; rpt.: Darmstadt: Wissenschaftliche Buchgesellschaft, 1965).

Schäfer, Dietrich. "Consilio vel judicio = mit minne oder mit rechte." *SB der königlich-preußischen Akademie der Wissenschaften* (1913). 719-733.

Scherer, Wilhelm. *Geistliche Poeten der deutschen Kaiserzeit. Zweites Heft. QF* 7. Strassbourg, 1875.

——————. *Geschichte der deutschen Dichtung im elften und zwölften Jahrhundert. QF* 12. Strasbourg, 1875.

Schilling, Otto. "Die Rechtsphilosophie bei den Kirchenvätern." *Archiv für Rechtswissenschaf* 16 (1922/23). 1-12.

Schmidt-Wiegand, Ruth. "Rechtswort und Rechtszeichen in der deutschen Dichtung." *FMS* 5 (1971). 267-283.

——————. "*Reht* und *ewa.* Die Epoche des Althochdeutschen in ihrer Bedeutung für die Geschichte der deutschen Rechtssprache." Ed. Rolf Bergmann et al. *Althochdeutsch.* Heidelberg: Winter, 1987. Vol. II, 937-958.

——————. "*hantgemælde* (Parzival 6, 19): Rechtswort und Rechtssinn bei Wolfram von Eschenbach." Ed. Kurt Gärtner and Joachim Heinzle. *Studien zu Wolfram von Eschenbach. Werner Schröder Festschrift.* Tübingen: Niemeyer, 1989. 333-342.

Scholem, Gershom. "Offenbarung und Tradition als religiöse Kategorien im Judentum." *Über einige Grundbegriffe des Judentums.* Frankfurt a. M: Suhrkamp, 1970. 90-120.

Schönbach, Anton. "Studien zur Geschichte der altdeutschen Predigt. Erstes Stück: Über Kelle's 'Speculum ecclesiae." *SB der kaiserlichen Akademie der Wissenschaften* (Vienna) 135 (1896).

Schott, Claus-Dieter. "Freiheit und libertas." *ZRG (GA)* 104 (1987). 84-109.

Schröbler, Ingeborg. "Das mittelhochdeutsche Gedicht vom 'Recht.'" *PBB* 80 (1958). 219-252.

——————. "Von den Grenzen des Verstehens mittelalterlicher Dichtung." *GRM NF* 13 (1963). 1-14.

Schröder, Werner. "Der Geist von Cluny und die Anfänge des frühmittelhochdeutschen Schrifttums." *PBB* (Halle) 72 (1950). 321-386.

——————. "Mönchische Reformbewegungen und frühdeutsche Literaturgeschichte." *Zeitschrift der Universität Halle. Gesch.-Sprachw.* 4, 2 (1955). 237-248.

——————. "Armuot." *DVjs* 34 (1960). 501-526.

——————. "Zum Begriff der 'binnengereimten Langzeile' in der altdeutschen Versgeschichte" Ed. Hugo Moser et al. *Festschrift Josef Quint*. Bonn: Emil Semmel, 1964. 194-202.

——————. "Versuch zu metrischer Beschreibung eines frühmittelhochdeutschen Gedichts mit einer forschungsgeschichtlichen Vorbemerkung." *ZfdA* 94 (1965). 196-213; 244-267.

——————. "Zu alten und neuen Theorien einer altdeutschen 'binnengereimten Langzeile." *PBB* 87 (1965). 150-165.

——————. "Kontinuität oder Diskontinuität in der Frühgeschichte der deutschen Literatur." *ZdfA* 100 (1971). 195-213.

Schulze, Hans K. "Rodungsfreiheit und Königsfreiheit. Zur Genese und Kritik neuerer verfassungsgeschichtlicher Theorien." *HZ* 219 (1974). 529-550.

——————. "Reichsaristokratie, Stammesadel und fränkische Freiheit." *HZ* 227 (1978). 353-373.

Schützeichel, Rudolph. *Das alemannische Memento mori. Das Gedicht und der geistig-historische Hintergrund*. Tübingen: Niemeyer, 1962.

——————. "Justitiam vendere." *Literaturwissenschaftliches Jahrbuch NF* (1964). 1-12.

——————. *Althochdeutsches Wörterbuch*. Tübingen: Niemeyer, 1981.

Schweikle, Günther. *Neithart*. Stuttgart: Metzler, 1990.

Searle, John R. *The Construction of Social Reality*. New York: The Free Press, 1995.

See, Klaus von. "Das Alter der Rígsthula." *Acta Philologica Scandinavia* 24 (1961). 1-12.

Soeteman, Cornelius. *Deutsche geistliche Dichtung des 11. und 12. Jahrhundert*. 2nd ed. Stuttgart: Metzler, 1971.

Southern, R. W. *The Making of the Middle Ages*. Tiptree, Essex: Arrow Books, 1959.

——————. *Saint Anselm and his Biographer*. Cambridge: Cambridge University, 1963.

Speicher, Stephan. *"Vom Rechte." Ein Kommentar im Rahmen der zeitgenössischen Literaturtradition*. GAG 443. Göppingen: Kümmerle, 1986.

Stahleder, Helmuth. "Zum Ständebegriff im Mittelalter." *Zeitschrift für bayerische Landesgeschichte* 35 (1972). 523-570.

Stenton, Doris M. *English Justice between the Norman Conquest and the Great Charter 1066-1215*. Philadelphia: American Philosophical Society, 1964.

Stosch, (Johannes). "Noch einmal mhd. *gelouben*." *ZfdA* 34 (1890). 77-78.

Tellenbach, Gerd. *Church, State and Christian Society at the Time of the Investiture Contest*. Trs. by R. F. Bennett. Oxford: Blackwell, 1940.

Vollmann-Profe, Gisela. *Von den Anfängen bis zum hohen Mittelalter. Wiederbeginn volkssprachlicher Schriftlichkeit im hohen Mittelalter (1050/60-1160/70)*. Vol. I, Part 2 *Geschichte der deutschen Literatur von den Anfängen bis zum Beginn der Neuzeit*. Ed. Joachim Heinzle. Königstein/Ts: Athenäum, 1986.

——————. Trs. and ed. *Frühmittelhochdeutsche Literatur*. Stuttgart: Reclam, 1996.

Vollrath, Hanna. "Herrschaft und Genossenschaft im Kontext frühmittelalterlicher Rechtsbeziehungen." *HJ* 102 (1982). 33-71.

Voltelini, Hans von. "Der Gedanke der allgemeinen Freiheit in den deutschen Rechtsbüchern." *ZRG (GA)* 57 (1937). 184-185.

Walch, Doris. *Charitas. Zur Rezeption des 'mandatum novum in altdeutschen Texten*. GAG 62. Göppingen: Kümmerle, 1973.

Wallace-Hadrill, J. M. "The *via regia* of the Carolingian Age." Ed. B. Smalley. *Trends in Medieval Political Thought.* Oxford: Blackwell, 1965. 22-41.

Wehrli, Max. *Geschichte der deutschen Literatur. Vol. 1. Vom frühen Mittelalter bis zum Ende des 16. Jahrhunderts.* Stuttgart: Reclam, 1984.

Weitzel, Jürgen. *Dinggenossenschaft und Recht.* 2 Vols. Cologne: Böhlau, 1985.

Weller, Alfred. *Die frühmittelhochdeutsche Wiener Genesis nach Quellen, Übersetzungsart, Stil und Syntax. Palaestra* 123. Berlin, 1914.

Wells, David A. "Die Erläuterung frühmittelhochdeutscher geistlicher Texte." Eds. L. P. Johnson et al. *Studien zur frühmittelhochdeutschen Literatur. Cambridger Colloquium 1971.* Berlin: Erich Schmidt, 1974. 160-179.

White, Stephan D. "'*Pactum . . . Legem Vincit et Amor Iudicium*:' The Settlement of Disputes by Compromise in Eleventh-Century France." *American Journal of Legal History* 22 (1978). 281-308.

Zotz, Thomas. "Adel, Oberschicht, Freie: Zur Terminologie der frühmittelalterlichen Sozialgeschichte." *Zeitschrift für die Geschichte des Oberrheins* 125 (1977). 3-20.

Index

WITHDRAWN